Basic Concepts of Ancient Philosophy

Studies in Continental Thought

Martin Heidegger

Basic Concepts of Ancient Philosophy

Translated by
Richard Rojcewicz

Indiana University Press
Bloomington and Indianapolis

This book is a publication of

Indiana University Press
601 North Morton Street
Bloomington, IN 47404-3797 USA

http://iupress.indiana.edu

Telephone orders 800-842-6796
Fax orders   812-855-7931
Orders by e-mail iuporder@indiana.edu

Published in German as Martin Heidegger, *Gesamtausgabe,* volume 22:
Die Grundbegriffe der antiken Philosophie,
edited by Franz-Karl Blust

Manufactured in the United States of America

Library of Congress Cataloging-in-Publication Data

Heidegger, Martin, 1889–1976.
[Grundbegriffe der antiken Philosophie. English]
Basic concepts of ancient philosophy / Martin Heidegger ;
translated by Richard Rojcewicz.
p. cm. — (Studies in Continental thought)
Includes bibliographical references.
ISBN-13: 978-0-253-34965-1 (cloth : alk. paper)
1. Philosophy, Ancient. I. Title.
B113.H4513 2008
180—dc22
2007016095

1 2 3 4 5   13 12 11 10 09 08

CONTENTS

Contents

Contents

Contents

Contents

Contents

Contents

xi

Translator's Foreword

This book is a translation of a lecture course Martin Heidegger offered in the summer semester 1926 at the University of Marburg. The German original appeared posthumously in 1993 (with a second edition in 2004) as volume 22 of Heidegger's collected works (*Gesamtausgabe*).

The date of the course places it at a time when Heidegger was completing the last of the published divisions of his magnum opus, *Being and Time*. His work on that book affected both the content and form of these lectures. The content of the course, besides illuminating the ancient thinkers, also sheds light on many of the central concepts of *Being and Time* and shows how these have roots in the basic concepts of ancient philosophy itself. On the other hand, the close connection to *Being and Time* had a deleterious effect on the form of the lectures as we have them. What we possess are precisely lecture *notes*, the notes Heidegger wrote for himself and referred to in his oral delivery. He did not, beforehand or afterward, elaborate them into full sentences. The pressing need to complete *Being and Time* precluded it. Thus the main part of the present text is in style almost always sketchy and at times even cryptic.

To eke out these inchoate notes, the editor of the volume has appended excerpts from student transcriptions of the lectures as actually delivered by Heidegger. The editor did not weave this material from the students into the main text, because the transcriptions were not officially approved by Heidegger. Thus the transcriptions must be approached with caution, but that they stem from Heidegger is beyond doubt: as he himself once remarked regarding some passages of disputed authenticity in Aristotle, "No student could write like that." The appended texts provide the required elaboration of the lecture notes, and if I may offer a word of advice to the reader, it is to take up the various transcriptions and supplements exactly at the place they attach to the main text (as indicated in footnotes), rather than all at once at the end. Otherwise, the notes will seem like an overture without the opera, an announcement of motifs without development, and the transcriptions like an opera without the overture.

The present translation is a complete English version of the German of the *Gesamtausgabe* edition. In fact, it is more. The work is heavily laden with Greek (and some Latin) terms and quotations, and very many of these are left untranslated. I have provided, and inserted into the text, within brackets, an English translation of all this untranslated Greek (and Latin) material. For recurring Greek terms, I have translated them in the text only the first time they appear but have compiled a glossary of them, to be found at the end of the volume. I attempted to provide a translation of the Greek which would be consistent with Heidegger's interpretation of the ancient authors. In a few instances, I found, in other volumes of the *Gesamtausgabe*, Heidegger's own translations of Greek passages he also cites here. In the other cases, I tried to take inspiration from Heidegger's inimitable way of translating but did not stray very far from the conventional renderings.

Square brackets have been used throughout the book for my insertions into the text, and the few footnotes I introduced are bracketed and marked "Trans." Braces ({}) are reserved for the editor's interpolations. As a convenience to anyone wishing to correlate passages in this translation with the original, the running heads indicate the *Gesamtausgabe* pagination.

Richard Rojcewicz
Point Park University

Basic Concepts of Ancient Philosophy

PRELIMINARY REMARKS

§1. On the aim and character of the course.[1]

The first task is to become clear about the aim and character of the course.

Aim: a penetrating understanding of the basic scientific concepts, ones which not only have determined—decisively determined—all subsequent philosophy but which have also made possible Western science as a whole and today still provide that science its foundations.

Character: introductory. That is, we will proceed step by step toward what is meant in the concepts and toward the way they are formed and grounded. It will thereby become evident *what* these lectures are dealing with, their object, as well as *how* they interrogate and investigate the objects, the mode of dealing with them. Included will be an increasing clarification of the non-philosophical positive sciences. Introductory: but not a popularization designed to promote so-called general culture. Since philosophy does play this role in the popular consciousness, however, and since philosophy is even being officially degraded to such a function, we need to clarify how things do stand with philosophy.

§2. Preliminary determination of the concept of philosophy over and against the current views.

Point of departure: popular view of philosophy and of its role in higher education.

1. Philosophy deals with "universal questions," ones that can touch and interest every person.

1. Title on the manuscript: "Sketches for the course on the basic concepts of ancient philosophy. Summer semester 1926."

1

2. What philosophy inquires into can also be encountered in every science, indeed even outside the sciences.

3. Philosophy is something in which everyone is engaged, either constantly or occasionally, out of different motives, in diverse circumstances, and with various degrees of urgency.

Philosophy is something universal, not a special science. Therefore philosophy must also be universally accessible, universally understandable. Philosophy requires no specialized method but only the universally distributed thinking of sound common sense; every fully awake head must understand it, everyone has something to say about it.

If a classical philologist attends a lecture on the theory of functions and understands nothing, he finds that to be in order. If a chemist listens to a talk about Hindu philology and understands nothing, he finds that to be in order. If they both, along with their colleagues from whatever disciplines, hear a lecture in philosophy and do not understand it, then that is found not to be in order, since philosophy is indeed something universal and must be accessible to everyone in the universe. That which, in some way or other, touches everyone must also be understood by everyone. This is not only the opinion of the students in higher education but is also, in large part, that of their teachers. A college course in philosophy is an opportunity for everyone's intellectual sustenance, for the renewal and expansion of culture, perhaps even for edification or the imparting of world-views. It is considered a great value that philosophical instruction is tailored to the needs of the students.

These universally held positions on philosophy are truly appalling. The most radical science and, accordingly, the most difficult one has been debased to a matter of so-called general culture. The presentations of philosophy as well as its problematics are supposed to be tailored to the needs predominant at any time. We will not now inquire into the grounds of this state of affairs nor into the means that have allowed it to develop and to spread today more widely than ever. Over and against the popular conception, we want, instead, to take a positive approach and gain at least a preliminary understanding of the possible idea of philosophy and to see clearly the positive necessities of its study, necessities predelineated in that idea.

If the just-characterized popular conception of philosophy is a perversion and a corruption, then it might be concluded that philosophy is a special science, like any other, and is restricted to only a few persons. Most are excluded, because what is required by the content of their individual science makes it practically impossible for them to take up in addition the exertions involved in the study of this particular specialty.

Such an argument, however, is merely the obverse of the popular conception and shares with it the same basic unclarity regarding the essence and task of philosophy.

1. Philosophy indeed deals with something universal but is not universally accessible without further ado.

2. Philosophy is the science of the most proper domain of all and yet is not a specialty.

Regarding 1: It remains to be determined in what sense philosophy is universal and how something can be an object such that it is in a genuine sense universal.

Regarding 2: The kind of questioning and proving involved in philosophical research likewise remains to be clarified. Philosophy is not a specialty but, rather, deals with that whose very articulation first makes possible something like specialties, i.e., subject-matters delimited one against the other.

Philosophy is research that lies at the foundation of all the sciences and that is "alive" in all of them, however this statement may come to be determined more precisely. But we can already ask: if philosophy lies at the basis of the sciences, then can it be less scientific or must it satisfy, in an even higher and more radical sense, the idea of science? Obviously, the latter.

But if philosophy is the *most original science, science in the utterly proper sense,* then the study of it must come completely from *free choice.* This latter cannot in the least be determined through points of view such as that of occupation or training in a specialty. To choose and take up the study of philosophy means to choose between full scientific existence and manual, blind preparation for an occupation. To choose the study of philosophy, to penetrate into its problematics, does not mean to take up one additional specialty for the sake of completeness and to be well-rounded. Nor does it mean to register for a so-called comprehensive course. On the contrary, it means to *decide in favor of transparency in one's own scientific acting, forbearing, and existing at the university,* versus blind preparation for exams and non-deliberate nibbling on intellectual tidbits. To spend one's student days in this latter way does not at all differ from serving an apprenticeship as a handyman's helper; at most it differs by way of its greater capriciousness, which is customarily called academic freedom. But freedom is not the "indifference of caprice"; on the contrary, it is *letting advance the authentic possibilities of human Da-sein,* thus here it is letting *genuine scientific questioning* advance, not being content with accidental knowledge.

One has already become unfree, a slave to prejudice and indolence, if one makes the excuse: philosophy is too difficult and too much. It might seem that this excuse expresses modesty and prudence, but at bottom it signifies flight from the exertions of genuine scientific study. For philosophy is not something "more," a mere "addition" to something else, but is exactly what the specialized sciences are, only more radically and in a more penetrating understanding. "Too difficult": no science, as long as it remains moved by actual questioning, is easy. What alone is easy is mere erudition without understanding.

Freedom is letting advance the questioning that takes place in scientific research. And that requires a proper openness and an understanding of science in general and of what is at issue in science. The foregoing consideration is not meant to frighten away, nor to entice, but to open the possibility of free reflection.

§3. Preliminary determination of the object of philosophy over and against the positive sciences: philosophy as critical science.

Therefore a preliminary orientation regarding the essence and task of philosophy. These can be determined in several ways. In the course itself we will choose one way: we will trace philosophy's original breakthrough, its first, decisive formation. Preliminarily, however, we will take another path, the nearest one: what lies closest is the sphere of the non-philosophical sciences. It is versus them that we now wish to determine philosophy.

Striking: the other sciences, mathematics, physics, history, philology, linguistics, do not begin by asking what is mathematics, physics, philology; instead, they just set about their work, they plunge into their subject matter. Or, if not, then they merely make some brief, general, prefatory remarks. That is no accident; on the contrary, an essential characteristic of the sciences is here manifesting itself. If asked what mathematics is, what philology is, the mathematician or philologist answers by bringing forth his science, by posing and working through definite mathematical or philological problems. That is the best, and the only, way.

And yet, the question remains in a certain sense unanswered. If the mathematician wished to say what mathematics is, not by presenting mathematical problems and proofs, but by talking *about* mathematics, its objects and method, then he could no longer employ mathematical proofs and concepts, just as little as the physicist could employ experiments to show and prove the essence of physics. Likewise, with the philological method one cannot show what philology is. When scientists try to answer such questions, they are beginning to philosophize. There is no mathematical concept of mathematics, because mathematics as such is not something mathematical. There is no philological concept of philology, because philology as such is not something philological.

Whence stems this remarkable state of affairs? In the very essence of all these sciences, in the fact that they are *positive* sciences, versus philosophy, which we call the *critical* science.

Positive: *ponere*—"posit," "lay"; *positum*—what has been "laid down," what already lies there. Positive sciences are those for which what they deal with, what can become their object and their theme, *already lies there.* Numbers are already there, spatial relations exist, nature is at hand, language is present, and so is literature. All this is *positum*, it lies there. It is a being; everything uncovered in science is *a being.* Positive sciences are sciences *of beings.*

But is that not a determination pertaining essentially to every science, thus also to philosophy as critical science? Or is not that which philosophy makes its theme pre-given to it? Is its object—and that which is to become an object—first thought up, first posited, or even invented, in mere thought? Then again, are not the positive sciences also critical ones? Are they somehow uncritical, unmethodical? Does not critique pertain to every scientific method? Thus if philosophy, too, has a theme and is not capricious invention, is it indeed also a positive science? And conversely, is every non-philosophical positive science, as science, not uncritical but in fact critical science? What then happens to the distinction between positive and critical science?

If the distinction is justified, then "critical" must mean something other than "methodologically cautious and free from prejudice." And if philosophy, too, actually encounters its theme and does not invent it, then it must be possible for something to be made a theme that does *not lie there*, i.e., is *not a being.*

§4. The "critical" function of philosophy: to separate and differentiate beings from Being.

Critical: κρίνειν—"to separate," "to differentiate," in differentiating something from something to make visible both what has been differentiated and what differentiates it. To differentiate: triangle from square, mammal from bird, epic from drama, noun from verb, one being from another—every science is constantly differentiating such things and thereby determining what has been differentiated.

Accordingly, if philosophy is critical science, such that it is preeminently "critical" in character, then there takes place in philosophy a differentiating in a preeminent sense. But what can be differentiated from beings other than beings? What can we still say of beings? They *are,* and only beings are. They are; they *have Being.* From beings and in beings what can be differentiated is *Being.* This differentiation does not concern beings and beings, but *beings and Being.* "Being"—under that term nothing can be represented. Indeed beings; but Being? In fact, the common understanding and common experience understand and seek only beings. To see and to grasp Being in beings, to differentiate

Being from beings, is the task of *the* differentiating science, philosophy. Its theme is *Being and never beings.*

Positive sciences: sciences of beings. That which lies there for natural experience and knowledge. Critical science: science of Being. That which does not lie there for natural experience but, instead, is *hidden,* never lies there, and yet is indeed always already understood, even *prior to* every experience of beings: as it were, the most positive and yet at the same time the least {positive}.[2] *Being "is" not.* Philosophy is critical science, not critical philosophy understood as theory of knowledge, critique of the limits of knowledge.

To come so far that you can represent something under the term "Being," can grasp the differentiation at issue, and can actually carry it out—that is the beginning of scientific philosophy. To introduce you into this beginning, to lead and guide you in beginning—that is the task of this course.

Critical science carries out this differentiation and thereby gains as its theme not beings but, instead, the Being of beings. The concept of positive science can now be made more precise. The non-philosophical sciences deal with beings, with what lies there, i.e., with what is first experienced and known. And beings can be investigated without explicitly asking about their Being. All methods and concepts are tailored to suit the grasping and determining of beings. This {i.e., Being}[3] is, on the other hand, at first unknown, closed, inaccessible. To disclose it, i.e., to distinguish Being from beings, particular ways of research are required.

Positive sciences make assertions about beings exclusively, *never* about Being. That is why mathematics cannot be determined mathematically, nor philology philologically. The mathematician treats numbers, or spatial relations, not number as such, i.e., the Being of numbers, not space as such, the Being of space, what and how space is. The philologist deals with literature, with written works, not with literature in general, what and how it is and can be.

Philosophy is critical, the *Being* of beings, but it does not criticize; i.e., it does not at all criticize the results of the positive sciences. What philosophy "criticizes" in a higher sense, i.e., critically determines, is the Being of beings, which is what the positive sciences presuppose. The term "positive" thereby has its sense made more sharp: "positive" means absorbed in pre-given beings and not asking about their Being. Nevertheless, insofar as they deal with beings, the positive sciences always co-understand Being, although not explicitly. Conversely, Being is always the Being of some being.

Being is not given in experience and yet is co-understood. Every-

2. Editor's interpolation.
3. Editor's interpolation.

one understands when we say: the weather "is" dreary, the trees "are" in bloom. We understand "is" and "are" and yet find ourselves in a predicament if we have to say what "is" and "are" mean, what "Being" signifies. An understanding of Being, although no concept.

That is why positive and critical science are necessarily separate. Every critical investigation does look to beings, but in a different sense than do the positive sciences; it does not make beings its theme. All positive sciences co-understand Being in beings, but in a different sense than does the critical science. They do not make Being thematic, the concept of Being and the structures of Being are not made problems; on the contrary, the theme is the investigation of beings, such as those of nature or history.

We can now clarify *how* it is that philosophy deals with something *"universal."*[4] Being is universal with regard to all beings; *every* being *is*, every being, *as* a being, has *Being*. And this universality of Being with regard to every being is a preeminent one, for within the realm of beings themselves there also occurs universality. A law of mechanics is universal over and against particular driving forces and impacts, a law of any kind of motion is universal over and against particular physico-chemical laws. A particular Greek epic versus other Greek epics; Greek epic, German epic, epic in general. *Genitivus subjectivus, genitivus objectivus,* in German, in Latin, the genitive in general. Democratic constitution, aristocratic constitution, constitution in general. Above all of these there is still a being, although one of varying degrees of generality. But what is involved for there *to be* at all something like motion, law, nature, what pertains to poetry in general, what constitutes the Being of language in general—these are questions about the "universalities" that precede all general beings and that still determine their Being. The fall of a body, falling itself, motion in nature; nature in general, what pertains to it, the capacity to be something like that, what constitutes its Being. This latter lies at the foundation of every determinate, factual process and is co-intended in every general law of nature. Historical event, historical happening; history in general, what belongs to its Being.

Being of nature,
Being of history,   } various modes of Being
Being of numbers.

Being in general *lies beyond*. This lying beyond of Being and of the determinations of the Being of beings, over and above beings as such, is *transcendere*—"to surpass," transcendence. Not as supersensible, metaphysical in a bad sense, whereby what is meant is still a being.

The science of this Being, *transcendens*, contains propositions about

4. Cf. above, §2, p. 2f.

Being, ones which assert not truths about beings, but truths about Being, about that which is transcendent, *transcendens*. This truth (*veritas*) is transcendental. Philosophical truth is *veritas transcendentalis,* transcendental not in the Kantian sense, although Kant is indeed oriented toward this concept, even if he distorts is.

Being is closed off, "under this term nothing can be represented," it is at first and for the most part inaccessible. Seeking and uncovering {Being}[5]—that is what the critical science is devoted to.

Plato: αὐτὴ ἡ οὐσία ἧς λόγον δίδομεν τοῦ εἶναι καὶ ἐρωτῶντες καὶ ἀποκρινόμενοι[6]—"We make thematic beings themselves, whose Being we display and make manifest in our questions and answers." τῇ τοῦ ὄντος ἀεὶ λογισμῶν προσκείμενος ἰδέᾳ[7]—Task of the philosopher: "He is constantly devoted to casting his gaze on beings," i.e., on their Being, "in the mode of conceptual interpretation." Aristotle: Ἔστιν ἐπιστήμη τις ἣ θεωρεῖ τὸ ὂν ᾗ ὂν καὶ τὰ τούτῳ ὑπάρχοντα καθ᾽ αὐτό.[8] ["There is a science which specifically considers beings as beings and that which in these beings is already there in advance and indeed in themselves."[9]]

It {the critical science}[10] is not positive, because its object is not pregiven to it but, instead, must first be uncovered. Uncovering, disclosing, determining, and questioning about Being is σοφία ["wisdom"]. σοφός ["the wise one"]—the one who has the taste and instinct for what remains hidden to the common understanding. The σοφός knows at the same time that this entails special tasks and troublesome research. He does not simply and securely possess but, instead, seeks, and must constantly seek, that to which he is devoted, that which he "loves"—φιλεῖν. σοφία, the disclosure of the Being of beings, is φιλοσοφία ["philosophy"], the seeking and questioning for this disclosure, and, as such, places itself under the most radical critique.

§5. Aim and method of the course.

To make visible the differentiation, the beginning of philosophy, (differentiation regarding concept formation, questioning and investigat-

5. Editor's interpolation.

6. *Phaedo* 78D1f., in *Platonis opera,* ed. J. Burnet, Oxford, 1899, vol. 1.

7. *Sophist*, 254A8f.

8. *Aristotelis Metaphysica,* recogn. W. Christ. Leipzig, 1886 (henceforth, Christ), Γ 1, 1003a21f.

9. [This is how Heidegger translates the passage in *Platon: Sophistes, Gesamtausgabe* (henceforth, GA) 19, Frankfurt: Klostermann, 1992, p. 208. He provides a less literal translation later in the present course; see below, p. 215. —Trans.]

10. Editor's interpolation.

ing; not for the sake of extensity in knowledge of topics and materials but, instead, for intensity in conceptualization; secure grasp of the differentiation; nothing left to caprice and accident) specifically in this way, namely by participating in and, as it were, *repeating* the first decisive beginning of scientific philosophy. We will retread the path of the uncovering of Being out of beings; such uncovering is the most radical and most difficult task facing human knowledge. It is a task that has never yet been brought to its pure state and today is more misunderstood than perhaps ever before. In this light, we can measure the very meager forward steps taken by scientific philosophy since the beginning.

A running start was accomplished by the Greeks; since then only a rerunning that has long since covered over and deformed the original intentions. To become able to understand this philosophy concretely, *how* Being was investigated, how conceptualized, i.e., which concepts of Being and of its determinations were gained.

Modern erudition, the knowledge of everything and the discussing of everything, has lost its edge long ago and is now incapable of radically differentiating between what we do understand, in the genuine sense, and what we do not understand within the original domains of scientific questioning. This erudition has become much too clever and jaded, i.e., philosophically unproductive, and so can no longer appreciate the verve that animated the discoveries of Plato and Aristotle.

Method of this introduction: weight will be placed on acquiring substantive understanding. No intention of filling the class sessions with anecdotes about the lives and fates of the ancient thinkers or rambling on about Greek culture. There will be no mere enumeration of the titles of the writings of the ancient authors, no synopsis of contents which contributes nothing to the understanding of the problems. All that can be had cheaply in compendia available by the dozen. It might be important for a full historiographical comprehension of Greek civilization. But our concern is philosophical understanding; not historiography but, instead, philosophy. To be sure, that does not mean to interpret unhistoriographically. Historiographical comprehension is itself possible only if substantive understanding has already been gained. One can describe ever so thoroughly the relations of the philosophers and of the philosophical schools to the then-contemporaneous poetry, art, politics, and social conditions, these can be analyzed minutely, and yet that will never lead to an understanding of philosophy itself, its intention, its philosophical content, the sphere of its problematics, the level of its methodological accomplishment. Furthermore, such understanding is not a matter of becoming informed about opinions, tenets, views. What *is* necessary is that we co-philosophize, and the attempt to do so will itself claim the entire time of our sessions and all of our force.

The exoteric works {?}—easily available today in various forms. We will later name the most important resources.[11]

Our concern will be fourfold:

1. The *whole* of the problematics of ancient philosophy is to be brought to light: some few central problems which are still unresolved.

2. The *main lines of development* are to be worked out; not the mere succession of philosophers and schools, but the way the problems have arisen out of one another: what direction did the questions take, with what conceptual means were they answered. Bogging down of lines of questioning, motives of stagnation, causes of foundering.

3. To form a more penetrating understanding with regard to determinate, concrete, *basic concepts*: Being-truth, principle-cause, possibility-necessity, relation, unity, multiplicity, nature, life, knowledge, expression-proof.[12]

4. On the basis of this consideration, to cast a glance at contemporary problematics and to characterize the way ancient philosophy *played out* in the Middle Ages and in modern times. Necessary to pose the questions more radically than did the Greeks. Can do so only if we have already understood Greek philosophy entirely on its own and do not interpret modern problems back into it. To be sure, in order to understand it that way it must first be understood at all, the horizons of its problems worked out, its intentions followed to the end; otherwise, philosophical discourse says nothing.

On the whole, the principal aim: 1. Substantive understanding, not anecdotes. 2. Contact with the primary sources, not with the secondary literature and others' opinions.

Let these suffice as the most needed preliminary remarks. Something of the sort was required by the confusion over the essence and tasks of philosophy but would have been completely superfluous if the state of research in scientific philosophy were more or less in order. Accordingly, these remarks have merely a propaedeutic goal here. Now the substantive *issues* alone are to speak.

---

11. Cf. below, §6, pp. 11-13.

12. Mörchen transcription: "All this has its inner coherence, the basis of which we need to grasp." (Supplementing the main text, from which Heidegger lectured, are student notes taken by H. Mörchen and W. Bröcker. Transcriptions of those notes are presented in the appendix and will be referred to according to this example: See Mörchen transcription, no. 1, p. 168.)

§6. The most important resources for texts. Sources regarding the historical transmission. General presentations and the most important study aids.

a) The most important resources for texts.

F. W. A. Mullach, *Fragmenta Philosophorum Graecorum.* Coll. rec. vert. Vols. 1–3. Paris, 1860ff.

Historia Philosophiae Graecae et Romanae. Locos coll., disposuerunt et notis auxerunt H. Ritter et L. Preller. Gotha, 1838; many editions.

H. Diels, *Die Fragmente der Vorsokratiker.* Greek and German, 3 vols., 4th ed. Berlin, 1922. {6th ed., ed. W. Kranz. Berlin, 1951.}

W. Nestle, *Die Vorsokratiker.* Selections and German trans. Jena, 1908.

Die Ethika des Demokritos. Texte und Untersuchungen. P. Natorp. Marburg, 1893.

Socrates: material found in the monograph by H. Maier, *Sokrates. Sein Werk und seine geschichtliche Stellung.* Tübingen, 1913.

Plato: latest complete works, ed. J. Burnet, *Platonis opera.* Scriptorum Classicorum Bibliotheca Oxoniensis. Vols. 1–5. Oxford, 1899ff.; *Platons Werke.* Trans. F. Schleiermacher. 6 vols., in 3 Parts. 3rd ed. Berlin, 1855–1862.

Aristotle: at present there is no reliable collected works; in preparation at Teubner (Leipzig); English ed. of the *Metaphysics:* Ἀριστοτέλους τὰ μετὰ τὰ φυσικά. *Aristotle's Metaphysics:* A rev. text with intro. and comm. by W. D. Ross. 2 vols. Oxford, 1924; Ἀριστοτέλους περὶ γενέσεως καὶ φθορᾶς. *Aristotle on Coming-to-be and Passing-away:* A rev. text with intro. and comm. by H. H. Joachim. Oxford, 1922; from Academia Regia Borussica, *Aristotelis opera,* 5 vols., (vols. 1–2, ed. I. Bekker), Berlin, 1831ff.

Stoicorum veterum fragmenta. Ed. H. von Arnim. 4 vols. Leipzig, 1903ff.

Epicurea. Ed. H. Usener. Leipzig, 1887.

Philo: *Philonis Alexandrini opera quae supersunt.* Ed. L. Cohn and P. Wendland. 6 vols. Berlin, 1896ff.

Plotinus: *Plotini Enneades.* Ed. H. F. Müller. 4 vols. Berlin, 1878ff.; *Plotini Enneades.* Ed. R. Volkmann. 2 vols. Leipzig, 1883–1884; a new French edition has not yet been completed.[13]

b) The handing down of philosophy among the Greek thinkers themselves. (Sources regarding the historical transmission.)

Doxographi Graeci. Coll. rec. prolegomenis indicibusque instr. H. Diels. Berlin, 1879.

---

13. Presumably Heidegger is referring to: *Plotin, Ennéades,* 6 vols., ed. E. Bréhier. Paris, 1924.

Diogenis Laertii de vitis philosophorum libri X. Cum indice rerum. 2 vols. Leipzig, 1884. Biographies. (*Sexti Empirici opera.* Rec. H. Mutschmann. Vol. 1, Leipzig, 1912; vol. 2, Leipzig, 1914; vol. 3, ed. J. Mau, Leipzig, 1954.)

Commentaries by the Neoplatonics on Aristotle and Plato: *Commentaria in Aristotelem Graeca.* Ed. consilio et auctoritate academiae litterarum regiae Borussicae. 23 vols., 3 supplementary vols. *Inter alia*: Simplicius on Aristotle's *Physics: Simplicii in Aristotelis Physicorum libros commentaria,* ed. H. Diels. Berlin. Vol. 9, 1882; vol. 10, 1895.

c) General presentations.

E. Zeller, *Die Philosophie der Griechen in ihrer geschichtlichen Entwicklung.* 3 parts in 6 halves.[14] Leipzig. Newest edition begins 1892 (5th ed.). {6th ed., 1919ff.}

F. Überweg, *Grundriß der Geschichte der Philosophie des Altertums.* 11th rev. ed. Most complete book of bibliographical references. Not in the reading room.

W. Dilthey, *Einleitung in die Geisteswissenschaften. Versuch einer Grundlegung für das Studium der Gesellschaft und der Geschichte.* Leipzig, 1883. In W. Dilthey, *Gesammelte Schriften.* Leipzig, 1914ff. Appears as vol. 1, 1922.

W. Windelband, *Geschichte der abendländischen Philosophie im Altertum.* 4th ed., ed. A. Goedeckemeyer. Munich, 1923 (in I. von Müller: *Handbuch der Altertumswissenschaft.* Bd. 5, Abt. 1, t. 1).

H. von Arnim, "Die europäische Philosophie des Altertums." In: *Allgemeine Geschichte der Philosophie: Die Kultur der Gegenwart.* Ed. P. Hinneberg. Teil 1, Abt. 5. Berlin and Leipzig, 1909, pp. 115-287.

K. Joel, *Geschichte der antiken Philosophie.* Vol. 1 (*Grundriß der philosophischen Wissenschaften*). Tübingen, 1921.

R. Hönigswald, *Die Philosophie des Altertums: Problemgeschichtliche und systematische Untersuchungen.* 2nd ed. Leipzig and Berlin, 1924.

d) Encyclopedia articles.

Paulys Real-Enzyklopädie der classischen Altertumswissenschaft. New ed., with the collaboration of numerous specialists. Ed. G. Wissowa. Stuttgart, 1894ff. Beginning with the 13th half-volume, ed. G. Wissowa and W. Kroll. Stuttgart, 1910ff. In the reading room. Valuable articles (P. Natorp[15]).

Archiv für Geschichte der Philosophie. In affiliation with H. Diels, W. Dilthey, B. Erdmann, and E. Zeller. Ed. L. Stein. Berlin, 1888ff.

14. In the ms.: "3 vols. in 6 parts."
15. Cf. the article "Antisthenes," vol. 1, 2, columns 2538-2545.

e) General studies in the history of ancient thinking.

J. Burckhardt, *Griechische Kulturgeschichte*. Ed. J. Oeri. 4 vols. Berlin and Stuttgart, 1898ff.

E. Meyer, *Geschichte des Alterthums*. 5 vols. Stuttgart, 1884ff.

E. Rohde, *Psyche: Seelencult und Unsterblichkeitsglaube der Griechen*. Freiburg, 1894.

F. Boll, *Sternglaube und Sterndeutung. Die Geschichte und das Wesen der Astrologie*. Ed. C. Bezold. Leipzig and Berlin, 1918.

H. Diels, *Antike Technik: Sieben Vorträge*. 2nd ed. Leipzig and Berlin, 1920.

J. L. Heiberg, "Exakte Wissenschaften und Medizin." In: A. Gercke and E. Norden, eds., *Einleitung in die Altertumswissenschaft*, vol. 2, no. 5. Leipzig and Berlin, 1922, pp. 317–357.

For the individual philosophers, main texts and biographies will be included in the context of the respective consideration.

PART ONE
GENERAL INTRODUCTION
TO ANCIENT PHILOSOPHY

1

Working out of the central concepts and questions of ancient philosophy, with the first book of Aristotle's *Metaphysics* as guideline

§7. Epochs of ancient philosophy.

There is agreement regarding the main lines. But does not touch anything essential; presented merely for the sake of orientation.

We distinguish four epochs, and specifically according to the direction and the kind of questioning.

1. The question of the Being of the world, nature (Milesian philosophy of nature, up to the time of the sophists, thus 600–450. Outlying territories, colonies in Asia Minor and in Italy/Sicily).

2. The question of the Being of human Dasein and the more radical appropriation of the question of the Being of the world. Fundamental elaboration of the problems of scientific philosophy. Socrates–Plato–Aristotle, 450 to nearly 300. Athens is the center of Greek science and culture generally.

1 and 2: the norm {?} of purely productive science is worked out and fixed. All important horizons of the problematic are laid down. In the two subsequent epochs, there is a decline, weakening, and deformation of scientific philosophy through world-views and religion. Occultism, surrogates.

3. The practical/world-view philosophy of Hellenism. Stoics, Epicureans, Skeptics. In the philosophical schools a certain scientific life is preserved.

4. The religious speculation of Neoplatonism. Simultaneously, a re-appropriation of the scientific epoch. Commentaries without the force to radicalize the problematic. Intrusion of speculation deriving from Christian theology.

Ancient philosophy ends in AD 529. Through an edict of Justinian, the Academy in Athens is closed, its property confiscated. Study of Greek philosophy is forbidden.

The common divisions into periods diverge with regard to details. Sometimes four or three or even only two epochs are posited. Characteristically, Hegel accepts three epochs, so as to enforce his dialectical scheme. 1 and 2 are taken together as i): formation and development of the totality of the sciences. ii) (3): disintegration into oppositions and trends: Stoics (dogmatic) — Skeptics. iii) (4): re-appropriation of the oppositions in the absolute of religion. Zeller,[1] who comes out of the Hegelian school, has concretely carried out this scheme in a historiographical study, free from the violence, but also less penetrating.

§8. Methodological middle way: Aristotle as guide. Structure of the first book of the *Metaphysics*. Aristotle's *Metaphysics:* editions and commentaries.

Scientific apex of ancient philosophy: Aristotle. He did not solve all problems, but he advanced to the limits which Greek philosophy could reach, given its general approach and its problematics. He unified in a positive way the fundamental motifs of the previous philosophy; after him, a decline.[2]

Met. A 3-6: Presentation of the earlier philosophers.
Met. A 7: Critical summary.
Met. A 8-9: Aporias: philosophers of nature, Pythagoreans, theory of Ideas.
Met. A 10: Double of 7, unifies A 3-6 and leads over to B and to the emphasis on the ἀμυδρῶς [things said "obscurely"].[3] Cf. Jaeger.[4]

Commentaries:
Alexander of Aphrodisias, c. AD 200, *In Aristotelis Metaphysica commentaria*, ed. M. Hayduck. *Commentaria in Aristotelem Graeca*. Vol. 1, Berlin, 1891.

---

1. E. Zeller, *Die Philosophie der Griechen in ihrer geschichtlichen Entwicklung.* 3 parts in 6 halves. 6th ed., ed. W. Nestle in collaboration with F. Lortzing. Leipzig, 1919ff. (Henceforth, Zeller.) See part 1: General introduction: Presocratic philosophy. First half-volume, pp. 210–227, esp. 225–227.

2. The page which should now follow is missing in the manuscript; its contents are given in the Mörchen transcription, nos. 1 and 2. See esp. no. 1, p. 168.

3. *Met.* A 10, 993a13f.

4. See Mörchen transcription, no. 2, p. 168f.

Thomas Aquinas, *In XII libros Metaphysicorum (Aristotelis commentarium)*. *Opera omnia*. Parma, 1852ff. Vol. 20, pp. 245-654.[5]

F. Suarez, *Disputationes metaphysicae. Opera omnia*. Paris, 1856ff. Vol. 25. Ed. C. Berton.[6]

H. Bonitz, *Aristotelis Metaphysica*. Recogn. et enarr. H. Bonitz. 2 vols. (vol. 2: *Commentarius*). Bonn, 1848-1849.[7]

A. Schwegler, *Die Metaphysik des Aristoteles*. Greek and German. Text, trans., and comm., with clarificatory discussions, by A. Schwegler. 4 vols. Tübingen, 1847-1848.[8]

W. D. Ross, Ἀριστοτέλους τὰ μετὰ τὰ φυσικά. *Aristotle's Metaphysics*. Rev. text with intro. and comm. by W. D. Ross. Vols. 1-2. Oxford, 1924.[9]

Translations:

A. Lasson, *Aristoteles, Metaphysik*. German trans. A. Lasson. Jena, 1907.

E. Rolfes, *Aristoteles' Metaphysik*. Trans. with an intro. and clarificatory notes by E. Rolfes. 2 vols. Leipzig, 1904; 2nd ed., Leipzig, 1920-1921.[10]

H. Bonitz, *Aristoteles, Metaphysik*. Trans. H. Bonitz, from his literary remains ed. E. Wellmann. Berlin, 1890.[11]

§9. Various modes of disclosing and understanding (*Met.* A, chap. 1).

Here the basic traits of a general theory of science; oriented toward the idea of the fundamental science. All essential expressions for knowing, apprehending, understanding are now terminologically stamped, specifically over and against what had been the case earlier; i.e., these expressions now differentiate the matters at issue themselves.[12]

---

5. Mörchen transcription: "very valuable."

6. Mörchen transcription: "important, because here ancient ontology passed over from the Middle Ages to modernity."

7. Mörchen transcription: "without particular philosophical pretensions, valuable."

8. Mörchen transcription: "strongly under Hegel's influence."

9. Mörchen transcription: "merely a paraphrase, but the only generally accessible commentary."

10. Mörchen transcription: "adheres strictly to the text, essentially determined by the medieval conception of Aristotle."

11. Mörchen transcription: "best translation, edited from his literary remains by one of his students."

12. See Mörchen transcription, no. 3, p. 169f.

Concept of σοφία: περί τινας ἀρχὰς καὶ αἰτίας ἐπιστήμη[13] ["knowledge regarding principles and causes"]. σοφία: ἐπιστήμη pure and
simple; ἐπιστάτης: the one who stands [steht] before and over some
matter, who can stand at the head of it [vorsteht], who understands [ver-
steht] it.

Path of the investigation: apprehending and knowing are comportments of humans, possessions of humans. Humans are beings among
others. Lifeless—living. Living beings have determinate comportments;
animals—humans. The task is then to interrogate the latter with regard to
their comportments having something to do with knowing, understanding, apprehending, perceiving. Manifold of possibilities and of modes of
disclosing in a certain gradation: σοφώτερος ["wiser"] (cf. 982a13f.),
μᾶλλον σοφός[14] ["more of a wise man"], ἔνδοξον ["esteemed"]).

ἀληθεύειν:[15] "to take out of concealment," "make unconcealed,"
"dis-cover" what was covered over. Living beings: human Dasein is
that peculiar being which discloses other beings and itself, not simply
as a supplementary faculty but, rather, φύσει ["by nature"]. *By virtue
of its very Being, the world and itself are already disclosed to it*, though indeterminately, confusedly, uncertainly. World: what is closest, Being *in
the proper sense.*

ἀληθεύειν: "to disclose," apprehend, understand: truth; knowledge
as appropriated cognition: certainty. Modes of disclosing and understanding, pre-theoretically.

Gradation,[16] development of the circumspection required for free
motion:

αἴσθησις
μνήμη
ἐμπειρία
τέχνη
ἐπιστήμη
σοφία (φρόνησις)

αἴσθησις (cf. 980a22):[17] "sense perception," ἴδια–κοινά–κατά
συμβεβηκός ["proper-common-incidental"], because what is present
is in every case enclosed in relations {?}.

μνήμη (980a29),[18] "retention," "memory," knowledge of what is
not present or, rather, is again present; to have already apprehended.

13. *Met.* A 1, 982a2. Reading in Christ: περί τινας αἰτίας καὶ ἀρχάς.
14. *Met.* A 1, 982a15f.: μᾶλλον ... σοφίαν.
15. See Mörchen transcription, no. 3, p. 170.
16. See Mörchen transcription, no. 3, p. 170f.
17. See Mörchen transcription, no. 3, p. 170f.
18. See Mörchen transcription, no. 3, p. 170f.

Freer orientation, circumspection, to take in at a glance. More teachable, richer possibilities of taking in, not merely (perceptual) staring at, not simply bound to one and the same present {possibility}.[19] A certain understanding.

φρόνιμος ["the insightful one"] (cf. 980b21)[20]
μαθητικός ["the learned one"] (cf. 980b21)
φαντασίαι–μνήμη ["images–memory"] (cf. 980b26)

τέχνη–λογισμός (cf. 980b28),[21] "knowing one's way about"–"deliberation." {τέχνη:}[22] "understanding," title for a science: medicine; not "art," not dealing with the practical, but, instead, dealing with the theoretical, ἐπιστήμη (981a3).

ἐμπειρία (980b28) — ἀπειρία (981a5), "experience," not in the theoretical sense, distinguished from thinking, but the difference between being inexperienced and being experienced, practiced.

ἐμπειρία and τέχνη (cf. 981a4), "being experienced in . . . ," "knowing one's way about with understanding." ἐμπειρία has ἐννοήματα (cf. 981a6), taken cognizance of, deliberated, thought over in "many considerations." In each case: if this–then that, as often as this–so often that.

ἐμπειρία ἔχει ὑπόληψιν (cf. 981a7),[23] "also already has its anticipation." Being experienced in what is to be done in each case, καθ᾽ ἕκαστον (981a9). From many experiences arises a single anticipation. καθόλου (981a6), "in general," "on the whole," not in each case if–then, but, rather, because–therefore. The individual cases change: always if this–then that, ὅμοιον ["something alike"] (cf. 981a7). Something always remains the same, recurs, maintains itself throughout; therefore a persistent connection remains. τέχνη is not "in every case if–then," "as often as," i.e., finding the right thing to do from case to case, but is knowing *in advance*, everywhere such experiences have "one and the same outer look," κατ᾽ εἶδος ἕν (981a10), and specifically *because*. "If–then": here the "then" is ambiguous: (1) if–then; (2) because–therefore: delineation of the εἶδος, understanding the why. Being experienced, having cognizance: in every case if this–then that. ἔχει ὑπόληψιν ["has anticipation"] (cf. 981a7): knows in advance what? The *connection* of the if this–then that. Whence arises the possibility of *giving direction*. A healer. A machinist who looks after a machine. Connection of the sequence of processes. *Because* this is such and such, because the physiological state is such and such, *therefore*

19. Editor's interpolation.
20. See Mörchen transcription, no. 3, p. 170f.
21. See Mörchen transcription, no. 3, p. 171.
22. Editor's interpolation.
23. See Mörchen transcription, no. 3, p. 171.

this chemical intervention is possible and necessary. Not simply from case to case, but as an instance of something *universal,* an instance of a factual connection that holds without exception. The connection of the because–therefore is disclosed in this way: that which maintains itself in every case is explicitly seen, is seen *out of* the "empirically" given and is held fast. Thereby arises an understanding that, in a higher sense, is independent of the momentarily given. To this understanding, the being unveils itself more and more, just as it *always* and *properly* is. This is not simply understanding as the potential to understand, but is actually conceiving. He has a *concept.*[24] He can at any time exhibit the being as what it is and why it is such and such. τὸ ὅτι–τὸ διότι (981a29), "whereby"–"wherefore." Cognition, taking cognizance, knowing.

σοφώτερος (cf. 981a25f.):[25] κατὰ τὸ εἰδέναι μᾶλλον ["by seeing more"] (981a27), κατὰ τὸ λόγον ἔχειν ["by possessing the *logos*"] (981b6). ἔχειν λόγον, μετὰ λόγου ["with *logos*"]: "showing" of what something is in itself. τέχνη is therefore μᾶλλον ἐπιστήμη ["more of knowledge"] (cf. 981b8f). δύνασθαι διδάσκει (981b7), it is "able to teach," to show why this is so and that is otherwise, and indeed for all possible cases. αἴσθησις ["sense perception"], even though it grasps what is nearest and what is factual, just as it is at any time, is still not σοφία: for οὐ λέγουσι τὸ διὰ τί ["it does not tell us why"] (981b11f.).

§10. More precise characterization of σοφία
(*Met.* A, chap. 2).

Chap. 1: Idea of σοφία in general predelineated.
Chap. 2: How σοφία itself appears more precisely.
a) Everyday preconception of it;
b) interpretation of what is named in it;
c) its goal is not practical;
d) possibility of appropriating it, living in it: the most proper, most divine science; in it humans are most above and beyond themselves, highest possibility of their Being;
e) transformation of one's Being by possessing it.

Regarding a): Everyday preconception of σοφία[26]

Everyday view of understanding and science:
1. πάντα ["all things"] (982a8),

24. See Mörchen transcription, no. 3, p. 171f.
25. See Mörchen transcription, no. 3, p. 171f.
26. See Mörchen transcription, no. 4, p. 172; cf. GA 19, p. 94ff.

2. χαλεπά ["difficult things"] (982a10),
3. ἀκριβεστάτη ["most rigorous"] (cf. 982a13 and 25) — διδασκαλικὴ μάλιστα ["most instructive"] (cf. 982a13 and 28ff.),
4. ἑαυτῆς ἕνεκεν ["for the sake of itself"] (982a15),
5. ἀρχικωτάτη ["supreme"] (cf. 982a16f. and b4).

Regarding b): Interpretation of what is named in the everyday conception

In all the moments, it is the same thing that is meant. What satisfies the idea of σοφία, as meant in the enumerated characteristics, is the science that deals with the first principles and causes.

This interpretation of the average view of that science and of its proper sense is at once its concrete {?} determination, produced through a positive demonstration of its central motif.

Regarding c): Without practical purpose

οὐ ποιητική, {. . .} ἐκ τῶν πρώτων φιλοσοφησάτων ["not making anything practical, . . . from the first ones who philosophized"] (982b10f.); τὸ θαυμάζειν (982b11f.) — "to wonder" about something, i.e., not simply accept it as evident. Not to accept — the ground thereof is a claim to higher understanding, the will to go beyond mere recognition, not to be content with what is commonly taken as self-evident. τὰ ἄτοπα — "what is not in its place," what cannot be accommodated in one's greatest efforts at understanding, even if that which gives it its peculiarity may be clear to average knowledge. It lends itself to open-ended questioning. He alone wonders who: 1. does not yet understand, but 2. desires to understand. He seeks to escape from ἄγνοια ["ignorance"] (cf. 982b20) and thereby demonstrates that he desires νοεῖν ["apprehension"]. Whence arises διαπορεῖν ["to be at an impasse"] (cf. 982b15). Common sense believes it understands everything, because it is unaware of any higher possibilities of questioning. The one who wonders and questions further does not *make it through*, finds "no way out," ἀπορία (cf. 982b17). Therefore he must seek possibilities, work out the question, master the problem.

The scientific problem is not an arbitrary question, one randomly spit[27] out, but is a deliberately posed question, the predelineation and discussion of possible ways, means, and factual motifs, i.e., motifs offered by the interrogated object itself for its own determination. The most multifarious knowledge of everything possible is not yet science. What is essential (the problem) is a *capacity to question, drawn from, and developed in conformity with, the matter at issue itself.* Hence σοφία μόνη is ἐλευθέρα

---

27. Heidegger uses a word (*spatzen*) in the Swabian dialect that has this meaning.

(982b27), "σοφία alone is free," αὐτὴ ἑαυτῆς ἕνεκεν [existing "for its own sake"] (982b27f.). It is carried out in free openness to the matter at issue. Conformity to the matter at issue is its sole criterion.

Such comportment, i.e., such freedom as unbiased openness to the issues as they show themselves, is, however, something denied to humans. "That is why one might be of the opinion, and indeed justifiably," that σοφία οὐκ ἀνθρωπίνη {. . .} κτῆσις (982b28f.), that σοφία is "not a possible human possession" but is instead a mode of Being, a position toward the world, that humans cannot claim for themselves. For πολλαχῇ γὰρ ἡ φύσις δούλη τῶν ἀνθρώπων ἐστίν (982b29), "in many ways is the nature of man enslaved." Slave to prejudices, slave to prevailing opinion, slave to one's own dispositions, urges, and pretensions. Aristotle cites the poet Simonides,[28] who says it is not seemly for man to grasp after that to which the gods alone are privileged. Accordingly, if the poets are correct and the gods are jealous of presumptuous men, then it must be admitted that men who here venture too far are courting ruin. Neither are the poets correct, however, nor are the gods jealous.[29]

Regarding d): The most proper and most divine science

Once and for all: σοφία is the highest instance of understanding and is science in the proper sense. It is the most divine science. A science is divine insofar as: 1. it is such that God possesses it most properly, and 2. it relates to something divine. Both of these hold for the science of the first principles and causes: 1. God is for all things something like their origin and cause; 2. this science is an absolute and free mode of consideration and thus befits God most of all, who is himself the pure and eternal gazing upon beings and is the "gazing upon this very gazing," νόησις νοήσεως (Met. 1074b34). σοφία is θεολογική ["theology"] (cf. Met. 1026a19).

The highest science is without practical purpose. All the others are therefore, as regards practical life, more urgent and more necessary. But none is of a higher rank with respect to the meaning and the possibility of understanding.

Regarding e): Transformation of one's Being by possessing σοφία

The possession of such knowledge ushers in the state diametrically opposed to un- and pre-scientific comportment. What the common

---

28. Simonides, Ἐπίνικοι. In Poetae Lyrici Graeci, rec. Th. Bergk. 4th ed. Vol. 3: Poetae Melici. Leipzig, 1882. Frag. 5, v. 10, p. 388: θεὸς ἂν μόνος τοῦτ᾿ ἔχοι γέρας, ἄνδρα δ᾿ οὐκ . . . ["God alone would have this privilege, not man"].

29. See Mörchen transcription, no. 5, p. 172f.

understanding wonders at has now become transparent; what the common understanding does not find wonderful becomes for the researcher a problem in the proper sense.

§11. On the concept of ἀρχή and of αἴτιον in Aristotle.

a) On the character of Aristotle's presentation of the previous philosophies: orientation with respect to the guideline, namely Aristotle's theory of the causes. Taking a position on the reproach of proceeding unhistorically.

The object and theme of the most proper science are the first principles and causes, their πλῆθος ["number"] and εἶδος ["outward look"] (983b19).[30] Which are these causes? If this is the most rigorous science, then their number is restricted, even narrowly restricted: *four*.[31] Why this many and why these particular ones? Nowhere is a strict proof given; perhaps the methodological possibilities for such a proof are not even available. Nevertheless, Aristotle saw clearly that something remains open here. He attempts an indirect proof by showing that these four, and no others, were disclosed one after the other. He hopes that this insight will give us a higher πίστις, trust, in the necessity and the character of these causes.

Inquiry concerning those πρότερον {. . .} φιλοσοφήσαντας περὶ τῆς ἀληθείας (983b1ff.) — misleading to say, "those who were first to philosophize on the truth," rather: "those who philosophized on *beings themselves as beings*." φύσις ["nature"], περὶ φύσεως ["on nature"] (983a34f.) — that is, what in anything always already lies at the foundation, what from out of itself is always already present.

The consideration in the subsequent chapters [of the *Metaphysics*] is guided[32] by the working out of the four causes, i.e., by the elaboration of one determinate problem. The charge has therefore been made: Aristotle is proceeding unhistorically. Yes and no. Yes, inasmuch as he applies his own concepts. Culmination: what had previously been unclear, undetermined in its conceptual limits, is now separated out and differentiated. The ones who come afterward do not necessarily understand their predecessors better. They might not understand them at all; but if they do understand them, then in fact better. Better: to pursue to the end the very intentions expressed by the predecessors. In this way, Aristotle is

---

30. On ἀρχή and αἰτία: *Met.* Δ 1 and 2; *Aristotelis Physica.* Rec. C. Prantl. Leipzig, 1879, B 1, 192b8ff., and B 3, 194b16; *Posterior analytics,* B 11, 94a20ff.

31. See Mörchen transcription, no. 6, p. 173.

32. See Mörchen transcription, no. 7, p. 173.

indeed unhistorical. He does not simply report the opinions of his predecessors letter for letter and at the same level of understanding but, instead, tries to comprehend those opinions. This procedure, considered carefully, ought not be called unhistorical; on the contrary, it is *historical* in the *genuine* sense. It would be at variance with the research that is most properly attributable to our predecessors and to the ancients if we were to let that research ossify in the state we received it instead of grasping it *more radically* out of new possibilities.

The unhistoricality of Aristotle's procedure also shows itself in the fact that in his interpretation of the earlier philosophers he works with a concept quite unknown to them: that of ἀρχή. Even the word is rare among them and then simply means "beginning."

In the subsequent chapters, Aristotle does not carry out a full *interpretatio,* but only an overview, a first understanding of the problem. We will begin with a general orientation regarding the concepts of ἀρχή and αἴτιον ["cause"].

b) Determination of the concept of ἀρχή in
Met. Δ, chap. 1.[33]

Word—sound, matter named, meaning, concept. A being is understood, the understanding finds its words, the meaning is explicitly stamped, the concept is formed. Concept formation according to the way the understood being is *determined:* λόγος ["discourse, meaning, definition"]. Catalogue of concepts: περὶ τοῦ πολλαχῶς ["of things said in many ways"], the title Aristotle often uses for it.[34] Basic concepts, and principal concepts, of his philosophical problematic.

The basic concepts, in accord with their high level of generality, are polysemic.[35]

ὁμώνυμον—*aequivocum,* "homonymous," ὄνομα μόνον κοινόν, {. . .} λόγος {. . .} ἕτερος ["only the name in common; the *logos* is different"] (*Cat.* 1, 1a1-2).

33. See Mörchen transcription, no. 8, p. 173f.

34. He also uses the title περὶ τοῦ ποσαχῶς: see W. Jaeger, *Studien zur Entstehungsgeschichte der Metaphysik des Aristoteles.* Berlin, 1912 (henceforth, Jaeger, *Studien*), p. 118f. Jaeger cites the following passages: *Met.* E 4, 1028a4ff.; Z 1, 1028a10f.; Θ 1, 1046a4f.; Θ 8, 1049b4; I 1, 1052a15f.; I 4, 1055b6f.; I 6, 1056b34f.; cf. also *Diogenis Laertii de vitis philosophorum libri X.* Cum indice rerum. Leipzig, 1884, V, 23: Περὶ τῶν ποσαχῶς λεγομένων.

35. Cf. M. S. Boethius, *In Categorias Aristotelis libri IV.* In Boethius, *Opera omnia. Tomus posterior. Patrologia Latina.* Acc. J.-P. Migne. Vol. 64. Paris, 1891, pp. 159-294; P. Abelard, *Glossae super Praedicamenta Aristotelis. Die Glossen zu den Kategorien.* Ed. B. Geyer. In *Beiträge zur Geschichte der Philosophie des Mittelalters.* Texts and investigations. Ed. C. Baeumker. Vol. 21, pt. 2. Münster, 1921, pp. 111-305, esp. 117-118.

συνώνυμον — *univocum*, "univocal," ὄνομα κοινόν {. . .} λόγος {. . .} ὁ αὐτός ["the name in common and the same *logos*"] (*Cat.* 1, 1a7).

παρώνυμον — *denominativum*, "derived in meaning," ὅσα ἀπό τινος διαφέροντα τῇ πτώσει τὴν κατὰ τοὔνομα προσηγορίαν ἔχει ["deriving its name by changing the inflection of a related word"] (*Cat.* 1, 1a12f.), γραμματικὸς ἀπὸ γραμματικῆς ["'grammarian' from the word 'grammar'"] (cf. *Cat.* 1, 1a14).

The ambiguity in the basic concepts, what it signifies and why it is necessary, is not given its own theoretical consideration. Aristotle merely exhibits it factically, though indeed not in an arbitrary enumeration, but by proceeding from the closest, everyday meaning and ascending to the principal meanings, while also fixing the respects in which those meanings are articulated.

ἀρχή — here Aristotle gives the term a much broader and more diverse meaning, on a background which was clarified in *Met.* A.

1. The beginning, that with which something takes its departure, the beginning of a way, of a footpath (1012b34–1013a1).

2. The correct first step, the starting point for learning something, which does not lie in what is highest (the principles) but in what is closest. Examples (1013a1–4).

3. That with which the emergence of something starts, the "foundation" for a building, the keel for a ship, the groundwork, ἐνυπάρχον ["constituent principle"] (cf. 1013a4), specifically such that this "beginning" remains in the thing, is an integral part of it (1013a4–7).

4. That from which the motion emanates, something which is not itself what is in motion or becomes, which remains outside and does not co-constitute the being itself, μὴ ἐνυπάρχον ["not a constituent"] (cf. 1013a7), but which does cause the motion: the impetus. Father and mother for a child, strife for a battle (1013a7–10).

5. That which, by its own decisions and plans, brings something else into motion, thus by leading, guiding, directing, dominating. Such are kings and tyrants, also sciences higher in rank than others, πολιτική ["politics"], ἀρχιτεκτονική ["architecture"] (1013a10–14).

6. That from which something is primarily known. In a proof, the axioms, the principles (1013a14ff.). That which is common:[36] the first, the whence, in a particular sense the earlier than, τὸ πρῶτον εἶναι ὅθεν ["to be the first whence"] (1013a18), in the various orders of Being and of becoming, emerging, coming to be known. Formal concept of ἀρχή: the *first* "whence" . . . , the *last* "back whither." That structure: formal sense of orienting, directing, starting, determining.[37] Cf. *Met.* Δ 17, 1022a12: ἀρχή is πέρας τι, "limit."

36. See Mörchen transcription, no. 9, p. 174.
37. See Supplement no. 1, p. 159.

§12. The question of the causes in the previous philosophy.

a) The working out of the ἀρχή-character of ὕλη in the previous philosophy.

There indeed a questioning of the ἀρχαί ["principles"], but the problem is not explicitly formulated as such; left implicit. περὶ φύσεως (983a34f.): beings in themselves, whence and how they *are, beings in their Being.* περὶ φύσεως,[38] περὶ φύσεως ἱστορία ["research into nature"].[39] οἱ ἀρχαῖοι φυσιολόγοι ["the ancient investigators into nature"] (cf. 986b14). λόγος–φύσις, exhibition of beings in themselves; not a consideration of the possibility and necessity of a knowledge of nature, but a consideration of nature itself. Not simply the reason and cause of the world. Mythical genealogies and cosmologies.[40] The theogony of Hesiod, the cosmogony in Pherecydes of Syros: telling stories about beings; succession.

φύσις: φύειν — "to engender," φύεσθαι — "to grow." 1. the ever enduring,[41] 2. the becoming.[42] Both.[43] The essential: what of itself is always already present without human or divine involvement. The first-named meaning comes closest to the philosophical-ontological signification.

Cause:[44] what is already, first and foremost; what always is. 1. sought in general; 2. what is taken for such. ὕδωρ ["water"] — Thales; ἄπειρον ["the indeterminate"] — Anaximander; ἀήρ ["air"] — Anaximenes. Here cause comes into question in the sense of what is, and remains, always already; but without a concept of cause, without being able to decide what would satisfy this sought cause, and without understanding whether thereby the question of the *Being* of beings has already been answered or indeed has even merely been posed. ὡς τῆς τοιαύτης φύσεως ἀεὶ σοζωμένης φύσις σώζεται, "a being which, from out of itself, is always already there saves itself ever," (983b12f.), the constancy of what is always already present. The gaze of those who were seeking was aimed at that (though without genuinely seeing it), in-

38. See Mörchen transcription, no. 10, p. 174f.

39. Cf. Plato, *Phaedo*, 96a.

40. Cf. E. Cassirer, *Philosophie der symbolischen Formen*, vols. 1–3. Berlin, 1923ff. Vol. 1: *Die Sprache*, p. 13; vol. 2: *Das mythische Denken*, p. 57.

41. J. Burnet, *Early Greek Philosophy*, 3d ed. London, 1920 (henceforth, Burnet), p. 10: "everlasting"; p. 206 and n. 4, p. 205: "which does not pass away"; p. 228. [These quotes from Burnet are in English in Heidegger's text. — Trans.]

42. K. Joel, *Geschichte der antiken Philosophie*. Vol. 1 (*Grundriß der philosophischen Wissenschaften*). Tübingen, 1921, p. 256. Also Joel, *Der Ursprung der Naturphilosophie aus dem Geiste der Mystik*. Basel, 1903 (henceforth, Joel, *Ursprung*), p. 44.

43. A. Lasson, *Über den Zufall*. Berlin, 1918, pp. 52, 58ff.

44. See Mörchen transcription, no. 10, p. 174f.

tended it, was on its way toward it, but was not in a position to grasp it. On the contrary, *a* being was made the ἀρχή of Being. To be sure, at first merely a being, but already precisely *as* a being, in the light of an idea of *Being,* even if this idea was unclear.

What the gaze first strikes, regarding what is constantly present, is that *of which something consists.* ἀρχή—ἐν ὕλης εἴδει (983b7f.), the "from which" in the form, the outward look, of what is material. ὕλη ["matter"]: ὑποκείμενον ["substrate"] (983b16). ὕδωρ—Thales (983b20f.);[45] ἀήρ—Anaximenes (984a5); πῦρ ["fire"]—Heraclitus (984a7f.); γῆ ["earth"] and other factors—Empedocles (984a8f.). Anaxagoras—ἀπειρία τῶν ἀρχῶν ["infinity of principles"] (cf. 984a13), τὰ ὁμοιομερῆ, σύγκρισις–διάκρισις, διαμένειν, ἀΐδια ["things of like parts, conjunction-disjunction, persisting, eternal"] (cf. 984a14ff.). {Stages of development:}[46]

1. Everything consists of one factor, which always already is. Moisture, breath, fire are mere variations. Merely changing aspects of the same thing.
2. Everything consists of several factors. Here already a coming together, combination and separation, connection. Here order and transformation.
3. Everything out of infinitely many factors. Since the causes always are and are everlasting, they are inexhaustible. Constant change and transformation, but indeed no coming to be or passing away. On the contrary, everything remains. Here the source, that which animates; thus change and the incalculable multiplicity are clarified. ὑποκειμένη ὕλη: μόνη αἰτία ["matter as substrate: the only cause"] (cf. 984a17).

b) The question of cause in the sense of the whence of motion. The cause as impetus. The notion of the immobility of all beings.

What has come into prominence thus far? That which always is, ὑποκείμενον, and change, appearing and disappearing; transformation, motion; the thing itself. That is what is given and encountered in causal investigation.

How does it happen that the ὑποκείμενον changes; to what is that indebted? To hold onto the ὕλη is indeed necessary, but not sufficient. ξύλον—κλίνη ["wood—bed"] (cf. 984a24), ἕτερόν τι . . . αἴτιον ["some other cause"] (984a25), thus τὴν ἑτέραν ἀρχὴν ζητεῖν ["to seek another cause"] (984a26), namely, the impetus.

Those who, at the very beginning, followed this path of causal re-

45. See Mörchen transcription, no. 10, p. 174f.
46. Editor's interpolation.

search were satisfied with the one cause. It seemed to them they had thereby achieved understanding. In fact, however, the understanding itself had not yet developed all its possibilities. Science is not the mere acquisition of cognitions, the piling-up of material; on the contrary, new possibilities of questioning constitute the proper development of science itself.

Others who limited their questioning to the ἕν–ὑποκείμενον ["one–substrate"] (984a28ff.) were, so to speak, conquered by this idea, overwhelmed by it. They then excluded not only coming to be and passing away but also any sort of becoming and change. If what is is what always is, then that whose determination lies in change cannot be, for what is changing is not yet and is no longer. ὅλη φύσις ἀκίνητον ["the whole of nature immoveable"] (cf. 984a31)—the entirety of what is, precisely because it is, exists without motion.

Parmenides alone, of these latter, also saw a second cause, though not on the basis of his central doctrine, but only inasmuch as he {assumed}[47] two causes.

Those who postulated many causes fare better in Aristotle's exposition. Fire is what moves, gives an impetus, propels; the other factors are the propelled.

c) The cause of motion in the sense of ordering and ruling.

Following, μετά (984b8), the procedure of these thinkers, and again under the constraint of truth, the second-named cause was also brought into question. For it too was insufficient in relation to the actual γεννῆσαι τὴν τῶν ὄντων φύσιν ["coming to be of the nature of things"] (984b9). It could not provide an understanding of the whence of beings, that beings are just as they are. ἀναγκαζόμενοι ὑπ᾿ αὐτῆς τῆς ἀληθείας (cf. 984b9f.), "constrained by the truth," i.e., by beings lying there uncovered before the eyes. What one then sees are not only what is present-at-hand,[48]change, transformation, impetus, but also beings that have changed in such and such a way, beings that are changing themselves in a particular way. τὸ εὖ ἔχειν (cf. 984b11f.), "in the correct way"; more generally, in a determinate way, not arbitrarily or chaotically. τὸ καλῶς γίγνεσθαι (cf. 984b11f.), "beautifully," in an ordered way. The world is a κόσμος ["order"], a τάξις ["arrangement"]. These determinations of beings themselves are not clarified by the two previously uncovered causes. But the questioning must take into account what shows itself in that way. Fire, or something similar, is not the cause of such determinations, οὔτε ["not so"] (984b12); that is not possible, nor did any of those thinkers believe it was.

---

47. Editor's interpolation.
48. See Mörchen transcription, no. 11, p. 175f.

Instituting the appropriate way, directing, overseeing, instructing, *prescribing*. Order, ordering, disposing, *guiding. Reflection*, sense, for definite reasons [*Gründe*], under the guiding line of a rule, "reason" [»*Vernunft*«[49]]. 1. νοῦν {. . .} ἐνεῖναι (984b15) — "there is reason [*Vernunft*] in this," 2. νοῦν {. . .} αἴτιον τοῦ κόσμου ["it is the cause of the order"] (984b15f.). The cause of order is the cause of beings in general and is what, as effective cause, gives the impetus. Yet the specific character of causality remained hidden to those thinkers.

Not only κόσμος, τάξις (984b34) but also ἀταξία ["disorder"], αἰσχρόν ["ugliness"] (985a1), and these indeed πλείω (985a1), "predominantly," "mainly." νεῖκος–φιλία, "hate and love."

Characterization of the way they worked with these causes: uncertainly, arbitrarily, haltingly (985a11ff.). ἀμυδρῶς μέντοι καὶ οὐδὲν σαφῶς (985a13) — "obscurely and without conceptual determinateness," no proper practice of the scientific method of investigation. Basically they did not go beyond two causes: ὕλη ["matter"] and ἀρχὴ κινήσεως ["impetus of the motion"] (cf. 985a11ff.), and that was reflected in their most advanced scientific interpretations of beings.

d) μὴ ὄν and διαφοραί as causes of ὕλη.

Leucippus, Democritus:[50] στοιχεῖα ["elements"]: τὸ πλῆρες—κενόν ["the plenum—the void"] (985b5). τὸ πλῆρες, στερεόν: τὸ ὄν ["the plenum, the solid: beings"] (985b6f.), τὸ κενόν, μανόν τὸ: μὴ ὄν ["the void, the porous: nonbeings"] (985b7f.). Nonbeings [μὴ ὄν] are, just as much as beings.

The differences in the substrates are the causes of the other things that show themselves. διαφοραί ["differences"]: αἰτίαι (cf. 985b13), σχῆμα—τάξις—θέσις (cf. 985b14f.), "configuration"—"order"—"position." ῥυσμός—διαθιγή—τροπή (cf. 985b15f.), "uniform motion, symmetry, proportion"—"touch"—"turning": directions of possible changes.

Higher generality sought, even if the gaze is restricted to material Being, to *mutual separation in space*. Materialists?

κίνησις ["motion"] itself is not a problem, although constant use is made of this phenomenon. ὕλη—ὅθεν ἡ κίνησις ["matter—the whence of motion"] (985a13).

Thus Aristotle does not merely pursue the question of what in each case was postulated content-wise as a cause but also asks about the extent of the understanding of the causal character as such, about the grasp in each case of the possible and necessary causal function of the cause.

---

49. ["Reason" can translate both *der Grund* (as in the principle of sufficient reason) and *die Vernunft* (the faculty of the soul). Whenever it translates the latter, the German word will be indicated. —Trans.]

50. See Mörchen transcription, no. 12, p. 176.

e) The coming to light of the cause as the τὸ τί in the number theory of the Pythagoreans.

Difficulty: τέλος, οὗ ἕνεκα ["the end, the for the sake of which"]. Not at all yet the τὸ τί ["the this"].[51] But the latter already in Greek science with Parmenides, the Pythagoreans (ἀριθμός ["number"]), and Plato (ἰδέα ["Idea"]).

οἱ καλούμενοι Πυθαγόρειοι ["the so-called Pythagoreans"] (985b23) had given themselves over to the mathematical sciences, had pursued them especially. Having become at home in them, they saw in mathematical principles at the same time the *principles and causes of beings as a whole*.

The Greeks and mathematics: no sources documenting the time and mode of the transmission from the Egyptians or Phoenicians through papyri. Yet the Greeks' ramified {?} commercial relations, as well as their colonies, throughout the Mediterranean area, and their voyages for purposes of trade, culture, and research all testify clearly enough that an exchange had taken place. μάθημα (cf. 985b24), "that which can be taught," what can be demonstrated, science in general. Not accidental: Thales, the first scientific philosopher is also, according to tradition, the first Greek mathematician. Practical as well as theoretical problem: terrestrial navigation, determination of the position of a ship, calculation of its distance from land by means of precise angular measurements.

Special cultivation of mathematics by the so-called Pythagoreans. The principles of mathematics are in the first place ἀριθμοί ["numbers"] (985b26). In them the Pythagoreans believed could be seen ὁμοιώματα πολλὰ τοῖς οὖσι καὶ γιγνομένοις (985b27f.), "many likenesses to things that are and are coming to be." In number they found, e.g., the properties and relations of harmonies. Thus ὑπέλαβον (986a2), "they assumed."[52] The likeness is easier to grasp if it is observed by being presented in the numbers themselves. Moreover, a number itself and its presentation are not sharply separated.

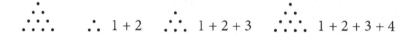

ὄγκοι ["magnitudes"], the series of natural numbers, form of the letter Δ. Numbers articulate and determine figures, space.

So the Pythagoreans tallied up everything in numbers and harmo-

---

51. See Mörchen transcription, no. 13, p. 176.
52. Namely, "that the elements of numbers were the elements of all things." See Mörchen transcription, no. 14, p. 176f.

nies that accords with the states of the heavens and with the universe in general. If some lacuna opened up, they did not shrink from artificial assumptions. For example: ἡ δεκὰς τέλειον (cf. 986a8), "ten," the "complete," "perfect" number. It contains the essence and Being of number in general. Therefore ten is also the number of the orbiting heavenly bodies. Yet only nine are evident in experience, and so διὰ τοῦτο δεκάτην τὴν ἀντίχθονα ποιοῦσιν ["they make the counter-earth the tenth"] (986a11f.).

Aristotle's goal in considering the doctrines and opinions of the Pythagoreans is to lay out which ἀρχαί they postulated καὶ πῶς εἰς τὰς εἰρημένας ἐμπίπτουσιν αἰτίας (986a15), "and how those relate to the four kinds of causes already named." Which of the latter are characteristic of numbers? Have the Pythagoreans said anything precise about that, or did they perhaps not make it clear?

The στοιχεῖα ["elements"] of number are the ἄρτιον ["even"] and the περιττόν ["odd"], the former πεπερασμένον ["finite"], the latter ἄπειρον ["infinite"] (986a18f.). ἕν ["one"] consists of both (986a19f.); it is just as much the former as the latter. Number arises ἐκ τοῦ ἑνός ["out of the one"] (986a20f.). The entire edifice of the world consists in numbers. This shows, according to Aristotle, that the Pythagoreans conceive of numbers as *causes*, specifically in the sense of that of which the world is made up, ὡς ὕλη ["in the sense of matter"] (cf. 986a17).

Other members of this school name ten principles, which they coordinate and place in series in various ways (cf. 986a22f.). Alcmeon of Croton, a younger contemporary of Pythagoras (cf. 986a27 and 29f.): ἐναντιότητες ["opposites"] (cf. 986a32), but ἀδιορίστως ["randomly"] (986a34). That is to say, the ἀρχαί are opposites without its being shown in determinate concepts how those principles and opposites lead back to the familiar four causes. Yet it is clear that ἐκ τούτων γὰρ ὡς ἐνυπαρχόντων συνεστάναι {. . .} τὴν οὐσίαν ["these, as constituent principles, compose what is present"] (986b7f.). This theory of opposites, however, is quite different from the doctrine of development {?} proposed by Empedocles (cf. 986b13ff.). ἴδιον αὐτῶν προσεπέθεσαν: τὸ πεπερασμένον, ἄπειρον ["specific to this school: the limited and the unlimited"] (cf. 987a15f.) were not themselves taken as beings beside other beings, nor as modifications of beings; on the contrary, the limited and the unlimited as such, and also *unity*, were taken as the *Being* of beings, as οὐσία. Therefore, number: οὐσία. This implies, however: περὶ τοῦ τί ἐστιν ἤρξαντο {. . .} λέγειν καὶ ὁρίζεσθαι ["they attempted to discuss and define the 'what'"] (987a20f.), they no longer questioned concerning the matter which things are made up of, nor concerning the impetus of motion, but, instead, they were concerned with what beings themselves are *as* beings, with the meaning of the Being of beings and of their being what they are and as such. Except that λίαν δ' ἁπλῶς ἐμπαγματεύθησαν (987a21f.), "their treatment of this question was, to be sure, still quite primitive." Only ἐπιπολαίως ["superficially"] (987a22, cf. 986b22f.) did they carry out the conceptual determinations. Example.[53]

Explicitly mentioned: Parmenides. Also a principle, consistent with Pythagorean theory, but he understood it in a different sense: τὸ κατὰ τὸν λόγον ἕν ["that which is one according to *logos*"] (cf. 986b19).

This consideration brings us to the problem-horizon opened by Plato in his appropriation of the essential impulses of his predecessors.

f) Plato's way of treating the problem of the causes
(*Met.* A, chap. 6): the Ideas as the Being of
beings, in the sense of the "what."

Plato's way of treating the basic problem (*Met.* A 6) is to determine the cause of the factual states, to determine beings in their principles. Following the Pythagoreans in many respects, but also some ἴδια ["idio-syncracies"] (987a31). In πολλά ["many things"] (987a30), Plato is determined by the Pythagoreans. At a young age, familiar with Craty-lus and the doctrines of Heraclitus: πάντα ῥεῖ, "everything is flowing." Firm tenet: the changing thing given in sense experience is not a pos-sible object of knowledge, not an ἀεὶ ὄν ["eternal being"]. What I know of such a being ceases at once to correspond with it; I no sooner utter the statement that it is such and such than my words have already be-come false.

Knowledge is of the ἀεί ["eternal"] and the κοινόν ["common"]: learned from Socrates, who was the first to direct the mind to the καθόλου ["universal"] and to strive for the ὁρισμός (cf. 987b3), the "delimitation" of the "what," the definition. περὶ μὲν τὰ ἠθικά (987b1), "in the realm of the acting, conduct, and behavior" of hu-mans. Plato is therefore basically of the opinion: the object of knowl-edge is ἕτερον, οὐ τῶν αἰσθητῶν ["other, not one of the sensibles"] (cf. 987b5). τὰ τοιαῦτα τῶν ὄντων ἰδέας ["these other beings are the Ideas"] (987b7f.).[54] τὰ αἰσθητὰ πάντα παρὰ ταῦτα—κατὰ ταῦτα λέγεσθαι πάντα (cf. 987b8f.), "what is seen at any time, the sensible thing beside them [i.e., beside the Ideas], is *addressed as what it is* ac-cording to them [the Ideas]"; ἄνθρωπος ["human being"]. The things seen do not exist in the mode of an ἰδέα (their Being is other) and yet their "what" is determined by (is according to) the ἰδέα. τὰ πολλὰ τῶν συνωνύμων (987b9f.), "the many things that have the same name" and the same λόγος, for example what are called humans and are determined by this "what," are that which they are κατὰ μέθεξιν

53. See Mörchen transcription, no. 15, p. 177.
54. See Mörchen transcription, no. 16, p. 177f.

(987b9), "by way of participation." Pythagoreans: μίμησις (cf. 987b11), "imitation," ὁμοίωσις ["assimilation"]. Plato merely changed the designation. What μέθεξις ["participation"] and μίμησις signify has not been clarified, not even today! The general thrust is insufficient!

εἴδη—αἰσθητά[55] ["ideas—sensibles"], μεταξὺ τὰ μαθηματικά ["mathematical things are in-between"]: ἀΐδια ["eternal"], ἀκίνητα ["unmoving"], but at the same time πολλά ["many"] (cf. 987b14ff.), whereas εἶδος αὐτὸ ἓν ἕκαστον μόνον ["the *eidos* itself in each case is single"] (987b18).

εἴδη: αἴτια {. . .} τοῖς ἄλλοις ["ideas: causes of all else"] (987b18.): στοιχεῖα τῶν εἰδῶν—στοιχεῖα πάντων ["elements of the ideas—elements of everything"] (cf. 987b19f.). οὐσία: ἕν ["what is present: one"] (cf. 987b21). ὕλη: πολλά: τὸ μέγα–μικρόν ["matter: many: the great-small"] (cf. 987b20). Through μέθεξις of these in the ἕν, ἀριθμοί ["numbers"] exist (cf. 987b21f.). Like the Pythagoreans: ἓν οὐσία ["the one is Being"] (cf. 987b22), not other beings among beings; ἀριθμοί are constitutive of beings (cf. 987b24f.). ἴδιον ["individual"] (987b27): (1) the ἄπειρον is itself articulated, doubled: μέγα–μικρόν (cf. 987b26); (2) ἀριθμοί are παρά ["beside"], not αὐτὰ τὰ πράγματα ["the things themselves"] (987b27f.).

The ἕν (οὐσία) and the ἀριθμοί, why are they παρά and in general why ἡ τῶν εἰδῶν εἰσαγωγή ["the bringing in of the Ideas"]?—διὰ τὴν ἐν τοῖς λόγοις {. . .} σκέψιν (987b31f.), "on the basis of a seeing within the λόγοι," because of looking at what, fundamentally, is always already meant in speaking about some thing; for example, bravery in the case of brave persons, science in the case of learned ones. This gaze directed at what is meant a priori is διαλέγεσθαι ["dialectics"] (cf. 987b32). Cf. *Sophist, Philebus.*

Why is the ὕλη doubled? Because from it numbers arise easily, with exception made for the primary numbers.

* * *

Parmenides is not touched on in the present context, because this discussion antedates Plato's turn to him. Specifically, it is only in Plato's later period that Parmenides comes to have special significance for him.

The fact that there breaks through in Parmenides that which came to light in later thinkers, namely in Plato and Aristotle, was seen by Aristotle himself, who stressed and clarified it in his characterization of Parmenides. He also noted a difference with all other preplatonic philosophers and with Parmenides' own students and successors: *Met.* A 5, 986b10-987a2. περὶ τοῦ παντὸς ὡς {. . .} μιᾶς οὔσης φύσεως

---

55. See Mörchen transcription, no. 16, p. 177f.

["about all things as beings of one and the same nature"] (986b11), but they also differ among themselves. The ἀκίνητον ["nonmoving"] (986b17) does not belong in the current discussion. That concerns another problematic.[56] ἔοικε τοῦ κατὰ τὸν λόγον ἑνὸς ἅπτεσθαι ["he (Parmenides) seems to have adhered to that which is one according to *logos*"] (986b19).

Critique of Plato (*Met.* A, chap. 9): οἱ δὲ τὰς ἰδέας αἰτίας τιθέμενοι ["those who put forth the Ideas as causes"] (990a34f.). Cannot go into the details of *Met.* A 8 and 9, since a presupposition for that is a more concrete knowledge of Plato's philosophy, which is precisely what we want to acquire.

56. See *Phys.* A 3.

2

The question of cause and of foundation as a philosophical question

§13. The unclarified connection between the question of cause and the question of Being: posing questions.

Basic problem: the question of the four causes of beings:

1. which are the causes;
2. what in beings themselves satisfies these causes in each case;
3. to determine beings themselves in all fundamental respects;
4. to determine the Being of beings in general;
5. in how many varied ways are beings spoken of.[57]

ὂν τὸ ἁπλῶς λεγόμενον[58] ["Being as said simply"]:[59]

1. ὂν τῶν κατηγοριῶν ["the Being of the categories"];
2. ὂν κατὰ συμβεβηκός ["Being as accidentally supervenient"] (cf. 1026a34);
3. ὂν ὡς ἀληθές ["Being as truth"] (cf. 1026a34f.);
4. ὂν δυνάμει καὶ ἐνεργείᾳ ["Being in the sense of the potential and the actual"] (cf. 1026b1f.).

These four basic meanings of Being were no more determined by Aristotle in their inner connection and their mode of origination out of the idea of Being itself than were the four causes. In no case do these four meanings of Being somehow correspond to the four causes, just as in general it must be said that there is fundamentally nothing here

---

57. Cf. *Met.* A 9, 992b18ff., to which special significance is attached.
58. See Mörchen transcription, no. 17, p. 178.
59. *Met.* E 2, 1026a33.

like a system in the sense of a unitary construction. The idea of system only since the advent of idealism, and behind it a definite notion of how things are laid out in advance. With Aristotle, just as with Plato, on the other hand, everything is open, under way, inchoate, still full of difficulties; nowhere the polish and settled character of a system. With respect to what has been discussed so far, the basic problem is this: why *these* four causes?[60] Why—from which being have the causes been wrested? How has that being been grasped in its Being? What is the connection between the Being of a cause and the Being of a foundation in general? Why do we ask about foundations, reasons? What is the origin and necessity of the "why"? Why do sciences particularly make reasons and causes their theme?

§14. The problem of foundation in modern philosophy.

Modern philosophy:[61] Leibniz: *Principium rationis sufficientis* ["principle of sufficient reason"]. No state of affairs and no event can have meaning without a sufficient reason for it, even if that reason is mostly hidden to us.

Leibniz: principle of sufficient reason:[62] no. 31: "our rational cognitions rest on two great principles: first, on that of contradiction, in virtue of which we designate as false everything that contains a contradiction, and as true everything that contradicts or[63] is opposed to the false" (*Theodicy*[64] §44; §169).[65]

No. 32: "Secondly, on that of sufficient reason, in virtue of which we assume that no fact can be true and existent, no utterance correct, without there being a sufficient reason why it is so and not otherwise, even if the reasons might in most cases be unknown to us" (§44; §169).[66]

Wolff: *Nihil est sine ratione {. . .}, cur potius sit, quam non sit.*[67] "Nothing is without a reason why it is and not rather is not."

60. See Mörchen transcription, no. 18, p. 178f.

61. See Mörchen transcription, no. 19, p. 179f.

62. Cf. *Monadologie* (1714), in: *Die philosophischen Schriften von G. W. Leibniz*, 7 vols., ed. C. J. Gerhardt (Berlin, 1875-1890). (Henceforth, Gerhardt.) Vol. 6, p. 607ff.; *Hauptschriften zur Grundlegung der Philosophie*, trans. A. Buchenau, ed. E. Cassirer (Leipzig, 1904-1906). (Henceforth, Cassirer.) Vol. 2, p. 435ff.

63. "Or" not in Cassirer.

64. "Theodicy" added by Heidegger.

65. Gerhardt, p. 612; Cassirer, p. 443.

66. Gerhardt, loc. cit.; Cassirer, loc. cit.

67. Ch. Wolff, *Philosophia prima sive ontologia*, 2d ed. Frankfurt and Leipzig, 1736. (Henceforth, Wolff.) §70, p. 47.

principium rationis sufficientis fiendi ["principle of the sufficient reason of becoming"],[68]
principium rationis sufficientis cognoscendi ["of being known"] (cf. §876, p. 649),
principium rationis sufficientis essendi ["of being"] (cf. §874, p. 648),
principium rationis sufficientis agendi ["of acting"] (cf. §721, p. 542).
τὸ πρῶτον {. . .} ὅθεν ἢ ἔστιν ἢ γίγνεται ἢ γιγνώσκεται ["the first whence of being or becoming or being known"] (*Met.* Δ 1, 1013a18f.).

Recapitulation

The previous sessions sketched the problematic that confronted the ancient philosopher: the disclosure of the Being of beings.

In Aristotle, the guidelines of the consideration: the four causes. We looked back on the main lines of pre-Aristotelian philosophy. At the end, we looked forward: the problem of foundations or reasons. Principle of sufficient reason, *principium rationis sufficientis. Nihil est sine ratione sufficiente, cur potius sit, quam non sit.*[69] "Nothing is without a sufficient reason why it is rather than is not." Self-evident principle of all research. How to understand it? Whence its necessity? Does the principle arise out of the very Being of that about which it speaks; i.e., from the idea of Being and nonbeing? To answer, we must understand Being itself.

Let us leave Aristotle's problematics in the background and listen now only to the questions raised, and answers posed, by the ancient thinkers themselves.

68. Cf. Wolff, §874, p. 648.
69. Cf. note 67 above.

PART TWO
THE MOST IMPORTANT GREEK THINKERS.
THEIR QUESTIONS AND ANSWERS

SECTION ONE
Philosophy up to Plato

Experience of beings,[1] understanding of Being in them. Concept of Being and thereby a conceptual-philosophical understanding of beings.

From beings to Being. Understanding, concepts; concept—λόγος. Truth. Addressing something *as* something, as *what* it is, which is not some being in it but is its Being, that which every being, as a being, always *"is."* λόγος is not αἴσθησις. σοφία, σοφόν of Heraclitus.

---

1. See Mörchen transcription, no. 20, p. 180f.

1

Milesian philosophy of nature

§15. Thales.[2]

The first philosopher and the "first mathematician," as reported by Proclus in his commentary on bk. 1 of Euclid's *Elements*.[3] Thales is supposed to have known certain geometrical theories, according to Eudemos, the first historian of astronomy and mathematics, and also according to Theophrastus (school of Aristotle), the first historian of philosophy.[4] On the construction {?} of triangles.[5] Thales used geometrical procedures to measure the distance of ships from land. The basics of surveying were known. Which is not to say that Thales himself must already have been explicitly cognizant of the theoretical presuppositions of such measurings. Knowledge of the rules of measuring does not require insight into the theoretical conditions of their possibility and necessity.

Aristotle, who obviously owes his historical information to the golden age of Plato's Academy, is the only source. (Theophrastus, Simplicius, and the doxographers all depend on him.)

1. The earth floats on water.[6]
2. Water is the (material) cause of all beings.[7]

2. Cf. Burnet, p. 40ff.

3. *Procli Diadochi in primum Euclidis elementorum librum commentarii.* Ex recogn. G. Friedlein. Leipzig, 1873 (henceforth, *Procli in primum Euclidis*), prol. 2, B, 38.

4. Cf. Burnet, p. 45, n. 4; *Eudemi Rhodii Peripatetici fragmenta.* Coll. L. Spengel. Berlin, 1864, frag. 94, p. 140; *Theophrasti Eresii opera omnia graeca* rec. lat. interpr. F. Wimmer. Paris, 1866, frag. 40, pp. 423–424.

5. Cf. *Procli in primum Euclidis,* prop. 5, theor. 2, B, 143; prop. 15, theor. 8, B, 171; prop. 26, theor. 17, B, 212.

6. Cf. Aristotle, *Met.* A 3, 983b21f.; *De caelo* B 13, 294a28ff.

7. Cf. Aristotle, *Met.* A 3, 983b21.

3. "All beings are full of demons."[8] "The magnet is alive, for it has the power to move iron."[9] Hylozoism: ὕλη–ψυχή ["matter-soul"], not matter to which is added spirit and life, but both still *unseparated!*[10]

Regarding 2: What is the world made up of? *Water;* from water and back into it. Water *perdures.* Its various states of aggregation: ice, liquid, vapor—understood meteorologically. The seed of all living things is moist: *moisture* is the principle of life. The constant, constancy, the never-changing.

§16. Anaximander.

Born circa 611. Theophrastus is the main source.

How[11] can what is original, lying at the foundation of all beings, itself be one of those beings?

1. Neither something determinate, a "this"; indeterminate in that respect, 2. it itself is not part of a conflict, not an opposite, 3. nor is it limited; instead, it is inexhaustible. φύσις.

The indeterminate,[12] whose essence is thus indeterminateness, cannot be determined more precisely than through the character of indeterminateness. Grounds for the introduction of the ἄπειρον: τῷ οὕτως ἂν μόνον μὴ ὑπολείπειν γένεσιν καὶ φθοράν, εἰ ἄπειρον εἴη ὅθεν ἀφαιρεῖται τὸ γιγνόμενον ["Coming to be and passing away never end, because that from which things come to be is interminable"].[13]

Oppositions: warm–cold, dry–moist, warm in summer—cold in winter. Injustice–impartiality; something prior to both.

Surrounding our world: κόσμοι[14] κατὰ πᾶσαν περίστασιν (πρόσω, ὀπίσω, ἄνω, κάτω, δεξιά, ἀριστερά) ["worlds in all dimensions (in front, behind, above, below, right, left)"],[15] innumerable "worlds," simultaneous. The unlimited which is outside this world "encompasses" all worlds. The worlds are "gods."[16] The philosophers deviate from the usual way of speaking: a god is not an object of adoration or the like but is, instead, a being in the most proper sense. Aristophanes in the

---

8. Cf. *Aristotelis de anima libri III.* Recogn. G. Biehl. Ed. altera curavit O. Apelt. Leipzig, 1911, A 5, 411a8.

9. Cf. *De anima* A 2, 405a20f.

10. See Mörchen transcription, no. 21, p. 181.

11. See Mörchen transcription, no. 22, p. 181.

12. Cf. Aristotle, *Phys.* Γ 5, 204b22ff.

13. *Phys.* Γ 4, 203b18ff.

14. *Phys.* Γ 4, 203b26.

15. *Phys.* Γ 5, 205b32ff.

16. *Phys.* Γ 4, 203b13.

Νεφέλαι [*Clouds*]: the philosophers are ἄθεοι ["atheists"].[17] Theory of the origin of the heavenly bodies, the earth, the moon, and the animals.

{Regarding the ἄπειρον:}[18] Not a sensible, determinate being, but something nonsensible, indeterminate; yet still *a being.*

Something unlimited, bodily in a spatial {?} sense. The exertion needed to grasp Being itself is expressed in the *infinity* of a being which is *prior* to all.

Aristotle always pays special attention to this thinker and often brings up his name. He tries to find in Anaximander a precursor of the idea of the indeterminate πρώτη ὕλη ["prime matter"]: ἀλλὰ καὶ ἐξ ὄντος γίγνεται πάντα, δυνάμει μέντοι ὄντος, ἐκ μὴ ὄντος δὲ ἐνεργείᾳ ["all things come to be out something, something that is potentially and not actually"].[19]

§17. Anaximenes.[20]

Circa 586–526. Theophrastus composed a monograph on him.

μίαν μὲν καί αὐτὸς τὴν ὑποκειμένην φύσιν ["also for him the substrate of nature is one"].[21] Each of his precursors is correct. Thales: a determinate matter; Anaximander: an infinite matter. {From both:}[22] the one determinate, yet infinite, material is always present and decides the essence of any modification. *Condensation-rarefaction,* not simply separation. All differences are now transformations of one homogenous matter, quantitative modes of it: ἀήρ, πνεῦμα—"air," "breath," wind, vapor, fog.[23] The primal matter has the same relation to the world as the breath (soul) has to human life. Idea of *animation, organism,* not mythical.

He had a much stronger influence than did Anaximander on the subsequent thinkers, especially on the Pythagoreans and Anaxagoras. The "philosophy of Anaximenes" came to designate the entire Milesian philosophy of nature.

17. Cf. *Aristophanis Comoediae.* Rec. F. W. Hall, W. M. Geldart. Vol. 1, 2d ed., Oxford, 1906–1907, (henceforth, *Aristophanis Comoediae*), vv. 367, 423, 1241, 1477, 1509.

18. Editor's interpolation.

19. *Met.* Λ 2, 1069b19f.

20. For texts see H. Diels, *Die Fragmente der Vorsokratiker,* Greek and German (henceforth, Diels 1). 4th ed. Berlin, 1922, vol. 1, chap. 3; 6th ed., ed. W. Kranz, vol. 1, chap. 13.

21. Diels 1, 4th ed., chap. 3, A. Life 5; 6th ed., 13 A 5.

22. Editor's interpolation.

23. Cf. Diels 1, 4th ed., 3 B 2; 6th ed., 13 B 2.

§18. The problem of Being. The question of the
relation between Being and becoming and the
question of opposition in general. Transition
to Heraclitus and Parmenides.

Disclosure of the Being of beings as a problem. Previously, *a* being, itself distinguished through the φύσις-character: ὕλη—ἄπειρον—
ἀριθμός. Implicitly an understanding of Being, but no concept. Ever
and again a foray, striving after Being, but always thrown back and
grasping it only as a being. If the Being of a being is not outside it but,
instead, belongs to the being itself, then does Being not again become
a being? Thereby, however, Being indeed becomes explicit and offers
itself as a problem, an ever more pressing one.

Being: what is *always present* and does not first become and then
pass away. On the other hand, in what is present there is also becoming and motion, ἔρως ["love"]. How to understand becoming itself? If
it is a mode of Being, then what about Being? The first thrust into the
domain of Being already introduces a new problematic (that of Being
and becoming), which it was necessary to work out once in an extreme fashion before a new solution could be thought. Not in a leap to
a new cause for explanatory purposes, but to assure oneself in a much
more penetrating way of how beings as a whole show themselves and
of what in them is problematic according to their basic constitution.

The opposition between the permanent and the changing is not the
only one; on the contrary, there are *"opposites"* within occurrences
themselves. Already the fact that opposition is standing out philosophically as such, and indeed not subordinate to something else, but
fundamentally, signifies a new level. At first, there is only an aware-
ness[24] of "now this, then that," a difference. The opposed is other and
yet the same; the most extreme integration into a whole. 1. Opposites
seen, 2. fundamentally grasped {?} as such in the natural, everyday
experience of Dasein: day and night, death–life, waking and sleep,
sickness–health, summer–winter. Not arbitrary, as for example stone
and triangle, sun and tree. Opposition is not mere difference; it is *counter-striving within a unity.* It is not the mere succession of changing
things; instead, *oppositionality* constitutes the very *Being* of the being.
The consideration thereby lies at a higher level.

Everything in the world is opposition:

1. the opposites *exclude one another;* the one *is not* the other; in what
is opposite is nonbeing, and thus the opposite is *not at all.* Only the
being itself is Being. Parmenides.

24. See Mörchen transcription, no. 23, p. 182.

2. they *condition one another;* the one *is also* the other; the counter-striving things harmonize, and thus opposition is the *essence of all things*. Only oppositionality is the true world. Heraclitus.

2

Heraclitus

Heraclitus ὁ σκοτεινός ["the obscure"],[25] born between 544 and 540.

---

§19. The principle of Heraclitean thought.

According to the testimony of Diogenes Laertius, Socrates already said: "You have to be a good swimmer to make headway here."[26]

Philosophy of nature: Stoa. Philo. Church fathers: Justin, Hyppolitus.[27] Gnostic interpretation.[28]

Usual view: 1. very close attachment to the Milesian philosophy of nature (cf. Aristotle: ὕδωρ, ἀήρ, πῦρ[29]), 2. *prior* to Parmenides. [But according to] Reinhardt: 1. *not* a philosopher of nature,[30] 2. *after* Parmenides, since he explicitly responds to the problem of opposition.[31] Thus he does not stand in the line of transmission of the doctrines of the Milesian philosophy of nature but, instead, in the line of Parmenides.[32]

---

25. See Mörchen transcription, no. 24, p. 182.

26. Cf. Diogenes Laertius, *Leben und Meinungen berühmter Philosophen.* Trans. and comm. O. Apelt. Leipzig, 1921, bk. 2, 22, and bk. 9, 11-12.

27. Cf. Hippolytus, *Werke.* Vol. 3. *Refutatio omnium haeresium.* Ed. P. Wendland. Leipzig, 1916, bk. 9, chaps. 9-10, pp. 241-245; Clemens Alexandrinus, *Stromata.* Ibid., vol. 2. Bks. 1-6, ed. O. Stahlin. Leipzig, 1906, bks. 2-6, pp. 117-435.

28. This partially still in Windelband's {?} history of philosophy: W. Windelband, *Geschichte der abendländischen Philosophie im Altertum.* 4th ed., ed. A. Goedeckemeyer. München, 1923.

29. *Met.* A 3, 984a7f.

30. K. Reinhardt, *Parmenides und die Geschichte der griechischen Philosophie.* Bonn, 1916, pp. 201-202.

31. Ibid., pp. 200-201.

32. Ibid., p. 202.

To resolve an ontological problem, that of opposition, by means of physics. The theory of opposition is not a side issue but is the *genuine problem*. Not a question in cosmogony: to lead over, by mechanical processes, from the original state to the current configuration of the world.

Change occurs by force of law, of ταὐτόν ["the same"].[33] Heraclitus's principle is not fire but, rather, ἕν τὸ σοφόν, λόγος ["one thing is wise, *logos*"]. Fire is only a form of appearance of cosmic reason [*Weltvernunft*]. πῦρ—πάντα ῥεῖ["fire—all things are flowing"]; instead, {?}: {?}[34] is change *and* permanence. This *Unity in what is opposed* is θεός ["God"].[35] Not πάντα ῥεῖ; *no* single fragment says: everything is mere transition and change, nowhere duration and perseverance. On the contrary, *perseverance in change*, ταὐτόν ["sameness"] in μεταπίπτειν ["alteration"], μέτρον ["measure"] in μεταβάλλειν ["change"]. Everything in the world is ταὐτόν; the warm cold, the cold warm.

§20. The main themes of Heraclitean thought.[36]

Opposition and unity, ἕν τὸ σοφόν ["one thing is wise"] (frag. 32), παλίντροπος ἁρμονίη, "counter-striving concord" (frag. 51). Fire as symbol. Reason [*Vernunft*]: λόγος. Soul: ψυχή.

Text: 126 fragments.[37] In what follows, a selection of the ones philosophically important for our problematic.

a) The question of oppositionality and unity.

The principle[38] is the One, the All-wise, θεός. Frags. 108, 67, 78, 102. Frag. 56: what is not to be seen or grasped as a being, as something present-at-hand, but can be apprehended only in the *understanding* and is *different from all beings*. Everything is opposition and tension; therefore oppositionality is not to be avoided in order to fasten onto one of the members. Instead, the *entire oppositionality itself*. Frags. 60, 61, 62. Frag. 126: everything becomes its opposite. Frag. 111.

Everything is *harmony*, ταὐτόν (and measure, limit). Frags. 88, 54, 51. Frag. 103: κύκλος ["circle"]. Frag. 8.

Fire as symbol: frag. 90. Everlasting perdurance in change: frag. 30.

33. Cf. frag. 88.
34. The passage could not be deciphered.
35. Cf. the explication in §20a.
36. See Mörchen transcription, no. 25, p. 182ff.
37. In Diels 1, 4th ed., 12 B; 6th ed., 22 B.
38. See Mörchen transcription, no. 25, p. 183f.

Sextus Empiricus: οὐσία κρόνου σωματική ["the bodily presence of time"].[39] The true essence is time itself. Hegel: abstract intuition of the process; the intuited becoming. Harmoniously out of what is absolutely opposed.

b) λόγος[40] as principle of beings.

ἓν πάντα ["all things one"]: frags. 50, 41.
  Frag. 1: λόγος:

1. Speech, word: a) the disclosed, λεγόμενον ["the uttered"], what *is* in the proper sense, what is understandable, the meaning. The manifested being itself as manifest; binding on everyone as this *very thing that has become understandable.* b) the disclosing, λέγειν. Not yet mere foundation, but that itself which *makes* something like a foundation *accessible.*
2. Reason [*Vernunft*].
3. Foundation: ὑποκείμενον.
4. What is addressed as something, in relation to, relatedness, proportion. Euclid.

Frag. 2, frag. 114: λόγος is *common*, withdrawn from the arbitrary, from random opinion. Frag. 29.

c) Disclosure and determination of the soul.[41]

ψυχή: frags. 115, 116, 45. Understanding, insight. What alone makes beings accessible in their Being. The soul augments itself, uncovers from itself, and pursues what is still covered up, unfolding out of itself the richness of meaning.

d) Assessment of Heraclitus's philosophy and transition to Parmenides.

All this amounts to a new position: the Being of beings, and sense, law, "rule." Penetration into Being: the common, that which lies beyond every being, but which at the same time is in λόγος. Understanding.

Parmenides: Aristotle: ἀδύνατον {. . .} ταὐτὸν ὑπολαμβάνειν εἶναι καὶ μὴ εἶναι ["impossible to accept the same thing as being and not being"].[42] {Heraclitus:}[43] The oppositional *is*, conflict; the dialectical itself in the Hegelian sense. The movement of constant opposition

---

39. Cf. *Adversus mathematicos* 10, 217/1. In *Opera.* Ed. H. Mutschmann, vol. 2. Leipzig, 1914 (henceforth, *Adversus mathematicos*), p. 348.
40. See Mörchen transcription, no. 26, p. 184.
41. See Mörchen transcription, no. 27, p. 184f.
42. *Met.* Γ 3, 1005b23f.
43. Editor's interpolation.

and sublation is the principle. Therefore Hegel already places Heraclitus *after* Parmenides and sees in him a higher level of development.[44] Being and nonbeing are abstractions. Becoming is the first "truth," the true essence, time itself.[45]

The higher level of the analysis of beings is accompanied by a more original grasp of λόγος and spirit, understanding. With Parmenides, who advances conceptual work, specifically in connection with a new solution of the problem, it is the same; indeed not λόγος–ψυχή, but that at which all cognition and conceptualization as such aim. *Truth* itself steps into the ambit of reflection, specifically in the strictest connection with the problem of Being. From this point on, the position remains unchanged until we arrive at the thesis: Being is only in consciousness and is unthinkable otherwise.

Back {to Heraclitus}:[46] the problem of opposition is his accomplishment. In opposition there is negativity, nonbeing, and thus opposition itself is not a being. Heraclitus has taken nonbeing itself ontically and has understood this ontic determination as an ontological one.

44. Cf. G. W. F. Hegel, *Vorlesungen über die Geschichte der Philosophie.* Ed. K. L. Michelet. Vol. 1, *G. W. F. Hegel's Werke* (henceforth, Hegel *WW*). Vol. 13. Berlin, 1833, pp. 327-328.

45. Ibid., pp. 334, 338-339.

46. Editor's interpolation.

3

Parmenides and the Eleatics

Reinhardt's investigations[47] unsettled the earlier approach to the interpretation, not only with respect to the relation of Parmenides (of Elea, born 540) to Heraclitus, but also with respect to the position of Parmenides within Eleatic philosophy itself: Xenophanes was taken to be the teacher, Parmenides the student who supposedly de-theologized the former's theological speculations.[48] One forgets that scientific and philosophical questioning never arises from without {?}, as if it were produced by simply continuing something else, but instead requires an independent questioning. And in this domain belief and superstition come to an end—in the Being of autonomous questioning and of concepts in general {?}.

§21. The problem of the relation between the two parts of Parmenides' didactic poem.

Parmenides: his didactic poem περὶ φύσεως ["On nature"].[49] Problem: Being. Only unity, the non-oppositional, *is*. And Being is graspable in νοεῖν ["apprehension, understanding"]; the way of understanding, the only true thing, truth.

But the didactic poem also has a second part:[50] on the world of becoming, φύσις, that which is not, the mere object of δόξα ["opinion"]. How can Parmenides treat of this and even want to clarify it and thus provide its "truth"? The connection of the two parts is a much-discussed problem in the history of philosophy.

47. Cf. above, §19, n. 5.

48. Joel, *Ursprung*, p. 83.

49. In Diels 1, 4th. ed., 18B; 6th ed., 28B. Also printed separately: H. Diels, *Parmenides, Lehrgedicht*. Greek and German. Berlin, 1897. (Henceforth, Diels, *Lehrgedicht*.)

50. Cf. frag. 8, vv. 50ff.; frag. 1, vv. 28ff.

Zeller,[51] Wilamowitz:[52] in the second part Parmenides is not offering fully valid truth but the *most probable hypothesis* that would make becoming understandable. This interpretation, however, comes out of the horizon of nineteenth-century natural science and overlooks the fact that it is precisely Parmenides who emphasizes that, with respect to truth, there are no degrees, no partaking in the one side as well as the other. On the contrary, truth, just like Being and nonbeing, is absolute. Either-or: truth or mere semblance.

Diels,[53] Burnet:[54] Parmenides is not offering here his own opinion and clarification but is only *reporting* the opinions of others, the Pythagoreans. Against this, it has rightfully been objected that Parmenides would have to understand these opinions precisely as opinions, i.e., for him, as nonbeing. How could he possibly report on futile human delusions, especially in the very context of a doctrinal presentation of truth!

Joel:[55] the second part only a *disputational exercise,* mere eristics. For what purpose? An opportunity for a discussion that merely teaches how to gain one's point and refute others. But are we supposed to believe that a thinker of Parmenides' rank would stoop to this activity and would lend his support to such goings-on?

Reinhardt drove these conceptions from the field, convincingly proving them to be impossible. At the same time, he made a positive contribution by indicating a new possibility, though he did not touch the heart of the genuine problematic. According to him, the second part is an essential component of Parmenides' theory of knowledge. "Theory of knowledge" in Greek philosophy—beware! Problem of truth in the strictest connection to the problem of Being. To the *Being* of *truth* belongs *essentially* the *untruth.* Proof that error has its foundation, in whatever way it has entered the world. For Parmenides, the most proper possibility of truth presupposes untruth. Not change and becoming, but *doxa itself* as *belonging to truth.*[56] More precision in the actual interpretation.

Truth-Being: the most intimate connection. Being and knowledge, Being and consciousness. ὄν–λόγος–ἰδέα–εἶδος–λόγος ["Being-discourse-Idea-outward look-discourse"]. *Through and in the one truth, the one Being; and only in Being, truth.*

The goddess of truth shows and leads the way to the disclosure of

51. Zeller, part 1: *Allgemeine Einleitung. Vorsokratische Philosophie.* First half-volume, pp. 725-726.

52. U. v. Wilamowitz-Moellendorf, "Lesefrüchte." In *Hermes: Zeitschrift für Classische Philologie.* Ed. G. Kaibel and C. Robert. 34, 1899, p. 203ff.

53. Diels, *Lehrgedicht,* p. 63, 101.

54. Burnet, pp. 184ff.

55. K. Joel, *Geschichte der antiken Philosophie.* Vol. 1. (*Grundriß der philosophischen Wissenschaften.*) Tübingen, 1921, pp. 435-436.

56. Cf. Plato, *Theatetus,* 183Ef.

Being as such. She keeps him far from the other way. But he must still understand that other way at the same time. Thus it is clear: the cause of error is not overcome through refutation and proof of impossible consequences, but only if error is understood in its origin.

Two ways:[57] explicit and constant emphasis on the ὁδός–μέθοδος ["way-method"].

The *way of semblance:* semblance is what merely appears outwardly to be such and such but is not so. Semblance is the rival of that which *shows itself.* What of itself compels on this path is always already the πολύπειρον ἔθος (cf. frag. 7, v. 3), the "habit of those with much experience," the usual, that which is commonly known and said about things. ἀκουή–γλῶσσα–ὄμμα ["hearsay-tongue-eye"] (cf. frag. 7, v. 4f.), immediate appearance. We are always already on this necessary way. Insofar as Dasein is, it is also already in the untruth. This way is not something that simply lies off the beaten track, to which one occasionally strays; on the contrary, Dasein is already on this way, insofar as Dasein is under way at all.

κρίνειν λόγωι (cf. frag. 7, v. 5), "to distinguish and decide in and from reflection" on the two possibilities. Then all that will remain is to resolutely follow one of the ways. Free openness to the things and not mere chatter. Science is not arbitrary, taken up on a whim, but is a choice on the basis of reflection; that only in *conceptualization,* λόγος.[58]

§22. Interpretation of Parmenides' didactic poem.

a) The first part of the didactic poem: the way of truth.

Which is the attitude corresponding to the way of truth, what is the proper mode of research, and what shows itself there? λεῦσσε {. . .} νόωι (frag. 2 {4}, v. 1), "see with reason [*Vernunft*]," ask, how beings are in themselves, and do not adhere to what is said about them!

ὅμως ἀπεόντα λεῦσσε παρεόντα βεβαίως, "as to what is nevertheless absent, see it with a sure gaze as present in its presence, for this gaze will not sever beings from their context" (cf. ibid., vv. 1-2).[59] Such a gaze does not see any isolated being, which, as this, is not that, but sees only the one Being itself. This gaze does not veil reality. It sees what every being is, it has Being present to it, whether the being is absent and removed or not.

---

57. Diels 1, 4th ed., 18B1, vv. 28ff.; 6th ed., 28B1; cf. frags. 4, 6 and 7. The numeration of the 6th ed. will henceforth be placed in braces ({}) when it diverges from that of the 4th ed. used by Heidegger.

58. Cf. the first lecture; see above, p. 3.

59. See Mörchen transcription, no. 28, p. 185.

ὄν is ξυνόν (frag. 3 {5}, v. 1), beings are "syncretic" [»zusammensei-end«], ἔχεσθαι ["holding together"] (frag. 2 {4}, v. 2), συνεχές ["self-co-hesive"] (frag. 8, v. 6). Every being, *as* a being, is the One, the Whole, Being. *Unity* and *wholeness of Being;* "oppositionlessness." *Presence* of a being, even if it may be absent. Accessible in νοεῖν (frag. 2 {4}, v. 1: νόωι), in "perception," in reflection on the being and on its sense, i.e., on *Being.* It is not a matter of a peculiar faculty, an occult science, an insight occasioned by some special technique, nor is it mystagogy or theosophy; on the contrary, it is the way of the closest-lying conceptual work.

The two ways are now to be determined more precisely. The first: νοῦς, conceptual determination; the One, the Whole, Being. What beings are in themselves, undistorted; truth, Being. The other: δόξα, "semblance," idle talk; the multifarious in what is otherwise, the equivocal {?}, opposition, nonbeing. Semblance distorts, since the many individuals are not the One.

Correlation of truth, reflection, and Being; they belong together, they are the same. Only in reflection does Being offer itself, and it *is* only what is grasped of it in reflection. *Identity of thinking and Being!* Idealism. Beings are not that which clarifies.

| Beings are. | Being is. |
| Nonbeings are not. | Nonbeing is not. |

Nonbeings are, nonbeing is: as possibility and modality of Being. Explicit affirmation: it cannot be proved that nonbeings are (frag. 7, v. 1). Plato's problem: whether nonbeings might not indeed be.[60]

There remain only the beings of the first way; taking that path, the result is: beings are (frag. 8). On that path occur many σήματα (frag. 8, v. 2), "signs," in which *Being* becomes visible, *shows itself.* In carrying on to the end the pure, unfalsified reflection, one that is not diverted as a method into reports and stories about beings but, instead, asks about Being itself, then this latter shows itself in the following characters:

ἀγένητον   (frag. 8, v. 3) — "unborn"; it did not ever first come to be, at no earlier time was it not.

ἀνώλεθρον   (ibid.) — "undying"; it will never pass away, at no later time will it not be.

οὖλον   (v. 4 in 4th ed.[61]) — "a whole"; it is not patched together from parts, ones that could be added or subtracted.

60. Plato, *Sophist,* 241D.

61. Instead of οὖλον and the next character, μουνογενές, W. Kranz, the editor of the 6th ed., follows the reading of Plutarch and Proclus and substitutes: ἔστι γὰρ οὐλομελές ["for it is whole"].

μουνογενές	(v. 4 in 4th ed.[62]) — "unique"; there are no more of the same, for whatever else could be or is, is uniquely *Being*.
ἀτρεμές	(v. 4) — "unshakable"; Being cannot be taken away. Being is nothing further than, and nothing other than, the fact that it *is*.
ἀτέλεστον	(ibid.) — "without end"; not a thing that somewhere or in some way comes to an end or to limits. Being has nothing against which it could be delimited as a being.
οὐδέ ποτ᾽ ἦν	(v. 5) — "never was it"; in it there is no past, nothing that once was present earlier.
οὐδέ ποτ᾽ ἔσται	(v. 5: οὐδ᾽ ἔσται) — "never will it be"; in it there is no future, nothing that will only later be present.
ἐπεὶ νῦν ἔστιν ὁμοῦ	(ibid.) — "because it is the now itself"; only the now, *constant presence* itself.
πᾶν	(ibid.) — "altogether"; through and through only now.
ἕν	(v. 6) — as this, it is pure now and nothing else. *One*, never other, no difference, no opposite.
συνεχές	(ibid.) — "self-cohesive"; in every now as now, in itself as itself.

Verses 5 and 6 of frag. 8 provide the most pointed interpretation of Being. It is telling that this interpretation is carried out with the help of *time and its characters,* indeed to the effect that the *now alone is,* along with whatever is in the now. The now, however, is always constant in every now. Being is *constant presence*. The now is the same in every now. Being is, in what it is, constantly without opposition or difference.

This connection, namely that in the determination of Being there is also a determination of time, has never been heeded previously, or has only been noted superficially. Differences of Being with respect to time: temporal Being: the real; non-temporal Being: the ideal; super-temporal Being: the metaphysical. Why and whence this connection, with what justification? How does time come to serve as criterion to differentiate the various modes of Being? We see already a first attempt by philosophy to gain a concept of Being by referring to time, though without explicitly naming and analyzing time itself. Something compelled by the factual connection between Being and time, obscure for the Greeks and still obscure today. In our interpretation we must emphasize the orientation toward the phenomenon of time and make clear that only in this perspective do the peculiar predicates applied to Being become understandable.

62. See previous note.

It is neither to be expressed nor maintained: Being ever once was not. To say that Being is *not* is precisely to say: *Being is*. What could it have been that impelled Being to come forth out of nonbeing? Being either is or is not. γένεσις ἀπέσβεσται (frag. 8, v. 21) —"all becoming (change) and difference have been obliterated." ἄπυστος ὄλεθρος (ibid.) —"passing away has disappeared." Change and difference are not.

Unity and self-sameness are explicitly effected anew. οὐδὲ διαιρετόν (v. 22) —"not to be split asunder." The now is always the now. If we, so to speak, divided the now and set off small moments in a now, they would always only be nows, always the now itself: seconds, thousandths of a second, millionths of a second are, when they are, the now. The now is constantly in every now. The non-now is not now and never is now; on the contrary, what is is always only the now.

ἐπεὶ πᾶν {. . .} ὁμοῖον (v. 22) —"for in the whole thoroughly homogeneous"; it does not become other, of another genus than the now.

Not μᾶλλον (v. 23) —not "more" now, and not χειρότερον (v. 24) —not "less" now. The now has no degrees, is never more weakly or more strongly the now, but is always only uniformly the now.

πᾶν δ᾽ ἔμπλεόν ἐστιν ἐόντος (ibid.) —Being "is entirely full of Being." The now consists of nothing other than the now.

ἐὸν γὰρ ἐόντι πελάζει (v. 25) —"one being abuts another," "comes close," is most close. One now abuts another, without a break. ξυνεχές (ibid.) —everything is in the now and is itself the now.

ἀκίνητον (v. 26) —"without motion"; it is always the now, the constant which stays. Kant, who understands time as the order of succession, the way all his predecessors did, also claims: time stays.[63] Time is only in the now. The now is constant, it stays; time stays. "Without beginning or end, because coming to be and passing away are precluded from it" (v. 27f.). ἀπῶσε δὲ πίστις ἀληθής (v. 28) —"the adherence to what shows itself uncovered in itself, as a being," which sees only *the now*. ταὐτόν τ᾽ ἐν ταὐτῶι τε μένον καθ᾽ ἑαυτό τε κεῖται (v. 29) —"the same, remaining in its self-sameness, lies there constantly present in itself." The now *is* in every now constantly itself.[64]

To determine Being more precisely and to take up anew the abovementioned thesis: *identity of Being and thinking*. "The perceptual-reflective apprehension of beings is the same as that on account of which the apprehended is what it is" (v. 34). What is apprehended is beings; to them apprehension as an apprehension of . . . is necessarily related. "You will not find an apprehending without the beings" which it apprehends and "in which it is expressed" (v. 35f.), which it manifests. What is apprehended, what is sought, is what is expressed about beings. *The apprehend-*

63. *Kritik der reinen Vernunft*, B 224-225.
64. See Mörchen transcription, no. 28a, p. 185f.

ing of . . . is *essentially related to beings.* It exists only through and with them. It itself is precisely what beings are: Being. Being and apprehending: apprehending is apprehension of beings, is itself *Being! Intentionality.*

"Like a well-rounded sphere" (v. 43), determined in itself and thus without end, "equally expansive from the middle in all directions" (v. 44). Uniform, now and only now, constant. σφαῖρα ["sphere"] (cf. v. 43): revolution of the sun, of the heavens. χρόνος ["time"]!

b) The second part of the didactic poem: the way of semblance.[65]

The second part: "theory of knowledge." Text: frag. 19: κατὰ δόξαν (v. 1), it only appears outwardly as a being, for now it is and already it is no longer. And it is, so to speak, captured in the names, which remain, whereas the thing named passes away. Thus people's words are empty sounds, empty husks, that provide nothing of reality. So there is no relying on things said.

Solely Being itself is. All δόξα adheres to the changeable and the changing, namely what is not now, not yet, or not anymore.

The power of reflection on Being, unprecedented certainty in linguistic formulation.

Parmenides: unity, uniqueness, wholeness, and immutability of Being. *Positively* on the basis of the phenomenon of time.

Zeno: if one accepts the opposite, viz., plurality and becoming, then arise contradiction and absurdity. *Negatively* on the basis of consequences.

§23. Zeno of Elea.

Born 489. εὐμήκη δὲ καὶ χαρίεντα ἰδεῖν—"tall and of pleasing appearance."[66]

a) Zeno's attempt to provide arguments contradicting the possibility of plurality and motion.

It is in dialogue with Socrates that Zeno clarifies the aim of his treatise:[67] "In truth my writing means to lend support to Parmenides' thesis by arguing against those who undertake to ridicule it and who claim to show that, if Being is one, many laughable things follow, including ἐναντία αὐτῷ (128d2), things that 'contradict the thesis itself.' My writing is directed against these people and gives them back an even stronger dose of their own medicine by seeking to demonstrate that their ὑπόθεσις, approach, basic thesis, εἰ πολλά ἐστιν ["if there are

65. See Mörchen transcription, no. 29, p. 186.
66. Plato, *Parmenides*, 127B4f.
67. Cf. *Parmenides*, 128C6–D.

many things"] (128d5f.), leads to even greater absurdities ἢ ἡ τοῦ ἓν εἶναι (128d6) — 'than does the thesis of the unity and uniqueness of Being,' as long as one investigates the matter with sufficient rigor."

εἰ πολλά ἐστιν, what then? He pursues the consequences of this ὑπόθεσις, on the basis of Parmenides' conception of Being. ὑπόθεσις: setting forth a contention as a problem to resolve. If τὰ συμβαίνοντα ["the consequences"] are impossible, then the ὑπόθεσις is destroyed. Zeno does not provide a new positive clarification of the philosophy of Being but only argumentation to overpower the denial of Parmenides' thesis.

Zeno's proofs regarding unity and multiplicity were preserved by Simplicius.[68] Those regarding motion: Aristotle, *Physics* Z 9.[69]

Combating a science of multiplicity and motion. Dialectical subversion of the idea of multiplicities as integrated out of unities. *Against* the Pythagoreans: the principle of beings is number, the presupposition and determination of ἁρμονία ["harmony"]; number is discrete multiplicity. {Zeno}:[70] inconsistency of this idea itself. (Against the unity of oppositionality, Heraclitus!) The whole is put together out of parts, their result. How are these, as parts, supposed to confer on the whole, as a whole, a quality, wholeness, they themselves do not possess?

1. The problem of spatial magnitudes.
2. The idea of quantitative relations in general.
3. The problem of motion.

Regarding 1:[71] a) The elements of spatial magnitudes are non-spatial. How is space supposed to arise through an agglomeration of non-spatial elements? b) The elements themselves are spatial, in a place in space. Everything that is, is in space. But then space, too, is in space, and so on *in infinitum*.[72]

Regarding 2: Putting together Pythagorean elements yields either a) no determinate magnitude at all, or b) an infinite one. Regarding a): out of sheer ciphers no magnitude can come to be. Regarding b): if out of magnitudes, ὄγκοι, then between any two there are always further magnitudes, *in infinitum*.[73] Nothing determinable: nothing. Indeterminate: nothing.

Regarding 3: *Motion:* a) broken down into elements which do not

68. Diels 1, 4th ed., 19B2 and 3 {29B2 and 3}.
69. 239b9ff. in Diels 1, 4th ed., 19A25–28 {29A25–28}.
70. Editor's interpolation.
71. See Mörchen transcription, no. 30, p. 186f.
72. Diels 1, 4th ed., 19A24 {29A24}.
73. Cf. Diels 1, 4th ed., 19B1 {29B1}.

move; b) broken down into elements in which the μεταβολή ["change"] is preserved.

Regarding 3a: Motion: totality of positions in space. Is that motion or not rather its opposite? A juxtaposition of locations results in rest! In every now a here; in every now, in the whole of time, a totality of heres will never yield motion.

Regarding 3b: Motion put together out of very small motions. Smallest transition from one motion to another; but within these transitions themselves are always more transitions. The closest nearness still infinitely distant. Prior to every place that needs to be traversed there always lies another one. The moving body does not at all advance. Therefore slower and faster cannot be distinguished. The fastest can never catch up to the slowest.

b) Four examples refuting the possibility of motion.

1. στάδιον: "You can never reach the end of a racecourse" (οὐκ ἐνδέχεται {. . .} τὸ στάδιον διελθεῖν[74]).
2. Ἀχιλλεύς: Achilles will never catch up to the tortoise.[75]
3. ἡ ὀϊστὸς φερομένη ἕστηκεν: "The flying arrow is stationary" (Phys. 239b30).
4. χρόνος (cf. Phys. 240a1).[76]

Regarding 1: "You can never reach the end of a racecourse." You can never traverse an infinite number of points in a finite time. You must traverse half of a given distance before you can traverse the whole. That goes on ad infinitum, since an infinite number of points are in any given distance; and you cannot, in a finite time, touch an infinite number of points, one after the other. a) a given distance (racecourse): breaks down into an infinite number of points; b) to traverse an infinite number of nows (each of which can also be infinitely divided!). No moving object, however fast it moves, can traverse any distance at all. Neither the spatial interval nor the temporal span, neither space nor time, but the *continuum* as such, συνεχές. As the continuum, it is the indeterminable nothing; how can it be determined, illustrated, finitely?

Regarding 2: Achilles will never catch up to the tortoise. He must first reach the place from which the tortoise has set out. During this time the tortoise will have advanced over a further portion of the way. Achilles must now cross this portion, but the tortoise will again be further off. He is always coming closer to the tortoise but never reaches

74. Aristotle, *Topica cum libro de sophisticis elenchis.* E schedis J. Strache ed. M. Wallies. Leipzig, 1923, Θ 8, 160b8f.

75. Cf. Aristotle, *Phys.* Z 9, 239b14ff.

76. Cf. Burnet, p. 291, n. 3; pp. 319-320.

it. Some distance always remains. No matter how slow the tortoise moves, it always traverses an infinite distance, and so Achilles can never catch up, for even a small and ever-diminishing distance remains infinite and cannot be crossed in a finite time.

Regarding 3: The flying arrow is stationary (stopped). For if a thing is stationary as soon as it occupies a place equal to itself, and if what is in flight does always occupy, at every moment, a place equal to itself, then it cannot move. Every moment, every now, is a here. The whole of time, the sum of the nows of motion, is a sum of heres. No "from here to there," since this again is an infinite sum of heres.

The arrow never "is" at a point of its trajectory. Being = presence, for "now" here, "now" there; since flight—trajectory. Being = presence, standing, standing over (object), standing against (resistance).

Regarding 4:[77] "Half of a time can be equal to the whole."[78] Let there be three series, A, B, and C, of ὄγκοι. Let B and C move with equal speed in opposite directions. The moment all three series line up, B has passed twice as many points of C as of A. Therefore

t_C here $= t_A$. But $t_C = t_B = \dfrac{t_A}{2}$

$t_C = t_A$

	Starting position:		*End position:*
(Stationary).	. . . .	A	. . . . A
(Moving)	. . . .)	B	. . . . B
(Moving)	(. . . .	C	 C

A given distance in an infinite number of points; cf. the example of the racecourse. An infinite number of points can be illustrated by means of various finite numbers, although here indeed it is presented by an oval.

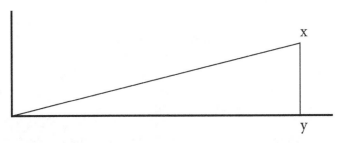

Between all the points of two line segments of different lengths there exists a univocal and reciprocal correlation.

77. See Mörchen transcription, no. 31, p. 187f.
78. Literally translated: "be equal to its double."

In spatial distance,[79] in motion, in "time." The same phenomenon not from space qua space, motion qua motion, time qua time, but from the fact that all these phenomena include a *continuum*, an actual infinity of "points," units. If this continuum is grasped as multiplicity, agglomeration, then nonsensicalities follow. Therefore it must be grasped as an *original unity and wholeness* which is prior to this infinite, endless divisibility. Unity, wholeness, ἀδιαίρετον ["indivisible"], συνεχές, continuum, Being itself.

B. Bolzano, *Paradoxien des Unendlichen*. Ed. from the author's literary remains by F. Přihonsky. Leipzig, 1851.

G. Cantor, *Grundlagen einer allgemeinen Mannichfaltigkeitslehre. Ein mathematisch-philosophischer Versuch in der Lehre des Unendlichen*. Leipzig, 1883.

H. Weyl, *Das Kontinuum. Kritische Untersuchungen über die Grundlagen der Analysis*. Leipzig, 1918.

B. Russell, A. N. Whitehead, *Principia mathematica*, vols. 1-3. Cambridge, 1910-1913.

c) Evaluation of Zeno's philosophy.

The difficulty does not lie in time, nor in space, but in the continuum. Continuum: *Being*. But this latter is identified with time. Yet Being is prior to space, time, magnitude, and so cannot be interpreted through time. "In time": here "time" itself as a being, οὐσία: Aristotle. When we say that Being is connected to time, we are intending "time" in an *original* sense, from which the time of the *common* understanding is *derived*, originated, without this origination ever being clear.

While Zeno's arguments are indeed negative in form, yet upon closer inspection they do bring Being itself into sharper relief. The continuum is a phenomenon that lies equally at the foundation of magnitude, space, and common time.

§24. Melissus of Samos.[80]

Above all, frag. 7:[81] Being is an utterly homogenous mass, without any distinction between the dense and the rare, the full and the empty; nothing "next to" it or "outside" it, "no limits."

Frag. 8[82] returns to, and sharpens, the *propositio* regarding αἴσθησις and δόξα, namely that these do not at all allow one to penetrate into

---

79. See Mörchen transcription, no. 31, p. 188.
80. See Mörchen transcription, no. 32, p. 188f.
81. Diels 1, 4th ed., 20B7 {30B7}.
82. Diels 1, 4th ed., 20B8 {30B8}.

the Being of beings. Nevertheless, with this extreme consequence Melissus touches on the intention of the basic possibilities, and of the conditions, that must be satisfied by a science of these multiplicities.

Problem of Being: critical science is ontological, positive science is ontic. To penetrate through to Being, yet all the while clinging to beings. Simultaneously the impossibility of a science of this {viz., Being}[83] and yet advancements in researching it.

83. Editor's interpolation.

4

The later philosophy of nature:
Empedocles, Anaxagoras, and atomism

§25. Being and the multiplicity of changing beings
in the later philosophy of nature.

Science[84] of beings, taking them in the sense of the multiple and the changing—impossible as ἕν: unity and uniqueness, wholeness, immutability. Unity and wholeness are to be maintained, as well as the ontological intention of characterizing Being, and yet there still is found a way to investigate beings. The idea of Being is preserved. The question is whether beings themselves can be grasped in a structurally more rich way, so that, as grasped in this way, they might satisfy, in their ontological concept, the Eleatic idea of Being. This idea of Being is the guideline. νοεῖν, λόγος, is the κριτήριον ["criterion"] for what is and what is not. But at the same time there is the intention of σῴζειν τὰ φαινόμενα, "saving the phenomena," i.e., restoring its proper rights to that which shows itself in itself and indeed as it shows itself. To this corresponds a more precise understanding of experience, of *sense perception*, namely an understanding that the senses, and indeed every sense, have their rights.[85]

On the other hand, Anaxagoras emphasizes the fundamental limits of the senses and the priority of νοῦς and λόγος. ὑπ᾽ ἀφαυρότητος αὐτῶν οὐ δυνατοί ἐσμεν κρίνειν τἀληθές[86]—"On account of their weakness, they do not allow us to grasp beings themselves in their differentiations."

---

84. See Mörchen transcription, no. 33, p. 189f.
85. Diels 1, 4th ed., 21B4, v. 9ff. {31B3, v. 9ff}.
86. Diels 1, 4th ed., 46B21 {Diels, vol. 2 (henceforth, Diels 2), 59B21}.

Leucippus.[87] For Parmenides, opposition and unity are mutually exclusive. For Heraclitus,[88] they are united. For both, however, no concrete science of beings: Parmenides does not have any beings in the strict concept of Being, whereas Heraclitus has nothing but beings in the strict concept of Being. Striking: previously the description concerned either only Being or only beings. The earlier philosophy of nature indeed asked about origins, but not at the level of an ontological problematic. In characterizing Aristotle's survey, we referred to the *principle of sufficient reason*, the basic principle of research, why something is and not rather is not.[89] We were already referring implicitly to Leucippus: οὐδὲν χρῆμα μάτην γίνεται, ἀλλὰ πάντα ἐκ λόγου τε καὶ ὑπ᾽ ἀνάγκης[90]—"Nothing arises by chance; on the contrary, everything comes from definite foundations and by force of necessity." αἰτιολογία ["aetiology"],[91] regard toward the nexus of foundation: foundation and the founded; only within this nexus can we grasp beings in their Being. φαινόμενον ["phenomenon"]: what shows itself is a being; as such it is founded with respect to its Being. Not the pure opposite of Being, sheer semblance, but a being in its Being. Not Being in itself, in detached tranquility, but the *Being of beings*. In the sense, however, of the *Greek* idea of Being: *constancy, constant presence*, now understood as the *constant foundation of change*.

a) This foundation is not identified with Being; instead, it provides something constant to underlie change, *"elementum,"* στοιχεῖα.[92]

b) Change itself not as coming to be and passing away; now instead, with respect to the elements, as a constant mixing and separating. Conservation of the whole in a multiplicity of possible transformations. Cf. Empedocles, frag. 8;[93] Anaxagoras, frag. 17.[94]

Being pertains most properly to the elements. But even becoming is understood as a mixing and separating of those elements, as their blending and segregation. Thereby the elements are original and constant; blending and separating are mere possibilities.

ῥιζώματα,[95] "roots," σπέρματα,[96] "seeds," στοιχεῖον ["element"]. Foundation and element are formal; the concretions are sundry. In

---

87. Diels 2, 4th ed., 54A7 {67A7}: Aristotle, *De generatione et corruptione* A 8, 324b25ff.; cf. *Phys., Met.* A; see Mörchen transcription, no. 33, p. 190f.

88. See above, p. 46f.

89. See above, §13 and §14, p. 37ff.

90. Diels 2, 4th ed., 54B2 {67B2}.

91. Cf. Diels 2, 4th ed., 55B: Democritus, frag. 118 {68B118}.

92. Plato, *Theatetus,* 201Eff.

93. Diels 1, 4th ed., 21B8 {31B8}.

94. Diels 1, 4th ed., 46B17 {59B17}.

95. Empedocles, Diels 1, 21B6 {31B6}.

96. Anaxagoras, Diels 1, 46B4; {2, 59B4}.

both ideas nothing is pre-delineated. Empedocles: fire, water, earth. Air.[97] Anaxagoras: every being passes over into the other. "Everything comes from everything."[98] *Qualities*, not materials, infinitely many and of infinitely many kinds. Every individual thing is in truth only a *determinate constellation* of the whole, of the totality of present, possible qualities. It is to these present constellations that names accrue.

πανσπερμία,[99] "totality of all seeds."

Democritus: σκοτίη ["obscure"], "inauthentic" knowledge; γνησίη ["lawfully begotten"], "authentic" knowledge.[100]

Atoms: σχῆμα, τάξις, θέσις ["shape, arrangement, position"].[101]

Element, foundation, relation. Empedocles: love–hate,[102] Σφαῖρος[103] –κόσμος.[104]

Anaxagoras: νοῦς.[105]

Atomism: ὑποκείμενον. Ordered whole of possible positions, the *void*.[106] This order of positions is also a being; it is the void, wherein this or that can move. ὑποκείμενον and κενόν, "substrate" and "dimension" are necessary components of change and motion. Even the κενόν has ὑπόστασις ["foundation"] and φύσις. Democritus: μὴ μᾶλλον τὸ δὲν ἢ τὸ μηδὲν εἶναι ["there is no more existence in something than in nothing"][107] (δείς, δέν / οὐδείς, τίς ["something, one thing / nothing, anything"]).

Here, sequent to Parmenides' idea of Being, everything that belongs to a possible nature is placed in Being; thus arises something like a schema of nature in general. It is not that Parmenides sees only the individual thing and Democritus the system; on the contrary, Parmenides also grasps the whole, but only in the pure, undifferentiated sameness of presence. Democritus, on the other hand, articulates even the constitutive moments of motion.

What makes the presentation difficult is the fact that these philosophers occupy an intermediary position between Parmenides' doctrine of Being and the speculation about beings in the older philosophy of

97. Diels 1, 4th ed., 21B17 {31B17}.

98. Diels 1, 4th ed., 46B6 {2, 59B6}.

99. Cf. Diels 1, 4th ed., 46A45 {2, 59A45}: Aristotle, *Phys.* Γ 4, 203a21f.

100. Cf. Diels 2, 4th ed., 55B11 {68B11}.

101. Cf. Diels 2, 4th ed., 54A6 (Leucippus) {67A6}: Aristotle, *Met.* A 4, 985b13ff.

102. Diels 1, 4th ed., 21B17 {31B17} and 4th ed., 21B26 {31B26}.

103. Diels 1, 4th ed., 21B27 and 28 {31B27 and 28}.

104. Cf. frag. 26, v. 5; see above, n. 102.

105. Diels 1, 4th ed., 46B12 {2, 59B12}.

106. See Mörchen transcription, no. 33, p. 190f.

107. Diels 2, 4th ed., 55B156 {68B156}. [For Heidegger's translation of frag. 156, see the Mörchen transcription, no. 33, *ad finem.* —Trans.]

nature, as well as the fact that it is easy to say either too much or too little about every concept here: danger of assimilating these concepts to those of modern natural science or of crudely identifying them with those of Thales and the like. People used to seek to characterize what is peculiar here by asking how that which beings themselves exhibit as their ontological structure does nevertheless not reach the ontological determinateness attaching to, for example, the ἕν of Parmenides.

§26. The problem of knowledge in the later philosophy of nature.

λόγος[108] is the court of appeal for determining genuine apprehension, but αἴσθησις has its own rights. The function of λόγος and νοῦς was seen, but their mode of Being was not conceptualized: here lies rather a basic difficulty in systematizing. Knowledge would be possible only through an *assimilation of the same by the same.* (Cf. Parmenides: the being as known and the Being of knowing are the same.[109]) Counteraction. Empedocles: we know only that which we ourselves are alike physically.[110] Democritus: εἴδωλα ["images"][111] – ἐπιρυσμίη ["floating"].[112] Frags. 7, 8, 9, 10.[113] Repercussion of the mode of Being of the knowable being on the Being of knowledge: knowledge is itself only matter, fire atoms, of the highest mobility. Knowledge itself is merely a process in the factual universe, of the same mode of Being as it.

Thus here a regression. But, in another respect, a further penetration into the structure of beings, even if, at the same time, a mistaking of the Being of this penetration. Whence we see that the functional achievement of νοῦς and λόγος is grasped, but their *Being is not conceptualized.* This discrepancy continues into the future, where the mode of Being of knowledge and of all comportments comes more directly into view. Descartes, Kant, Hegel.

108. See Mörchen transcription, no. 34, p. 191f.
109. Diels 1, 4th ed., 18B5 {28B3}.
110. Cf. Diels 1, 4th ed., 21B109; cf. 21B106 {31B109; cf. 31B106}.
111. Cf. Diels 2, 4th ed., 55B10a {68B10a}.
112. Diels 2, 4th ed., 55B7 {68B7}.
113. Diels 2, 4th ed., 55B7-10 {68B7-10}.

5

Sophistry and Socrates

§27. General characterization of sophistry.

1. Question of the Being of the world, nature. 2. Question of the Being of human Dasein.[114]

Sophistry marks the transition from 1 to 2. A backward glance shows that the division into periods means, as regards content, only that an emphasis is placed respectively on the world or on Dasein, for even in the case of the former there is already νοῦς, λόγος, knowledge, apprehension, spirit, soul. Truth. Wherever philosophical reflection exists, there is manifestly always a questioning of world and Dasein, Dasein and world. The more radical the one, the more clear the whole.

In sophistry, reflection moves from a consideration of the world to an interpretation of Dasein, specifically of Dasein's possibilities of knowledge and comportment, morally and politically. Truth and falsity, justice and injustice: decisions about them a matter of subjective conviction. Indeed this interpretation is still carried out using the means offered by the previous philosophy of nature, as formulated in Heraclitus, for example, or in the Eleatics. We already saw the constant repercussion of the idea of Being on the conception of knowledge itself. Sophistry is not in a positive sense scientifically productive. It does not yet make the Being of Dasein an explicit theme of investigative work. It draws on its predecessors but brings into view a new possible thematic field for cultural consciousness. Distinction: pre-scientific interest in cognition and culture and scientific thematization. Sophistic science belongs to period 1; in view of the emphasis on Dasein, sophistry belongs to 2; in fact it is neither, transition.

Main exponents of the *older* sophistry:[115]

---

114. Cf. the division into periods in §7, p. 17f.
115. Full materials on the older sophistry in Diels 2, 4th ed., 73bff. {79ff.}.

68

Protagoras of Abdera

Gorgias of Leontini (Sicily)

Hippias of Elis

Prodicus of Ceos

Anonymus Iamblichi (extract of his writing in the *Protrepticus* of the Neoplatonic Iamblichus)

Δισσοὶ λόγοι (Διαλέξεις) ["Double arguments (Discourses)"]

From the *later* circle of sophists: Antiphon (᾽Αλήθεια ["truth, disclosedness"])

σοφιστής ["sophist"] —"the one with expert knowledge," "the one who understands," cf. σοφός ["wise man"], σοφία ["wisdom"].[116] At first, not a designation for a philosophical trend or school, but also not a pejorative connotation. Only circa 450 was the meaning restricted, not on account of a new theoretical determination of the concept, but because experts acquired special importance in science and in practical, political affairs. The rise of democracy after the Persian wars not only opened to the individual new possibilities of participating in community affairs but at the same time also required a higher and more secure education. And that required teachers. These teachers were the sophists. They imparted not only theoretical cognitions, but also practical, political, and historical knowledge, and, above all, the skill needed for public effectiveness: speech. Thereby the importance of rhetoric: in the public assembly, in debates, but also in court, in the great political processes. Closely connected to rhetoric was eristics, the technique of disputation. And both require a mastery of λόγος, διαλέγεσθαι, dialectic. Here the sophists accomplished positive tasks and did positive work, not only for the spread of culture but also for an increase in general vitality, for *new questions,* for *critique.*

Characteristic of their philosophical instruction: imparted for payment, whereas it was otherwise free of charge. From the point of view of the philosophers, the sophists appeared as mercenary peddlers of pseudo-wisdom, as self-extolling tempters of youth, trappers, fishermen. Plato's philosophical critique thrust the positive merit of the sophists to the background. They appear only as corruptors of youth, of true culture, and of morals. Sophistry: arbitrarily, on false grounds, refuting something true, making it totter, or proving what is false, making it plausible.

Meditation on life and guidance not through oracles, mores, passions, and the disposition of the moment but, instead, through *thoughtful reflection.* No longer to believe and imitate, but to form opinions for oneself and make one's own way. Against νόμος, "convention," and for φύσις, "constant change." Enlightenment, education, παιδεύειν. Eloquence, rhetoric. Topics: the various points of view, τόποι, from which an issue

116. Cf. above, §9, p. 20.

can be conceived and grasped. Dialectics: to view something from various sides, not to absolutize one side. Ὑμεῖς δέ ["You, on the other hand"] . . . The one who lies says what is not; but what is not cannot be said; therefore no one can lie.[117] The teaching activity was soon carried out in this form: to hoodwink through clever talk and artifices and to palm off on the hearers definite opinions and purposes.

§28. Protagoras.

Homo-mensura ["man-the-measure"] principle: πάντων χρημάτων μέτρον ἄνθρωπον εἶναι, τῶν μὲν ὄντων ὡς ἔστι, τῶν δὲ μὴ ὄντων, ὡς οὐκ ἔστιν ["The human being is the measure of all things: of beings, as they are, and of nonbeings, as they are not"].[118] ἄνθρωπος ["human being"] understood as the individual, not humanity versus animals. Substantial rationality, self-conscious reason [*Vernunft*] in humans. Cf. Plato, *Theatetus:* οἷα μὲν ἕκαστα ἐμοὶ φαίνεται τοιαῦτα μὲν ἔστιν ἐμοί, οἷα δὲ σοί, τοιαῦτα δὲ αὖ σοί· ἄνθρωπος δὲ σύ τε κἀγώ ["each thing is to me just as it appears to me and is to you just as it appears to you: both you and I being humans"].[119] A wind makes one person cold, another not. Therefore we cannot say the wind in itself is cold or not cold. πρός τι ["to someone"], what shows itself in each case to any individual is the truth, the being itself; and everything shows itself differently to different individuals. Heraclitus: since everything, including the individual Dasein, is constantly changing, both in itself and in its relation to others. Not only are the objects of knowledge constantly changing, but so is knowledge itself. The mode of Being of knowledge is the same as the Being of the beings to be known.[120] Frag. 7: "The lines given in sense perception are not of the same kind as those the geometer has for an object; in this way nothing can be experienced as straight or curved. The circle does not touch the tangent at only one point."[121]

The αἴσθησις-doctrine of Protagoras is taken up positively in Plato's *Theatetus.*[122]

Dialectic,[123] rhetoric.

Linguistic critique (ὀρθοέπεια).[124] Classification of the genera of names and propositions: διεῖλέ τε τὸν λόγον πρῶτος εἰς τέτταρα

---

117. Plato, *Euthydemus,* 283C8ff.
118. Diels 2, 4th ed., 74B1 {80B1}: Plato, *Theatetus,* 152A2–4.
119. Plato, *Theatetus,* 152A6–8.
120. See Mörchen transcription, no. 35, p. 192.
121. Diels 2, 4th ed., 74B7 {80B7}: Aristotle, *Met.* B 2, 997b35ff.
122. Plato, *Theatetus,* 152Aff.
123. Cf. Aristotle, *Met.* Γ 4, 1007b22f.
124. Cf. Diels 2, 4th ed., 74A26 {80A26}: Plato, *Phaedrus,* 267C6.

["into four"]: εὐχωλήν (petition), ἐρώτησιν ["question"], ἀπόκρισιν ["answer"], ἐντολήν (command). According to others, there are seven forms.[125] Πρωταγόρας τὰ γένη τῶν ὀνομάτων διήρει, ἄρρενα καὶ θήλεα καὶ σκεύη ["Protagoras divides nouns into the classes of masculine, feminine, and neuter"].[126]

Elucidation: περὶ μὲν θεῶν οὐκ ἔχω εἰδέναι, οὔθ᾽ ὡς εἰσὶν οὔθ᾽ ὡς οὐκ εἰσὶν οὔθ᾽ ὁποῖοί τινες ἰδέαν· πολλὰ γὰρ τὰ κωλύοντα εἰδέναι ἥ τ᾽ ἀιδηλότης καὶ βραχὺς ὢν ὁ βίος τοῦ ἀνθρώπου. ["I have no knowledge of the gods, neither that they are, nor that they are not, nor what sort of *eidos* they have: for there are many impediments to knowing them, such as their obscurity and the shortness of human life."][127]

---

§29. Gorgias.

Περὶ τοῦ μὴ ὄντος ἢ Περὶ φύσεως ["On nonbeing, or, On nature"].[128] Opinions diverge regarding the content and aim of this text. Some believe that presented here is merely an example of the most overdone dialectics and sophistry; others find positive and serious deliberations, to be sure not without a strong influence from the art of formal argumentation. Aristotle wrote Πρὸς τὰ Γοργίου ["Against the views of Gorgias"],[129] and we can assume Aristotle would not do battle against a mere babbler.

The content of the text in three theses:[130] 1. There is nothing. 2. But if there were something, it would be unknowable. 3. If there were something and it were knowable, then the knowledge of this being would be incommunicable and could not be expressed or interpreted.

The Being of beings, the knowability of Being, and the communicability of what is known are denied.

---

125. *Diogenis Laertii de vitis IX,* 53 and 54, in Diels 2, 4th ed., 74A1, p. 220 {80A1, p. 254}.

126. Aristotle, *Ars rhetorica.* Ed. A. Roemer. Leipzig, 1914, Γ 5, 1407b6ff. in Diels 2, 4th ed., 74A27 {80A27}.

127. Diels 2, 4th ed., 74B4 {80B4}. [For Heidegger's translation of frag. 4, see the Mörchen transcription, no. 35. —Trans.]

128. See Diels 2, 4th ed., 76B3 {82B3}: from Sextus Empiricus, *Adversus mathematicos* 7, 65ff.; see Mörchen transcription, no. 36, p. 192f.

129. *Opera.* Ex recogn. I. Bekkeri. Ed. Academia Regia Borussica. Berlin, 1831, vol. 2, 979a12–980b21; F. W. A. Mullach, *Aristotelis de Melisso, Xenophane et Gorgia disputationes cum Eleaticorum philosophorum fragmentis.* Berlin, 1845, pp. 62–79; "Aristotelis qui fertur de Melisso Xenophane Gorgia libellus." Ed. H. Diels. In: *Abhandlungen der Königlichen Akademie der Wissenschaften zu Berlin aus den Jahren 1899 und 1900.* Berlin, 1900, Philosophisch-historische Classe, Abh. 1, pp. 1–40.

130. Sextus Empiricus, *Adversus mathematicos* 7, 66.

Regarding 1: Being. εἰ γὰρ ἔστι (τι) — "if Is."[131] There is nothing. a) What is not is not. b) Beings are not either: aa) eternal, or bb) produced by becoming, or cc) both at once. c) Beings must either be one or many; but they can be neither. d) Likewise, both the one and the many cannot be at the same time.

Regarding 2: What is thought of would have to be; nonbeings could not be thought of.

Regarding 3: Every sign is different from what is signified. Words are something other than colors. The ear does not hear colors. How is the same intended thing supposed to be in two different "subjects"?

§30. Further exponents of sophistry.

a) Hippias of Elis.

Famous for his mathematical, astronomical, and geometrical knowledge. He was well versed περί τε γραμμάτων δυνάμεως καὶ συλλαβῶν καὶ ῥυθμῶν καὶ ἁρμονιῶν ["in letters, syllables, rhythms, and harmonies"].[132] Transmission of Greek culture. In his basic moral-political notions he was not as extreme as one might expect from the dialectical and theoretical declarations of the other sophists.

b) Prodicus of Ceos.[133]

Distinction between words of closely allied meaning; problem of signification; expression.[134] Socrates several times called himself, even if not with full seriousness, a student of Prodicus.

He handed down characteristic theses of the enlightened position of sophistry:

What people find *useful* they worship as divine: sun, moon, rivers, fountains, bread, wine, water, fire.[135] Rudiments of this can be found in the critique Empedocles and Democritus make against popular religion.

Fear of death is unfounded. For death is something that concerns neither the living nor the dead; not the first, because they are still alive; not the second, because they are no longer alive. As long as the living being is alive, death is not present; when that being is not alive, death cannot possibly be present to it.

131. G. W. F. Hegel, *Vorlesungen über die Geschichte der Philosophie.* Ed. K. L. Michelet, vol 2; Hegel *WW,* vol. 14. Berlin, 1833, p. 37ff.

132. Plato, *Hippias major,* 285D1f.

133. Cf. Plato, *Protagoras,* 315D1ff.

134. Cf. Plato, *Euthydemus,* 277E3ff.

135. Diels 2, 4th ed., 77B5 {84B5} from: Cicero, *De natura deorum* 1, 118; Sextus Empiricus, *Adversus mathematicos* 9, 18.

c) Anonymus Iamblichi.[136]

Outworn, would-be enlightened wisdom without philosophical significance; merely characterizes the process by which the propositions of the sophists were increasingly popularized.

d) Δισσοὶ λόγοι.[137]

Theses, counter-theses: ταὐτόν—οὐ ταὐτόν ["the same—not the same"]; regarding the ἀγαθόν ["good"] and the κακόν ["bad"]: sickness is bad for the one who is sick, good for the doctor. Relativity of the consideration.

Teachability of virtue: the counter-arguments do not stand.

It is clear: the sphere of questions Socrates posed in his own way was already known.

§31. Socrates.

a) Biography and sources.

Born circa 470. Son of the sculptor Sophroniscus and the midwife Phainarete. Aristophanes' Νεφέλαι [*Clouds*] in 427; Socrates a personality well known in the city. Three military campaigns; poor; refused to hold any public office.

Indicted by Anytus, Meletus, and Lycon in 399. {Charges:}[138] corrupting the youth. Disbelief in the gods of the city. Belief in new daemons. In court, he refused to make any concessions. Then he would not flee from prison, though his friends had prepared an escape. In their presence he drank the cup of hemlock, after convincing them of the necessity of his action.

There is no clear and unanimous view of Socrates, even today. The reason is the variety of sources: 1. Xenophon's *Memorabilia*,[139] *Apology, Symposium*.[140] 2. Plato's dialogues.[141] 3. Some indications in Aristotle. 4. Aristophanes' *Clouds*.[142]

136. Diels 2, 4th ed., 82 {89}.
137. Diels 2, 4th ed., 83 {90}.
138. Editor's interpolation.
139. In: *Xenophontis opera omnia*. Recogn. E. C. Marchant, vol. 2, Oxford, 1900ff.
140. Ibid.
141. In: *Platonis opera*. Recogn. I. Burnet. Oxford, 1899ff.
142. Νεφέλαι. In: *Aristophanis Comoediae*.

K. Joel[143] on Aristotle's view, E. Dühring[144] on Xenophon's, J. Burnet[145] on Plato's, H. Maier[146] a mediator.

b) The significance of Socrates for the understanding of Dasein in general.

Distinction[147] between what we actually understand and what we do not understand. Ignorance versus omniscience and versus the hastiness of common sense. Appropriation of *genuine knowledge* versus superficial chatter. Questioning what is most evident and closest versus arcane sagacity. Without a preconceived thesis regarding *knowledge itself:* what it is, what is its scope. Concept.

Intention to justify knowledge as such, positive. Even here an orientation toward what is closest, the activity of handcraft, ποίησις–τέχνη–εἶδος, ἔργον μετὰ λόγου ["making–know-how–essence, product accompanied by *logos*"]. *Production* had been the guideline for the interpretation of the world. Now it becomes the point of departure for the knowledge residing in it. Something in its ground, why and how it is such and such, on the basis of *what* it is, the τί. What something, prior to all actuality, already was in its potentiality is its *essence.* The τί (εἶδος) is what is primarily disclosed; from it all other beings and all comportment toward them receive their sureness and transparency.

All action, so as not to be blind, requires *transparency.* Regard toward, and sight for, the *"for the sake of which."* Thereby possibilities are understood, the *respective potentiality-for-Being,* the suitability, "virtue," ἀρετή. Self-knowledge in the current situation, taking into account the circumstances. The potentiality-for-Being and the understanding exist only as this knowledge. Virtue is knowledge, ἀρετή is φρόνησις.

c) The significance of Socrates for scientific-philosophical research.[148]

Socrates: always, fundamentally and essentially, attempting to achieve this knowledge, awakening of an understanding of it, implanting an instinct for it. No new contents or domains, no new trend in philosophy. He left everything in its place, and yet he shook all things right to their

143. K. Joel, *Der echte und der Xenophontische Sokrates.* 3 vols. Berlin, 1893-1901, vol. 1, pp. 203-312.

144. E. Dühring, *Kritische Geschichte der Philosophie von ihren Anfängen bis zur Gegenwart,* 3rd ed., Leipzig, 1878, pp. 81-82.

145. J. Burnet, *Greek Philosophy.* Pt. 1: Thales to Plato. London, 1920, pp. 128, 149-150; J. Burnet, *Platonism.* Berkeley, 1928, pp. 18-19.

146. H. Maier, *Sokrates. Sein Werk und seine geschichtliche Stellung.* Tübingen, 1913, pt. 1: "Die Quellen," pp. 4-156.

147. See Mörchen transcription, no. 37, p. 193f.

148. See Mörchen transcription, no. 38, p. 194f.

foundations: a new *possibility* and thereby a radical summons to knowledge and to the *grounding* of knowledge. Fact: no scientific results and yet a revolution of science, such that Plato and Aristotle became possible on account of him. The significance of *methodological* determination was here demonstrated once and for all in the history of knowledge and research. Method is not technique; on the contrary, it means to look to the ground of things and thereby grasp the possibility of apprehending and determining them.

Socrates' method, according to Aristotle:[149] 1. ἐπακτικὸς λόγος ["*logos* that leads on"] (cf. 1078b28), ἐπαγωγή, "to lead over," in λέγειν to what something is addressed as, a primordial coming to visibility of the τί. 2. ὁρίζεσθαι καθόλου (1078b28f.), to "circumscribe" what has been set forth and to determine its current constitution and structure.

Maieutics: emptiness to be exposed for what it is and others to be helped to *deliver* the possibility of understanding teeming in them. Maieutics is the antithesis of the *imparting* of cognitions.

Indeed there had already been proofs, grounding, reflection on cognitive comportment, but now the *concept* as such is explicitly made prominent and understood precisely *as* concept. λόγον διδόναι, to investigate and pose the ground expressly as ground. To grasp the essence is not to run about and gather properties found haphazardly; on the contrary, it is *to grasp the a priori.* What maintains itself throughout variation and modification. Apprehension itself; the "general," καθόλου, the universal—itself a being, or not? Only a signification? What does that mean? λόγος: concept, signification, meaning. *Being* and *meaning.*

Socrates was not a moralist who disdained the philosophy of nature. On the contrary, his concern was the *understanding of Dasein's knowledge and action in general.* He was no more concerned with determinate domains of the knowledge of nature than he was with ethical principles of delimited content or even with a special value system and its particular hierarchy of values. Socrates thought much too radically for such contingent matters to hold him fast: theoretician, practitioner, dialectician, moralist, prophet, philosopher, religious personality. Socrates comes into focus through the work of Plato and Aristotle, and through a comparison of their philosophical problematic versus the previous philosophy, much more clearly than if we tried to build up an image of him on his own.

149. *Met.* M 4, 1078b27ff.

SECTION TWO
Plato's Philosophy

1

Biography, secondary literature, and general characterization of Plato's questioning

§32. Biography, sources, and secondary literature.

Biography in bare dates: 427, born in Athens. Son of Ariston and Periktione. Composed plays in his youth. Active in politics. Philosophy {was first taught to him by}[1] Cratylus, the Heraclitean. Circa 406, met Socrates. Minor dialogues. 399, death of Socrates. To 388, various travels: Megara (Socratics), Egypt, Italy, Sicily. Mathematics and medicine. 387, founding of the Academy. 366–365, 361, two further travels to Syracuse, in order to implement his political ideas. 347, death.

Writings: the *Apology*, thirty-four dialogues, a series of letters, some poems.

Questions surrounding him: genuineness of the dialogues, establishment of their time of composition, their chronology; problem as regards content: Plato's philosophical development.

Transmission:
1. Numerous papyri, of great antiquity, show only that the text, as given in the newest manuscripts, reaches back very far in time. Here already substantial corruptions.
   2. Medieval manuscripts.
   3. Indirect transmission: cited in the scholiasts, in commentaries.

Editions:
Henricus Stephanus, *Platonis Opera quae extant omnia,* ex nova Joannis Serrani interpretatione, perpetuis ejusdem notis illustrata. Geneva,

---

1. Editor's interpolation.

1578. Page numbers of this edition used in citations: e.g., *Phaedrus* 275D.

New complete editions:
Platonis Dialogi graece et latine. Ex rec. I. Bekkeri. 8 vols. in 3 parts. Berlin, 1816–1818, with commentary and scholia (commentary 2 vols. Berlin, 1823).
Platonis dialogos selectos. Rec. et comm. in usum scholarum instr. G. Stallbaum. Starting with vol. 4, pt. 2: *Platonis opera omnia.* 10 vols. Gotha and Erfurt, 1827–1860.
Platonis dialogi secundum Thrasylli tetralogias dispositi. Ex recogn. C. F. Hermanni. 6 vols. Leipzig, 1869ff.; new ed. by M. Wohlrab. Leipzig, 1877–1887.
Burnet, I., *Platonis opera.* 5 vols. Oxford, 1899–1906. Best critical edition.
Croiset, M., et al. *Platon, Oeuvres complètes.* Texte établi. Collection des universités de France. 13 vols. Paris, 1920ff.

Letters:
Die Briefe Platons. Ed. E. Howald. Zurich, 1923.

Translations:
Platons Werke. Trans. F. Schleiermacher. 6 vols. in 3 parts. 3rd ed. Berlin, 1855–1862.
Platons Werke in Einzelausgaben. Trans. and notes O. Apelt. Leipzig, 1911ff.

Secondary literature:
Hermann, K. F., *Geschichte und System der Platonischen Philosophie.* Pt. 1: "Die historisch-kritische Grundlegung enthaltend." Heidelberg, 1839.
Windelband, W., *Platon.* 6th ed. Stuttgart, 1920. (Frommans Klassiker der Philosophie.)
Raeder, H., *Platons philosophische Entwicklung.* Leipzig, 1905.
Ritter, C., *Platon. Sein Leben, seine Schriften, seine Lehre.* 2 vols. Munich, 1910 (vol. 1), 1923 (vol. 2).
Natorp, P., *Platos Ideenlehre. Eine Einfiihrung in den Idealismus.* Leipzig, 1903, 2nd ed., 1921.
von Wilamowitz-Moellendorff, U., *Platon,* 2 vols., vol 1: *Leben und Werke;* vol 2: *Beilagen und Textkritik.* Berlin, 1919, 2nd ed. Berlin, 1920.

§33. General characterization of Plato's questioning.

The theory of Ideas.[2] That characterizes Plato's philosophy. From the term itself, it would appear that something completely novel is emerging here. But that is mere appearance. What is new is that the old intention of the previous philosophy is taken up more radically. Socrates: asking for the essence, concept. τί ἐστιν; This or that being, "What is it?" Plato: what is a being at all? Asking for the essence of beings as beings, asking for Being!

εἶδος, "outward look," what something in itself shows itself as. What do beings as beings show themselves as? Investigation into the Ideas: asking for the Being of beings. That is the substantive content of the problem of the Ideas. Not the theory of Ideas for itself as a special philosophical opinion, in order then to join it to the previous philosophy, but the old question taken up on the more transparent basis provided by Socrates' questioning. Only from this point of view, from the substantive content of the "theory of Ideas," the Being of beings, can it be understood how and why there arose what is usually considered the problem of the Ideas.

Motifs: the working out of the question of the Being of beings is *universal* and, equally, occurs at the level of *principle:* the totality of beings in their Being; and it is specifically in this respect that they are to be *known.* The result is that such a task is determined: 1. from the mode of the experience of beings in general, 2. from the directions of the theoretical knowledge of beings, and 3. from the ruling and available understanding of Being in general.[3]

Why εἶδος, "outward look," Gestalt?[4]

1. On the basis of *apprehension;* people who are "all eyes." Primacy of showing.

2. Gestalt: that which holds all together, not a sum of the conglomerated parts, but rather the very law of the conjoining. *Earlier than.*

3. What every individual Gestalt configures. Impressing of order. Ruling, and specifically its *principle, measure.* The *constant.* μέθεξις ["participation"]. E.g., health.

4. Thus, however, the universe of beings. Sky, globe, orbit of the stars. All beings have in this way an original impress. *Universality, determinateness.*

5. This is what remains *unchanged.* The *knowable.* Mathematical science holds for nature and yet has not been obtained from it or in it as such.

2. See Mörchen transcription, no. 39, p. 195.
3. See the recapitulation below, p. 80.
4. See Mörchen transcription, no. 39, p. 195f.

6. Itself *something*, a τόπος—ὑπερουράνιος ["a place beyond the heavens"],[5] something *transcendent*. Being of beings.

Ideas: χωρισμός ["separation"], ὄντως ὄν ["the being that most is"]. The Being of beings is itself a being, and indeed the most proper being. Thus beings in general are derived; relation between both.

Platonism:[6] questioning, theory, and world-view, oriented toward this basic opposition, which it holds fast to or seeks to reconcile.

Becoming, change	— (Being) Constancy
The individual	The universal
The accidental	Law
Nature	Spirit
The temporal	The eternal
Sense perception	Logical-conceptual cognition
The conditioned	The unconditioned

Two-world theory, μέθεξις, μεταξύ ["between"].

Recapitulation

Idea: interpretation of beings with respect to their Being. The theory of Ideas is ontology, *eidos:* eidetics, "eidetic reduction,"[7] phenomenology. The expression "eidetics" taken over from psychology, has there nothing to do with the problematic of philosophy.

Motives for eliciting the εἴδη ["Ideas"], according to the meaning in each case: Gestalt, law, ordered whole, norm, what is constant. χωρισμός, μέθεξις. Platonism.

---

5. Cf. *Phaedrus,* 247C3.

6. See Mörchen transcription, no. 39, p. 196.

7. Cf. E. Husserl, *Ideen zu einer reinen Phänomenologie und phänomenologischen Philosophie. Jahrbuch für Philosophie und phänomenologische Forschung,* vol. 1, Halle/Saale, 1913, p. 4.

2

More concrete determination of the problem of Being in Plato's philosophy

After this general characterization of Plato's questioning, we want to grasp it more determinately. Three issues:

1. Ground and domain of the problem of Being.
2. Center of the problem of the Ideas.
3. The basic problem of ontology.

§34. Ground and domain of the problem of Being.[8]

a) The apprehension of beings and the understanding of Being in the *Republic*.

The question of Being includes: 1. experience of beings, 2. consideration of Being.

Regarding 1: to experience beings: which beings? The entire realm of beings?

ἐπιστήμη —	Mathematics, medicine:	Nature
ποίησις —		World of work as a whole
πρᾶξις —		Action, history
πόλις —	The concrete and the state	

Everywhere in beings are "Ideas"; i.e., insofar as we *experience* beings as beings at all, and are not blindly delivered over to them, there is al-

---

8. See Mörchen transcription, no. 40, p. 196f.

ready an understanding of Being. No accident that the *Republic* contains reflections such as those on the classification of beings and of the possible modes of the apprehension of beings.[9]

πολλὰ καλά ["many beautiful things"], πολλὰ ἕκαστα ["many individuals"]. αὐτὸ καλόν, "the beautiful itself as such"; κατ᾽ ἰδέαν μίαν ["according to one Idea"]; ὃ ἔστιν—"what it is." ἕκαστον—"the present individual," the This.

ὁρᾶσθαι	νοεῖσθαι
Seen with the eyes	Apprehended, grasped in the understanding
ἀκοή ["hearing"], αἴσθησις in general	
αἰσθητά ["perceived things"]	
αἴσθησις – αἰσθητά	
τρίτον ["third thing"] in ὄψις ["sight"] (507E1f.)	καταλάμπει ἀλήθειά τε καὶ τὸ ὄν ["shining on truth and Being"] (508D5)
φῶς ["light"] (507E4)	what illuminates both disclosedness and Being
ἥλιος ["the sun"] (cf. 508A7)	what illumines through the *understanding of Being*
ὄψις–ἡλιοειδέστατον ["most sharing in the *eidos* of the sun"] (508B3)	
αἴτιος ὄψεως ["cause of vision"] (cf. 508B9)	ἡ τοῦ ἀγαθοῦ ἰδέα ["the Idea of the good"] (cf. 508E2f.)
τοῦ ἀγαθοῦ ἔκγονον ["offspring of the good"] (508B12f.)	ἀλήθειαν παρέχει ["furnishing truth"] (509A7)
ἀνάλογον ἑαυτῷ ["analogous to itself"]	(508B13) ἀλήθεια, ἐπιστήμη (cf. 508E3f.), ἀγαθοειδῆ ["of the same *eidos* as the good"] (509A3)
ὁρατόν ["visible"] (509D4)[10]	νοητόν ["intelligible"] (509D4)

"Cuttings": τομή (cf. 510B2), τμήματα (509D7)

1. εἰκόνες (509E1)—"images," νοητὸν {. . .} εἶδος (511A3)
in which beings present
themselves. σκίας ["shadows"],
φαντάσματα (510A1)—"simulacra,"
reflections in water, on the surfaces
of dense, smooth, shiny bodies.

---

9. *Republic,* bk. 6, 507Bff.; see Mörchen transcription, no. 40, p. 197f.
10. See Mörchen transcription, no. 40, p. 198f.

2. ᾧ τοῦτο ἔοικεν (510A5),
   this thing itself,
τά τε περὶ ἡμᾶς ζῷα ["the
   animals round about us"]
   (510A5),
φυτευτόν ["plants"] (510A6),
σκευαστὸν ὅλον (510A6),
   "equipment."

μιμηθέντα (cf. 510B4), the   εἶδος ὁρώμενον ["visible *eidos*"]
   "imitated," now itself   (cf. 510D5)
   εἰκόνες, itself an "image."
τέτταρα {. . .} παθήματα ἐν
   τῇ ψυχῇ ["four dispositions
   in the soul"] (511D7)[11]

ἥλιος   ἀγαθόν
δόξα   νόησις

1. εἰκασία (cf. 511E2)   1. διάνοια (cf. 511D8)
   ("visual appearance")
                                   ὑποθέσεσι χρῆσθαι, οὐκ ἐπ᾽ ἀρχὴν
                                   ἰοῦσα ["employing hypotheses, not
                                   proceeding up to the beginning"]
                                   (cf. 511A3-5), as εἰκόσι χρωμένη
                                   ["employing images"] (cf. 511A6),
                                   which for their part were already
                                   imaged.

2. πίστις ["trust"]   2. νόησις (cf. 511D8), λόγος
   (cf. 511E1)   (511B4), οὐκ ἀρχὰς {. . .}
                                   ὑπόθεσις (511B5), "not the begin-
                                   ning as foundation," but merely as
                                   point of departure. ἀνυπόθετον
                                   ["non-hypothetical"] (cf. 511B6),
                                   τοῦ παντὸς ἀρχή ["the beginning of
                                   all"] (cf. 511B7).

New articulation of the kinds of apprehension, on the basis of a new classification of beings. Apprehension of beings in order to disclose them in their Being. Various modes of disclosability, disclosedness, truth. But not simply various forms of truth; instead, a hierarchy of those forms. Different truths, the difference according to the respective mode of Being of the disclosing comportment, of Dasein itself. Apprehension through αἴσθησις requires light; thus in general illu-

11. See Mörchen transcription, no. 40, p. 198f.

mination. According to the possible lighting, the kind and source of the light, there are various possibilities of access to the beings themselves. Difference in the source of light according to the mode of Being of Dasein: difference in the understanding of Being.

It is not unusual for Plato to present figuratively a basic problem he does understand but has not completely mastered.

b) The cave allegory: levels and relativity of truth.[12]

Cave:[13] image of our Being in the spatial surrounding world. The light in the cave. Outside the cave: the sun and the beings it shines on and whose growth it conditions and promotes, Being in the proper sense: image of the world of the Ideas, the sun represents the *highest Idea*. What in the allegory represents the highest, the world of Ideas, is in actuality, outside of the allegory, our spatial surrounding world, which is symbolized in the allegory by the cave. The spatial surrounding world, illuminated by the sun, has a double function: 1. as symbol: the highest; 2. as the actual world: the lower.

As a being,[14] that which in each case immediately shows itself. It is *assumed* as a being and *accepted* as a being, δόξα, δέχεσθαι (without proof). Insofar as Dasein is, it has a ἕδρα (cf. 517B2), a "seat" and a place and thereby has surroundings. A surrounding world, even if accessible only to a small degree, is already disclosed with Dasein. A light, an illumination is required for anything at all to be seen, even if only the shadows in the half-darkness of the cave. In other words, for a being to be experienced there must already be an illumination of Being. An understanding of Being. The light must shine, although it is not necessary that the light itself already be seen or even be grasped consciously at all. Those in chains know nothing about the light and can never know about it. The light is there, Dasein lives in an understanding of Being, without knowing about it.[15]

The first level of truth:

a) Pre-givenness of a world in general; seat.
b) Understanding of Being, inexplicit. Being is neither seen nor conceived.
c) A determinate mode of letting be encountered (εἰκασία ["image"]).
d) διαλέγεσθαι, "to speak all the way through," to speak about that, about beings.

---

12. *Republic*, bk. 7, 514Aff.; see Mörchen transcription, no. 41, p. 199f.
13. In the manuscript, this inserted page bears the title, "Cave allegory."
14. See Mörchen transcription, no. 41, p. 200.
15. See supplement no. 2, p. 159.

e) Dasein, to which this world is pre-given, to which the world itself
    is unveiled.

In unity with that, Dasein is also disclosed to itself. According to the
levels of disclosedness, Dasein sees itself only in terms of *what* it encounters, only in terms of the world. Those in chains see themselves
only as shadows.

How then is the transition to a higher level of truth carried out?
(Wherein resides what is essential to the differences in truth?) It is not
carried out by gaining more of the old cognitions, by having a richer
manifold of uncovered beings, since the mode of Being of Dasein allows only shadows to be seen.

The chained-up Dasein must be *released*, so that it can see in the
light itself, i.e., know about the light itself. But that means: the understanding of Being must become explicit and be transformed. As long
as that does not happen, i.e., as long as the released ones cannot see in
the light itself, they also cannot see the very beings that are directly
illuminated. On the contrary, in conformity with the understanding
of Being (shadowy, without light) still ruling at the earlier level, they
will take any being they now encounter, any thing itself—since it is
not shadowy—as a nonbeing. What is first needed is an acclimation to
the light; i.e., the formation of the new level of truth primarily requires a familiarization with the new understanding of Being. On that
basis, the things themselves can then be distinguished from their
shadows and semblances. Only from the higher understanding of
Being do the things that had been exclusively taken as beings now become comprehensible in their Being. That is to say, in order to survey
and understand all beings and their respective ways to be, what is required is the highest understanding of Being, the knowledge of what
Being properly means.

The transition to a higher level is always as follows: not by an extension of cognitions in the already given domain of experience but,
instead, primarily by being drawn more and more to the light. That is,
the development of the understanding of Being opens the gaze for beings and for their various ways to be. At issue is not a mere influx of
new cognitions, but an *overturning* of the entire current basic position
of Dasein itself with respect to what it takes at any level as a genuine
being. Thus truth is grounded in the respective mode of Being of Dasein—whether Dasein is imprisoned in the cave or not, whether Being
is determined according to the immediately given beings or according
to a universal concept of Being, one that is not restricted to a determinate domain.[16]

16. See supplement no. 3, p. 159.

Understanding of Being: ability to see the light, the one that illuminates beings as beings. No accident that Plato speaks figuratively, for the understanding of Being is to be clarified precisely with and through the problem of the Ideas. We know the inexplicit and non-conceptual meaning of Being for the Greeks: *everlasting persistence.*

There are shadows only as long as things are carried past the fire which is burning behind those who are in chains. The shadows are utterly fleeting, without persistence, whereas the things—even if not being carried past the light—*remain;* and, as remaining, they become apprehensible, provided I see the light itself, i.e., provided I take them, on the basis of this direct illumination, as no longer in the realm of shadows.

The things in the light have a different persistence (constancy) than do the shadows, and yet they are changeable: their Gestalt may be deformed and the same Gestalt may be multiplied in various modes. The more penetrating understanding of Being, the sight of what is *unchangeable,* the understanding of αὐτὸ τὸ τρίγωνον ["the triangle itself"], reveals them, the things themselves, as "images." It is the rise of mathematical-geometrical cognition that wins something constant in the genuine sense and thus first makes visible the inconstancy of the things that are constant in relation to their shadows. But these mathematical cognitions for their part still have need of images, sensuous representations. They are not yet pure Being itself; the latter is first given with the ἰδέαι as such, with the highest ἰδέα: ἡ ἀγαθοῦ ἰδέα ["the Idea of the good"].[17]

This highest Idea is determined as follows:

1. ἐν τῷ γνωστῷ τελευταία (end and completion) καὶ μόγις ὁρᾶσθαι ["but scarcely to be seen"],[18]
2. πάντων αὕτη ὀρθῶν τε καὶ καλῶν αἰτία (517c2),
3. ἔν τε {τῷ} ὁρατῷ φῶς καὶ τὸν τούτου κύριον τεκοῦσα (517c3),
4. ἔν τε νοητῷ αὐτὴ κυρία λήθειαν καὶ νοῦν παρασχομένη (517c3f.),
5. ἡ τοῦ παντὸς ἀρχή (cf. 511b7),
6. ἔτι ἐπέκεινα τῆς οὐσίας (509b9).

Regarding 1) "In the field of the understandable, that which lies at the end," that which the understanding finally comes up against, whereby the understanding receives its completion, termination, conclusion. For the Greeks, πέρας, "limit," determinateness.

17. Cf. *Metaphysische Anfangsgründe der Logik im Ausgang von Leibniz.* Marburger Vorlesung Sommersemester 1928. GA 26. Frankfurt, 1978, p. 237.
18. *Republic,* bk. 7, 517B8f.

Regarding 2) "Cause of everything correct and beautiful," basic determination of all order—τάξις, put together, coexisting—its principle.

Regarding 3) The Idea of the good: it itself "begets both the light in the domain of what is visible as well as the lord of that domain" (the sun). Here the good is the *effective power* and source of all light. Even what is looked upon in sunlight and is visible to the eyes, even such a being is, as a being, graspable in its Being only through an understanding of Being.

Regarding 4) "In the field of what is understandable, it itself holds sway," determines everything, makes possible and "bestows truth, *disclosedness*, and *understanding*."

Regarding 5) "The ground and origin of all," of both beings and Being.

Regarding 6) It "yet lies beyond beings and Being." The question of Being transcends itself.

The understanding of Being[19] resides originally in the seeing of this Idea. Here is the *fundamental truth* itself, which makes possible all truths. (Later taken again in a purely ontic sense: Middle Ages, absolute spirit.)

Being is over and beyond all beings. Later Plato saw the distinction in a still sharper way, even if he did not follow it up.[20] But here the question has this orientation: beings are not interrogated so as to discover in what they consist, how they originated, but instead to disclose what "Being" signifies, what we mean in general by speaking of "Being." And that is obscure. The question of Being transcends itself. *The ontological problem turns around! Metontological;* θεολογική; beings as a whole. The ἰδέα ἀγαθοῦ: that which is utterly preferable to everything, the *most preeminent.* Being in general and the preferable. Something still *beyond* beings, belonging to the *transcendence* of Being, essentially determining the Idea of Being! The *most original possibility*! Originally *making possible* everything.

---

§35. Indication of the center of the problem of the Ideas.[21]

ὄησις–λόγος; ἰδέα–εἴδη–ἀγαθόν. Understanding of Being–ψυχή–ἀνάμνησις ["recollection"]. πᾶσα μὲν ἀνθρώπου ψυχὴ φύσει τεθέαται τὰ ὄντα[22]—"Every human soul has, by nature, already seen

19. See Mörchen transcription, no. 42, p. 200f.
20. *Sophist,* 242Cff.
21. See Mörchen transcription, no. 43, p. 201.
22. *Phaedrus,* 249E4f.

beings." The *soul* constitutes human Dasein: Dasein is already, in advance, such that it understands Being. Platonically: the most proper being is revealed to it: the ἀγαθόν.

Regarding ἀνάμνησις: νοῦς-λόγος, ἐπιστήμη.

Theatetus:[23] several issues simultaneously: 1. the Idea of science. In the background: the knowable in general. 2. Concrete presentation of the dialogical development of a problem. 3. Takes up an earlier position of Plato's and introduces the later one: the formation of the basic problem and of its methodology. Dialectics.

Regarding the ψυχή: *understanding of Being* in the Being of Dasein. Acting, doing, works. Being. Consciousness and Being; ego; subject; Dasein.

§36. Regarding the basic problem of ontology and regarding dialectics.

Ideas:[24] the One, the constant, versus the many and the changeable. But now there are many Ideas. τί—ἕκαστον ["this one—each"]. Difference, otherness, change, reversal, motion. Unity itself is something other than multiplicity; unity is other than otherness. The unity and connection of the Ideas themselves, συμπλοκὴ τῶν εἰδῶν. Only here is the domain of λόγος, of the original διαλέγεσθαι. To lead into this domain and to lead through it to Being itself and its structures. προσχρώμενος {. . .} εἴδεσιν αὐτοῖς δι᾽ αὐτῶν εἰς αὐτά, καὶ τελευτᾷ εἰς εἴδη ["employing Ideas themselves, going from Ideas to Ideas, and ending in Ideas"].[25]

Sophist, Parmenides, Philebus, Statesman; the *Theatetus* is preparatory.

Concept of dialectic: science of Being and of the connection of the structures of Being. σύνθεσις—διαίρεσις ["conjunction—disjunction"].

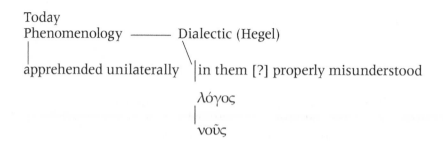

23. See below, chap. 3, p. 90ff.
24. See Mörchen transcription, no. 44, p. 202.
25. *Republic,* 511C1f. [For Heidegger's paraphrasing translation, see the Mörchen transcription, no. 44. —Trans.]

Logic — Ontology
|
|
Dialectical   Theology has nothing to do with this, at most
                negatively related.[26]

26. The remainder of the diagram on this page of the manuscript is largely
illegible.

3

Interpretation of the dialogue, *Theatetus:*[27] the connection between the question of the Idea of science and the question of Being

Content-summary and outline (142Aff.).[28]

Dialogue between Eucleides and Terpsion as prelude to the dialogue proper, chap. 1, up to 143C. Dialogue of Socrates with Theodorus and Theatetus. Introduction, chaps. 2–7, up to 151D. Fixing the theme: τί ἐστιν ἐπιστήμη; ["what is knowledge?"] (cf. 146C3), whether ἐπιστήμη is σοφία, whether "knowledge is understanding," what knowledge itself is.

First definition: ἡ αἴσθησις ἐπιστήμη ["knowledge is perception"], chaps. 8–30 (151D–187B).

1. Clarification of the definition through the theses of Protagoras and Heraclitus, chaps. 8–15, up to 161B.
2. Refutation of the objections against the thesis of Protagoras, and further clarification of its meaning, chaps. 16–21 (161B–169D).
3. Restriction of the validity of Protagoras's thesis to momentary perception, chaps. 22–26 (169D–179D).
4. Fundamental and conclusive refutation of Protagoras's doctrine of knowledge by testing its Heraclitean presuppositions, chaps. 27–29, up to 184A.
5. Refutation of the thesis of Theatetus: αἴσθησις = ἐπιστήμη, chaps. 29–39 (184A–187B).

Second definition: ἡ ἀληθὴς δόξα ἐπιστήμη ["knowledge is true opinion"], chaps. 31–38 (187B–201D).

27. See Mörchen transcription, no. 45, p. 202.
28. Cf. H. Bonitz, *Platonische Studien,* 3d ed., Berlin, 1886, p. 47ff.

1. τὸ δοξάζειν ψευδῆ ["false opinion"], chaps. 31–37. (clarification of the essence)

   a) Distinction between two possibilities: knowledge and non-knowledge.
   b) Distinction between momentary perception and memory.
   c) Distinction between the idle possession of knowledge and genuine employment of it.

2. Testing of second definition, chap. 38.

Third definition: ἡ δόξα ἀληθὴς μετὰ λόγου ["true opinion along with *logos*"], chaps. 39–43 (201E–210B).

1. General characterization of the thesis. Interpretation and denomination.
2. Clarification of the phenomenon of λόγος.

Result—negative!

§37. Prologue and introduction. Fixing the theme: what is knowledge?

a) Prelude: dialogue between Eucleides and Terpsion (142A–143C).

In Megara, Eucleides, arriving from the harbor, and Terpsion meet. Eucleides mentions that he came across Theatetus, and other wounded soldiers, who were being carried from Corinth to Athens. The discussion then turns to Theatetus. Eucleides recalls what Socrates said about him. Socrates once had a conversation with Theatetus and related it to Eucleides. This dialogue was written down by Eucleides, frequently consulting Socrates himself, and he now wants to have it read to Terpsion. He wrote it as a direct conversation, just the way the dialogue itself took place. Participants in the earlier dialogue, now to be read, were: Socrates, Θεόδωρος ὁ γεωμέτρης ["Theodorus the geometer"] (cf. 143B8) from Cyrene in North Africa, who is a friend of Socrates and of Protagoras, and Theatetus. For all practical purposes, only Socrates and Theatetus speak. Theatetus also appears in the *Sophist*; Theodorus in the *Statesman*.[29]

b) Introduction to the dialogue proper (143D–151D).

143D8–E1: Socrates addresses Theodorus, "Not a few seek your acquaintance, and rightly so." Socrates is looking for young people who offer a promise of exceptional accomplishments. Theodorus names Theatetus, who, while being described to Socrates, comes out of the gymnasium with friends. He has a snub nose and protruding eyes, just like Socrates, who wants to make his acquaintance and, by looking at Theatetus, see what he himself looks like. Theodorus calls Theatetus over to Socrates. 145B6f.: "It is time for you to present yourself and for me to examine you appropriately." 145C7: "Tell me, do you learn from . . . ?" Yet μικϱὸν δέ τι ἀποϱῶ (145D6), "there is one little thing in which I cannot make my way." Learning is gaining more understanding with regard to that which one learns. Simply to gain various cognitions, nothing controversial about that. On the other hand, misgivings regarding knowledge, understanding, itself, its truth: which comportment discloses beings as beings, which comportment leads to Being?

Theatetus begins to catch on to the method, and he himself brings up an example from the theory of numbers, but he still does not venture an answer to Socrates' question. Theatetus admits to having heard much of Socrates' way of questioning and the investigation of the εἶδος ἕν ["one *eidos*"] (cf. 148D6), though he himself has not mastered it. Nor has he been satisfied by the answers he has received from others. 148E–151D: Socrates encourages him and takes the occasion to offer a thorough presentation of his method. It would not be amiss to say that if Plato here once again portrays Socrates at length, he does it so as to convey his own method by contrast.

{Recapitulation:}[30]

Attempt at definition, abandoned. Correction by Socrates. New approach through geometry. Theatetus's {?} altered ways. Concession of non-knowledge. Socrates on pregnancy, labor pangs, and maieutics.

Acceptance of the theme and the question.[31]

§38. General discussion of the significance of the questioning in the *Theatetus* in the context of the Platonic problem of Being.

Before we attempt, by way of thematic discussions of the *Theatetus*, to characterize the central and fundamental problem of Plato's philoso-

---

30. Editor's interpolation.
31. See the following §.

phy, namely the ψυχή and dialectic, we need to recall once again the main points of the problem.

The *Theatetus* treats of αἴσθησις, δόξα, λόγος, ἐπιστήμη: modes of apprehension, modes of knowledge in the ontic sense, "statements" about known beings; thus it does not treat of Being and of beings as such. Viewed superficially, it seems indeed that this "epistemological" dialogue falls outside the theme we have made central to the entire lecture course and also to our presentation of Plato's philosophy: the question of the Being of beings itself and not the question of the apprehension of Being and beings. But it must be noted: αἴσθησις is related to becoming, and δόξα precisely to the Being which can also *not* be, thus to nonbeings. The fact that αἴσθησις and δόξα become problems signifies that Plato is placing himself on a path that will allow him to take up in a positive way the problem of becoming, change, and nonbeing.[32] With the level of the problematic attained at that time, it was much too difficult to gain direct access to nonbeings (becoming), provided it is in principle possible to do so at all. For the "not," negation, is always {dependent on}[33] the mode of apprehension. Perhaps there is no question of Being without a consideration of the mode of access to beings, and in the end the explicit question of knowledge may be nothing other than a sharpened formulation of the problem directed at the determination of Being. Knowledge is knowledge *of beings, disclosure of beings,* the possessing and preserving of beings as disclosed. "Knowledge of" is a *sharpened* relation to *beings;* according to the conviction of the Greeks, it is here that beings are accessible at all. *Sophist:* μὴ ὄν ["nonbeing"].

Hidden behind the problem of αἴσθησις and δόξα is the problem of μὴ ὄν and κίνησις ["motion"]. But that signifies something further: previously, Plato was essentially oriented toward the practical world of action and handcraft. Now coming into view are the beings of the world in the sense of nature. No accident that Theodorus and Theatetus, mathematicians, astronomers, masters of harmony, participate in this dialogue.

No epistemology in the *Theatetus.* It aims instead: 1. at nonbeing and becoming, whereby knowledge is co-discussed at the same time, 2. at a fundamental discussion of the problematic of Being, and 3. thereby at a transformation of this problematic itself.

αἴσθησις, δόξα, λόγος: Problem. Memory: *Republic:* δόξα—νόησις. New approach to the entire problematic concerns the problem of the Ideas and of Being. The Idea of the good: that on the basis of which anything becomes understandable, that toward which the various com-

---

32. See Mörchen transcription, no. 47, p. 203.
33. Editor's interpolation.

portments are striving, that for the sake of which something is, that to which something is appropriate and destined. With the *Theatetus*, the problem of Being begins, in a certain sense, to detach itself from the Idea of the good. Stenzel[34] has, with justification, taken that fact as a criterion for the detachment of Plato's philosophy from Socrates and from a specifically ethical orientation. Two periods: the *Republic* marks the termination of the first (cf. earlier[35]). New one begins with the *Theatetus*.

The detachment of the problem of Being from the Idea of the good is a fact. Yet in regard to it there remains a double problem: 1. why in general was it possible to understand Being in terms of the ἀγαθόν, and 2. why, even later, in Aristotle and beyond, is the ἀγαθόν understood as a basic determination of Being, *omne ens est bonum* ["every being is good"]. Accordingly, we will have to ask:

1. Is the orientation of the problem of the Ideas toward the Idea of the good merely a chance episode, or are there substantial motives residing in the content of the question of Being that have led to the ἀγαθόν?

2. Can this question itself be answered from the point of view of Plato's later period? In other words, does not that which was intended with the Idea of the ἀγαθόν also lie in the development of the genuine dialectic and in the conception of ψυχή, as these are found in the later period? And so does not the function of the ἀγαθόν return in the end?

Summary: How does the proposal of the Idea of the good go together with the task of dialectic? To what extent is there won, in both, a new way of posing the question of Being? What is the significance of Plato's philosophical work in terms of the basic problem of scientific philosophy, the question of Being in general? What is to be learned, in both a positive and negative sense, from this? In what follows we will try to answer these questions.[36]

---

34. J. Stenzel, *Studien zur Entwicklung der platonischen Dialektik von Sokrates zu Aristoteles: Arete und Diairesis. Mit einem Anhang: Literarische Form und philosophischer Gehalt des platonischen Dialoges.* Breslau, 1917, pp. 38–39.

35. Cf. §34b, p. 87.

36. See supplement no. 4, p. 160.

First definition: ἡ αἴσθησις ἐπιστήμη (chaps. 8-30)

§39. Knowledge is perception: clarification of this thesis through the propositions of Protagoras and Heraclitus (chaps. 8-15, 151D-161B).

From what has just been said we should not expect this passage to contain an epistemological discussion, much less a psychological one. It treats, instead, of Being[37] and becoming and, since Being = constancy, of constancy and becoming, wherein Being properly resides. The earlier opposition found in Parmenides and Heraclitus, but now raised to a new level, although not mastered. Yet central problems, the positive and actual questioning. Plato previously attributed motion, change, κίνησις to μὴ ὄν. Now a peculiar emphasis on κίνησις itself.

Knowledge comports itself to beings in the mode of perception. φαίνεται (151E2), "something shows itself"; what shows itself is a being. Apprehension of a being: to let it show itself in the mode of perception. But the same thing shows itself differently to different individuals. Αἴσθησις ἄρα τοῦ ὄντος ἀεί ["perception always perceives some being"] (152C5), an essential constatation. The very meaning of perception includes the opinion of apprehending a being in itself; this holds even for illusory perception and hallucination.

Clarification, fundamentals of the thesis: a double consideration: perception—the perceived, mode of Being of Dasein. Perception—the perceived: understood as a process occurring between present-at-hand things (the schema of the natural scientific explanation) and understood as a *phenomenological* state of affairs. This latter has the primacy.

The One (sameness) in itself, with respect to itself, is not. The determinations, "something" and "of such quality," cannot be attributed

37. See Mörchen transcription, no. 48, p. 204f.

95

to anything, for things are always only *becoming* (152D, cf. 157B). Against Parmenides. That which "is" moves. Then if knowledge *is*— i.e., if according to the thesis, there is "perception"—then it too must exist on the basis of motion and as motion. The principle still remains: nothing can in itself be *one*. κίνησις has the priority; τὸ μὲν εἶναι δοκοῦν {. . .} κίνησις παρέχει (153A6f.), "motion presents the very look of the Being of beings"; immobility, on the other hand, presents that of nonbeing. What lives and moves "is." κίνησις as εἶναι is ἀγαθόν. ἥλιος ["the sun"], περιφορά ["going round"] (cf. 153D1f.), is now, precisely as moved and moving, the foundation of beings.

In this ontological context: if χρῶμα λευκόν (153d9), "a white color," is something perceived—according to the thesis, a being—μὴ εἶναι αὐτὸ ἕτερόν τι ἔξω τῶν σῶν ὀμμάτων μηδ᾽ ἐν τοῖς ὄμμασι μηδέ τιν᾽ αὐτῷ χώραν ἀποτάξῃς ["is not another thing itself outside your eyes, nor inside the eyes, and is not to be assigned any actual place"] (153D9ff.), then it would indeed already be in some way and would not merely become. But it does become, and specifically: *perception*—προσβάλλον ["striking"], προσβαλλόμενον ["what is struck"], προσήκουσα φορά ["the appropriate motion"], μεταξὺ γεγονός ["arising in-between"], ἑκάστῳ ἴδιον ["peculiar to each perceiver"] (cf. 153E7-154A2). No certainty that it is the same for others, and indeed it is even different for the same perceiver at different times. If the προσβαλλόμενον itself, which we encounter, were warm or white, then it would not show itself differently to others, αὐτό γε μηδὲν μεταβάλλον ["as long as it itself did not change"] (154B3). If it (λευκόν ["white"]) were in itself that which measures and touches, then it would not become different when something else simply προσελθόν (cf. 154B5), "approached" it, without itself undergoing anything thereby. Accordingly, there must be *change* for perception to be possible, i.e., for the perceived to be a *being*, i.e., for something to be able to show itself to everyone (154B). Thus perception is reduced to the problem of κίνησις.

Theatetus does not comprehend this new step taken with regard to the presuppositions of αἴσθησις. Socrates explains with a παράδειγμα ["example"]: ἀστράγαλοι ["dice"] (cf. 154C1ff.). Let there be 6 dice. If you juxtapose 4 others, then 6 is greater, 1½ times greater. If you juxtapose 12 others, then 6 is smaller, ½ times smaller. 6 is both greater *and* smaller: 1½ and ½. Can something become greater without increasing? Can something be other than it is without changing? *No!* But with regard to the first question: can something show itself as other without having increased? *Yes;* for each perceiver the same thing is different, other.[38] How can these two results be reconciled? Which principles must be maintained, and what lies in the relations among

38. See supplement no. 5, p. 160.

the dice? 1. Never can something become greater or smaller, neither in extension or number, as long as it remains the same with itself. 2. That to which something is neither added nor taken away has neither increased nor decreased but, instead, remains the same. 3. If something was not earlier, and later is, that cannot happen without it becoming and having become. But if we consider the dice example, then the opposite seems to be the case. 1. 6 remains the same with itself! 2. Nothing is added to it, and yet it is not always the same. 3. First it was greater, then smaller.

Another παράδειγμα. "Now I am still bigger than you, but when you have grown I will be smaller. I will be later what I was not earlier, without having become." Theatetus: "I cannot stop wondering about these things; looking at them I become giddy." μάλα γὰρ φιλοσόφου (155C8ff.), that is "the proper attitude of the philosopher," to wonder. To investigate what lies at the basis of those theses, to uncover τὴν ἀλήθειαν ἀποκεκρυμμένην ["the hidden truth"] (155D10).

Relationality[39] and relativity as *ontological* problems. Relatedness of something to something, relation between. Problem of relation in general. Relation and Being, Being and otherness, not being such and such.

Plato looks still more closely into the problem. The principles. To test what these φάσματα ἐν ἡμῖν ["appearances in us"] (155A2) are all about. I become smaller by the fact that you have grown. I change, although I remain the same, by the fact that you have changed. I am later what I was not earlier, without having become so. "To become" through comparison, "to become" through change, "to be" in relation to. To maintain {?} the intentional view, through real change.

Otherness, other than, than what, in view of what. To take up a point of view with reference to something that remains the same. Large–small, more–less: essentially *relative*. Nothing in itself "is"; everything becomes. A being is only the act of becoming ({?}[40]) of the perceptual *process*. But the man who is all senses is precisely a *nonbeing*.

The principle of Protagoras: τὸ πᾶν κίνησις ἦν καὶ ἄλλο παρὰ τοῦτο οὐδέν ["everything is motion and there is nothing besides"] (156A5). δύο εἴδη κινήσεως ["two kinds of motion"] (cf. 156A5f.): ποιεῖν, "acting," and πάσχειν (156A7), "undergoing." Perceiving and the perceived, from their interplay a perception arises. Perception, motion, κίνησις, εἶναι.[41] And indeed neither of these two is for itself; rather, each is what it is in relation to the other (157A). But that is exactly what the just-cited principle states: "nothing *is* one in itself" (152D3). There is *no being* at all, *only becoming*. This designation, which

39. See Mörchen transcription, no. 49, p. 205.
40. Illegible.
41. See supplement no. 5, p. 160.

we have employed up to now only through custom and ignorance, is to be done away with. Nor can we say "something," "this," or "that." οὐδὲν ὄνομα ὅτι ἀν ίστῇ (157B4f.), "no name which congeals something," which signifies something standing still. We find only that which becomes, passes away, changes. Everything moves; *motion is Being.*

In order to hold to the main lines of the argumentation and allow the positive content of Plato's discussions to come forth, we will pass over the intermediate considerations and pick up the thread at 180C.

---

§40. Fundamental and conclusive refutation of Protagoras's doctrine of knowledge by testing its Heraclitean presuppositions (chaps. 27-29, 180C-184A).

Plato says here: "The problem has come down from the ancients" (180C7f.). The later ones have so popularized the thesis that every cobbler can understand it. "But I had almost forgotten" the counter-thesis that "all things are one and immobile and that there is no place for motion" (180D7ff.). "Without noticing it, in the course of our dialogue we have" ἀμφοτέρων εἰς τὸ μέσον πεπτωκότες ["fallen between the two factions"] (180E6). "We must resist and come to a decision about both parties": οἱ ῥέοντες (cf. 181A4), "the flowing ones," and οἱ {. . .} στασιῶται (181A6f.), the "immobilizers." Two things are evident: 1. μέσον ["middle"] (180E6), Plato consciously places himself in the middle, on neither side, without, however, denying either side. 2. Again the fundamental problem is that of Being. Perception as determined through ποιεῖν ["making"], πάσχειν ["undergoing"]. Motion is a phenomenon on that basis. Thus a radical understanding of both sides.

First the flowing ones, and {in the *Theatetus*}[42] only them. (The other side is taken up in the *Sophist,* in the context of the same problematic.) οἱ ῥέοντες: ἀρχή {. . .} σκέψεως ["for the flowing ones: the beginning of the examination"] (181C1). 1. φορά ["locomotion"] (cf. 181D6), 2. ἀλλοίωσις ["becoming other"] (cf. 181D5). Do all beings move in both ways or only according to one way? Obviously the flowing ones must say "in both respects," for if something moved only in one of the ways, φορά, then we would still have immobility. For example, something white, which changes its place, would remain the same, unchanged. If, as the thesis says, according to both ways, then the white must also change.

White, however, is something perceived, and as such arises in and through an interplay of acting and undergoing. That which undergoes becomes perceptive, but not a perception (182A). That which acts be-

---

42. Editor's interpolation.

comes a ποιόν ["of a definite sort"], but not a quality (182A). But if everything only becomes and is not, can we at all speak of a thing's determinate color? ἀεὶ λέγοντος ὑπεξέρχεται ἅτε δὴ ῥέον (182D7), "as something that is flowing, it ever withdraws from showing itself in naming and assertion." But if nothing perseveres, then we can also not say that *something* is seen. Yet perception is indeed supposed to be knowledge! The disclosure of the foundation of perception, κίνησις, leads to the conclusion that there is nothing stable to be grasped at all, that we cannot say "such and such" or "not such and such" (183A5f.). We must, as it were, invent a new language to be able to address and express what is ceaselessly changing. The most appropriate expression: ἄπειρον ["unlimited"] (Kant).[43]

The ontological problematic and the *impossibility* of perception as knowledge. It is not only the perceived object that is dissolved, but equally the perceptual process. The phenomenon of perception and knowledge is utterly reduced to motion; i.e., to inconstancy. This result is merely the ontological consequence of the fact that the perceived is different for every perceiver. It is obvious, however, that in this critique the *genuine phenomenon of perception* (intentionality) is lost. Perception is discussed in the same way as the perceived being (a thing in motion). The intentional structure of perception is leveled down to a present-at-hand interplay between perceived things, the effect of a collision. If the discussion stopped here, then Plato, with this "explanation" of αἴσθησις, would not have done justice to the phenomenon, the understanding of which was called for by Socrates. λόγος indeed is directed to a τι. This phenomenal state of affairs is not to be suppressed, but clarified. In other words, the demonstration that perception is knowledge, or, on the other hand, that it cannot be knowledge, must take its bearings from what perception itself is.

§41. Refutation of Theatetus's thesis: αἴσθησις = ἐπιστήμη (chaps. 29-39, 184A-187B).

Therefore only at 184B do we have a turn to a positive analysis of perception; αἴσθησις τινός ["perception of something"], indication of that *to which* it is directed, and *how*. Through this consideration, αἴσθησις in general is placed in the context of cognitive comportment and not taken up in isolation. Previously: individual cases of knowledge, {considered}[44] as beings themselves. Now we find a tracing back to that which lies at the foundation of all knowledge in accord with its most proper sense, to that which can be made visible from knowledge itself.

43. See Mörchen transcription, no. 50, p. 205.
44. Editor's interpolation.

Plato now seeks to show, on the basis of the structure of perception, that it cannot be knowledge. For perception does not grasp Being. But Being must be grasped if beings are to be disclosable, i.e., for disclosedness, truth, to be possible. Where Being is not understood and truth is not possible, there can be no knowledge. Knowledge is precisely the apprehension of beings as they *are*. This proof that perception cannot be knowledge, based on the intentional constitution of perception, is totally different from the earlier one, which was an ontological consideration that referred to the perceptual process and saw in it a constant flowing, inconstancy. (Yet even this earlier proof is not without aim {?}: emphasis on the movedness of the αἰσθητά.)

Perception; *with what?* Eyes, ears? No; on the contrary, *by means of* them, *with their help, through* them. They function in perception, they cooperate in it, but they are not what perceives (184B). Thereby, however, that which had earlier been the basis of the discussion is demoted. Brought to the foreground now are not the eyes, but that which uses them as visual organs, that which first *organizes them into organs*. It is not because we have eyes that we see; on the contrary, it is because we see, that we have eyes. This is expressed in the distinction between ᾧ ["with which"] and δι' οὗ ["through which"] (184C6). That *with* which we see is that which sees. That *through* which, the eyes, are not what sees. The essential in perception does not reside in the organs. They themselves are organized as organs, and placed into function, by the perceiver, in whom they have unity. No merely juxtaposed perceptions. πάντα ταῦτα συντείνει (184D3f.), "all these are directed together" to One. They are all perceptions of this perceiver, who is *prior* to the organs.[45] The organs as such are not decisive, and so neither is the interplay between them and the things that exercise effects on them. Such processes do not now enter the domain of the consideration.

τινι ἡμῶν αὐτῶν τῷ αὐτῷ διά ["something one and the same, within ourselves, through"] (184D7f.). 1. We ourselves are perception; it is what belongs to our most proper self, which 2. as such remains the same, constant, not inconstant. "I," as the same, now hear and see, 3. through something.

Nexus: two things must be noted:

1. The organs through which {are perceived}[46] the warm, the hard, the light, the sweet, are τοῦ σώματος ["of the body"] (184E5).

2. What is perceived through *one* faculty, e.g., color, is not perceived through the others.

The sounding clock is seen and heard. Seeing, hearing, touching; direction: beings. These moments are not differentiable as juxtaposed

45. See Mörchen transcription, no. 51, p. 205ff.
46. Editor's interpolation.

but as emerging *out of the unity of the intended being.* How is that? If I intend and determine something about two different perceptions, it is not through the one faculty perceiving what is perceived by the other. Not only do I not perceive what is perceived by the other, I also, and above all, do not perceive both together; "both," "together" (185A4). Then what do I mean in saying I perceive πρῶτον μέν ["in the first place"] (185A8) that they both are (185A9)? In the first place, before all else, I understand them already as *beings* (cf. 185C5). Each is, in relation to each, other; on the other hand, each is self-same.

The positive conclusion: ἀναλογίσματα ["analogizings"] (186C2f.) — λόγος (cf. 185E5) — κατηγορεῖν ["categorizing"]. Categories, discovery of the categorial versus the sensual. Already cited: Kant: sensibility-understanding. But beware of introducing here a critical interpretation of knowledge.[47] Prior to that, the substantive content of the problem: sensuous and categorial intuition.[48] The board is black. Assertion: black board, "which" is; black (adjectival) property. A being understood as a being in its Being.

In connection with αἴσθησις and on the basis of the question of Being.

47. I. Kant, *Kritik der reinen Vemunft,* A 51/B 75; see Mörchen transcription, no. 51, p. 205ff.

48. E. Husserl, *Logische Untersuchungen, II. Theil: VI. Untersuchung: Elemente einer phänomenologischen Aufklärung der Erkenntnis,* Halle/Saale, 1901.

Second definition:
ἐπιστήμη ἀληθὴς δόξα
(chaps. 31-38, 187B-201D)

§42. Proof of the thesis that knowledge is true δόξα by way of proving the impossibility of δοξάζειν ψευδῆ.

a) The path through the proof of the impossibility of δοξάζειν ψευδῆ as evidence for the intrinsic reference of this questioning to the problem of Being.

Truth only from the understanding of Being; the understanding of Being only from the soul itself, {which}[49] discloses it. The negative proposition, perception is not knowledge, states in a positive sense what necessarily belongs to knowledge: the disclosing of Being, understanding of Being, the soul itself, understanding, interpretation, λόγος; Being, beings, the perceived. Clarification of Being! That is, further, the soul is of itself; it is not something that merely comes to be given but, on the contrary, is an a priori of Dasein!

Being of the soul; comportment arising from the soul: to be of the opinion, assume as, hold in favor of, mean that such and such. Stated positively, knowledge, proceeding from the soul itself, very generally: δοξάζειν.[50] Earlier, δόξα was the opposite of νόησις: μὴ ὄν—ὄν. Now seen more positively: in it something that makes knowledge possible. δόξα is something over and above αἴσθησις. Thus oriented to ὄν.

δόξα, view, opinion. To knowledge belongs truth. Hence knowledge merely true δόξα? Is true δόξα knowledge? What is δόξα itself? What is δοξάζειν? These questions are part of the theme, but they are

49. Editor's interpolation.
50. See Mörchen transcription, no. 52, p. 207f.; see also supplement no. 6, p. 160.

102

investigated factically, in regard to a peculiar phenomenon, ψευδής δόξα ["false opinion"]. Not accidental:

1. At that time in history: οὐκ ἔστι ἀντιλέγειν, contradiction does not exist; there is nothing false, οὐκ ἔστι ψευδῆ λέγειν.[51]

2. *Sophist:* ψευδής λόγος is explicitly the theme and indeed within a delineation of μὴ ὄν, i.e., ὄν.[52] Plato notes expressly that it would in fact be necessary to investigate ἀληθὴς δόξα first of all, but here both are equivalent methodologically, since μὴ ὄν as well as ὄν, ψεῦδος, and ἀλήθεια formally become problems.

We see: αἴσθησις—problem of Being; also knowledge as ψευδής δόξα {is centered on the}[53] problem of Being; and specifically μὴ ὄν ["nonbeing"], ἕτερον ["otherness"], ἐναντίον ["opposition"]; κίνησις—to be other, to change. λόγος—δοξάζειν; ὄν—μὴ ὄν; ἕτερον, ἄλλο ["different"]; συνάπτειν ["conjoin"]—σύνθεσις ["combination"]. Dovetailing of utterly positive phenomena. In contrast, Natorp: "For the rest, this whole second part contains {. . .} only an overweening critique of others' opinions, whose contradictions, crude vicious circles, and question-beggings it playfully unfolds and thereby exposes the grotesque folly of their basic point of view in its primal dogmatism."[54] The motive for this interpretation is clear: critical (in the sense of epistemological critique) versus dogmatic conception of knowledge. Knowledge is the positing and determining of objects in thinking (Marburg School's view of Kant) versus a mere picturing of them.[55]

The critical analysis of δόξα versus δόξα ψευδής:[56]

1. 187B–189B: δοξάζειν ψευδές ["false opinion"] and δοξάζειν οὐδέν ["opinion of nothing"].

   a) 188A–D: εἰδέναι ["seeing"],
   b) 188D–189B: εἶναι ["Being"].

There is no such phenomenon at all.

2. δόξα ψευδής as ἀλλοδοξία ["mistaken opinion"], ἑτεροδοξεῖν ["opinion about something other"]: 189B–190C.
3. δόξα and σύναψις αἰσθήσεως πρὸς διάνοιαν ["conjunction of perception and thought"] (cf. 195D1f.), 190C–200D

51. Cf. Aristotle, *Met.* Δ 29, 1024b34.
52. *Sophist,* 260C2ff.
53. Editor's interpolation.
54. *Platos Ideenlehre,* 2d ed. Leipzig, 1921 (henceforth, Natorp), p. 119; see also Mörchen transcription, no. 52, p. 207.
55. Cf. Natorp, p. 112.
56. See Mörchen transcription, no. 52, p. 207f.

b) The carrying out of the proof of the impossibility of
δοξάζειν ψευδῆ (187B–189B).

Regarding 1: Two kinds of δόξα: ἀληθής, ψευδής. Does it hold for all things and for each, then, that we either know or do not know it? Obviously! That is a complete classification! Coming to know and forgetting, the μεταξύ ["the in-between"], we will for now leave aside (188A1ff., cf. 191C). What our opinions are directed at is then something we either know or do not know. To know something and not know it, or not to know something and at the same time to know it, is ἀδύνατον ["impossible"] (188A10f.). Plato must have already possessed the result of the *Sophist*! False opinion: to be directed to something that is given, something that one therefore does know.

a) What one has an opinion about and *knows*, but not taken as what one knows; instead, as some other thing that one also knows. Knowing both, one does not know both. Impossible.

b) Or, what the opinion is about is something one does *not know*, and with regard to it the opinion is likewise directed to something one does not know. Impossible.

Therefore one does not take what one knows for what one does not know, and vice versa.[57] To do so would be wonderful (188C)! Actually, this πάθος ["affect"] does reside in ψευδὴς δόξα (cf. 191B/C). From this standpoint, hence, false opinion is impossible. Either I know the thing, and then my opinion is true; or I do not know it, and then I cannot at all be directed toward it. To be directed to a nonbeing is nothing! Either I know that which I have an opinion about or not. But my opinion is indeed about something: μὴ ὄν–οὐκ ὄν–οὐδέν ["nonbeing–not a being–nothing"]. Knowing and not knowing are not the issue; on the contrary, at issue are *Being* and *nonbeing*. Can anyone have an opinion about nonbeings? Ὅταν ["Yes, whenever"] . . . (188D10ff.), if one indeed believes something, but this something is not true. To be directed to something, but not as something true, is nothing. Yet does it not sometimes happen that one sees something, but sees nothing?[58] If it is a thing, then it is a matter of some being—or not?

---

57. See supplement no. 7, p. 160.
58. See Mörchen transcription, no. 53, p. 208.

§43. Parenthetical discussion of the as-structure and otherness.

a) The as-structure of λόγος. The mutual exclusivity of Being and nonbeing in the Greek theory of λόγος.

δοξάζειν—(λέγειν) ψευδὴν δόξαν: λέγειν τὰ μὴ ὄντα ["false opinion: saying things that are not"].[59] λόγος: to interpret something by showing it *as* something. To draw out of beings something pre-given as such and such, *as that which* I determine it to be, but also to apprehend it on the basis of what is known and familiar. To understand some X as Socrates, as something it is not. Something, the pre-given, the encountered, as something, the determinant: different origin, the as-structure itself.

On the other hand, Antisthenes:[60] there is only the ἕν, only sameness and constancy. λόγος, λέγειν ταὐτόν ["to say the same"], A is A, A is in no way B. Something other and not the same: therefore nothing.

ψεῦδος: to distort, to show: 1. intentionality, 2. the as-structure. Not something as itself but, instead, to name *two:* one *and* the other, not only the one *for* the other. Seen more closely, the "as" is present even in identification.

b) The relativity of the μή in the sense of otherness in the *Sophist*.

ἕτερον ἕτερον ["the other is other"]: 1. One thing is the other one,[61] identical with the different one; 2. one thing is otherwise.

Something can show itself: 1. in itself, as itself;[62] 2. πρός τι ["related to something"], ἕτερον is πρός τι (cf. 255C13), not sameness. *Other than,* something *with respect to* something. ἀμφότερα (255B12f.).

Everything ὂν διὰ τὸ μετέχειν τῆς ἰδέας τῆς θατέρου ["participates in the Idea of the other"] (255E5f.). ἕτερον ["other"] is not ἐναντίον ["opposite"], but being-other (258B2f.), and is so on the basis of the κοινωνία ["commonality"] (cf. 256B).[63] The μὴ καλόν ["not beautiful"], originating from the καλόν ["beautiful"], co-posits the καλόν (257D10f.). The "not" belongs to the Being of beings,

---

59. Cf. *Sophist,* 260C3; see Mörchen transcription, no. 54, p. 208f.

60. Cf. F. W. A. Mullach, *Fragmenta Philosophorum Graecorum. Coll. rec. vert.* Vols. 1–3. Paris, 1860ff. (Henceforth, Mullach, *Fragmenta.*) Vol. 2, *Antisthenes,* frag. 47, pp. 282–283.

61. See Mörchen transcription, no. 55, p. 209.

62. *Sophist,* 255C12f.

63. See supplement no. 8, p. 160f.

κοινωνία. Versus ἐναντίωσις ["opposition"] is ἀντίθεσις ["contrast"] (257E6). The μή ["not"] is δύναμις ["possibility"] of the πρός τι, of the *being-toward;* it belongs to Being. ἕτερον is not exclusion, complete difference; on the contrary, something is retained in it. The μή is not excluded from beings but, instead, τὶ μηνύει (257B10) — "shows something," namely, that what it (the other) is, is not nonbeing. {The μή}[64] does not make disappear, does not bring us before nothingness, but ·instead, *lets something be seen.*

A is B: identical with, the same, Being is present with A. A is not B: not identical, different, excluding.

Every being that is, insofar as it is, differs from all the others. Every being is a one and, *as a one,* is still *different. Being-other belongs to Being,* i.e., not to be such and such. Structure of nonbeing. Then what does Being mean? Possible togetherness: togetherness—co-presencing. Whence this "co-"? Because "one thing" can be articulated only in something of a different kind, but, at the same time, only as access. In this something of a different kind, the other is precisely *there* as "*co-.*"

---

§44. ἀλλοδοξία as the ground of possibility of δοξάζειν ψευδῆ (189B-190C).

Regarding 2: ἀλλοδοξία ["mistaken opinion"].[65]

Opinion about . . . always about a being, but in this case about one instead of the other, in place of the other. To mistake beings, to be confused about that toward which the gaze is directed. But always intending *only one thing;* the other remains outside. Single-rayed intention. But the "in the place of" belongs essentially to the intended itself, on the basis of the "as."

Mis-taking: I take something ugly for something beautiful and vice versa. ἕτερον ἀντὶ ἑτέρου ["one thing in place of another"] (cf. 189C2f.). Something which I know I take for something else which I also know. But I cannot be mistaken about something I know. I always intend this being just as it is; in other words, even in such a case my opinion is true.

Theatetus taken as Socrates: not one instead of the other, as if we simply intended the wrong person; instead, necessarily both, but we name them falsely. Thus the one *for* the other; not "either-or," but "as well as," and indeed in a determinate structural form. Not only one instead of the other, but this one *for* the other, the one *as* the other:

---

64. Editor's interpolation.
65. Cf. *Theatetus,* 189B12, see above, p. 103; see Mörchen transcription, no. 56, p. 209f.

thus to interpret and understand, and always already to experience and apprehend, something *as* something. Experience is not limited to sensation, not only in also grasping beings and the determinations of Being, but also in always apprehending a being *as* such and such. It is pre-given (known) and *intended as* such and such, which it is *not*. But I know this, precisely not in making a false assertion but in my opinion that it is so.

Here the "other than it is" is interpreted as "one *instead* of the other." ἕτερον {. . .} ὡς ἕτερον (189D7), "the one for an other." "Instead of," but not "as."

διανοεῖν ["thought"] for δοξάζειν. The comportment of διάνοια (cf. 189D8, E1) in: the one for the other (189D7), both or only one (189E2). What is διανοεῖσθαι (189E2, middle voice)? λόγος ψυχῆς (cf. 189E6), earlier considered the first comportment of the soul, still undetermined, exhibited only in general, that which is beyond and transcends; but I do grasp Being, the categories. δοξάζειν–λέγειν (190A4), on the other hand, the conflict λόγος–δόξα. δόξα is λόγος εἰρημένος (cf. 190A5), something "spoken," i.e., the carrying out of a demonstration, the possession of what is asserted, of what is under discussion. In λόγος is εἶναι, demonstration, assertion; thus ἕτερον ἕτερον εἶναι ["saying one thing is another"] (190A9).

But is that actually the case; can we say the one *is* the other? Being: do they both have the same Being? Thus a person cannot say both, the one and the other, because λόγος is λέγειν τὸ αὐτό ["saying the same"]. Theory prior to the phenomena, although already an approach to them.

δόξα ψευδής is also not ἑτεροδοξεῖν ["opinion about something other"]; that is impossible. Impossible for the opinion not to be about both things; one is insufficient (190D4ff.). δόξα ψευδής is not ἀλλογοξία (cf. 190E). Positively: λόγος, "showing," although not known in its structure.

---

§45. δόξα and the conjunction of perception and thought (διάνοια) (190C-200D).

Before the discussion progresses, once again the *genuine* phenomenon[66] of false opinion breaks through, specifically in an example: it may happen that I know Socrates and yet at times take someone (who is not Socrates) approaching me out of the distance for Socrates: ᾠήθην εἶναι Σωκράτη ὃν οἶδα ["suppose to be Socrates, whom I know"] (191B4f.). Here the phenomenon is explicitly described, the

---

66. See supplement no. 9, p. 161.

phenomenon of *mis-seeing*. I falsely take someone for another. At issue is basically the interpretation of this phenomenon.

The adequate interpretation, however, is hindered by the preconceived theory. How is the mis-seeing *interpreted:* the mis-seeing implies the knowledge of Socrates, implies that I know him. I mis-see, take for Socrates, and I identify that which I know (Socrates) with that which I do not know, X. Thus the mis-seeing implies that: ἃ ἴσμεν ἐποίει ἡμᾶς εἰδότας μὴ εἰδέναι (191B7f.), "what we know turns our knowing into non-knowing." The known becomes the unknown. That is impossible.

1. I do not identify the known with the unknown; on the contrary, the known (Socrates) is that *as which* I *interpret* what is given.

2. The X whom I encounter is not what is unknown, but what is given; and in the sense of the mis-seeing it is precisely what is *known*. My opinion is that I see Socrates in this X.

The *Greek* interpretation falls outside of the phenomenon and characterizes it through its objective results. In other words, it sees in the phenomenon the objective state of affairs, that X is not Socrates and that I do not recognize X as X (as the one he actually is).

The *phenomenon* implies precisely that I *have the opinion: it is Socrates.* Contained in the phenomenon is the circumstance that it is factually not Socrates. The mis-seeing is a matter of my apprehending something, not as that which it is not, but as that which I presume it to be. Something unknown does precisely not enter in. At issue is not simply identification, but something *as* something; not something unknown as known, but *the perceived as presumed to be such and such.*

Something in relation to something, something as something. But in the present context, that is understood only in this sense: not that I hold a known something to be something I do not know, neither a matter of perception nor representation; but, instead, *the perceived taken as the represented.* Different modes of possessing a being. I know something perceived, I know something represented, knowing in λόγος. Knowledge is not at all univocal; *a being and its Being are different.* To attribute, to the given, something that is not given (perceived) but is, as such, known: a stranger *as* Socrates. Or, to take someone (Socrates) whom I do not know as such, but perceive as approaching me, *for* Theodorus. Now no longer the "in the place of," not a matter of identification, but instead a matter of "taking *for*," and both *given differently.*

On the basis of the dogmatic thesis of λόγος–λέγειν ταὐτό and on the basis of the unclarity in the mode in which what is pre-given is given and what is determining is presumed to be, this interpretation of the ψευδὴς δόξα is rejected as well.

Regarding 3: The third {interpretation}[67] now tries to gain clarity, precisely in this direction.

The example of mis-seeing shows: I know something or other. Socrates is known to me, even if I am not looking at him. The knowledge of him is retained in me (cf. 192D).

1. It is possible at times to perceive, and at times not to perceive, that which one knows. Knowledge of something, something learned, without having seen for oneself.

2. What one does not know can probably never be experienced, and often never is, or is experienced only to be forgotten right away. Having seen, one no longer knows how it looks.[68]

Examples:

1. I know both Theodorus and Theatetus, but I do not perceive either of them. Then I will not take the one for the other.

2. I know the one but not at all the other, and I do not perceive either of them. Also in this case, I will not take the one I know for the one I do not know. What is determining is completely unknown to me.

3. I know neither, and I perceive neither. Then it will a fortiori be impossible for me to take the one I do not know for another I also do not know. Nothing is pre-given, and nothing that determines is known.

It follows that the ψευδῆ δοξάζειν consists only in this: "I know both of you," ἔχων {. . .} τὰ σημεῖα (193B10f.), "I have impressions of you," "signs," "I have an inkling of you." "I see both distantly," μὴ ἱκανῶς (193C2), "not sufficiently." I see and want to "recognize" what is there. I try τῇ οἰκείᾳ ὄψει (193C3), "to attribute to the one who is currently seen, in accord with his outward look," the "signs" that pertain to him. Thereby I mistake what is determinant, the "signs" that pertain to what is currently seen, and I take Theodorus for Theatetus, and vice versa. τὼ σημείω μὴ κατὰ τὴν αὑτοῦ αἴσθησιν ἑκάτερον ἔχειν (194A1f.), "the signs are not attributed to the perceived object to which they currently correspond," their attribution does not correspond, i.e., the signs do not actually pertain to the perceived object to which they are attributed.

For this mistaken attribution to be possible, however, something must be perceived, and, on the other hand, something must be known. Where there is neither knowledge, familiarity, nor perception, there is also no mis-seeing and (false) mixed-up opinion (194B). The essential (cf. 195C7): not a simple identification of the known with the unknown, but at once something perceived, given, and known in itself,

---

67. Editor's interpolation.
68. See Mörchen transcription, no. 57, p. 210f.

as well as something only represented, known only in an inkling, and indeed their σύναψις ["conjunction"] (cf. 195D1).[69]

Then where perceptions are not involved, where they play no part, there could not be mis-seeing: e.g., in calculation, in counting sums. Indeed we do in fact make mistakes in counting. But there it cannot be a matter of a false relation between what is retained in thought and something perceived. Thus this interpretation is *not tenable*. Thereby what is scandalous about our procedure comes to light: we are seeking to clarify knowledge and false knowledge, without knowing what knowledge itself is (196D10).

---

§46. Testing the second definition (201A–D).

From the second to the third definition. True opinion = knowledge.[70] But one can have true opinion *without* knowledge. The grounds for this assertion can clarify what is meant by knowledge. Jurors judge on the basis of a true opinion they have formed regarding the case (201Bf.). But they did not see the criminal act itself, they were not present. So they have no knowledge. Which implies for this concept: they have not made accessible to themselves, in their own experience, the being about which they are rendering a decision. If correct opinion and knowledge were identical, then a competent juror never has a correct opinion without having knowledge at the same time. Thus they are different, and knowledge is to be distinguished from true opinion—in virtue of what? What is the distinguishing moment?

69. See supplement no. 10, p. 161.
70. See Mörchen transcription, no. 58, p. 211.

Third definition of ἐπιστήμη: ἀληθὴς δόξα μετὰ λόγου (chaps. 39–43, 201E–210B)

§47. General characterization of the thesis: knowledge is true δόξα μετὰ λόγου. Interpretation and denomination.

μετὰ λόγου ["with *logos*"],[71] that is to say, in such a manner that the showing of the beings themselves is present *for* the soul itself, or in such a manner that the soul itself makes manifest beings in their disclosedness, thus beings as actually being, as being such and such, beings *as*. That is the substantive meaning, which, admittedly, is not prominent, since Plato does not succeed in grasping λόγος itself univocally. Yet a definition in the *Meno*.[72] It has already been indicated that Plato submits his own definition to critique. But λόγος indeed has another meaning: simple grasp of the *what*, Socratic λόγος. Now, however, taken positively!

The discussion of ψευδὴς δόξα shows: in the background stands the problem of the ἕτερον, something in place of the other, something as something else, μὴ ὄν, and specifically in relation to λόγος. Antisthenes: identification, tautology of the subject with itself;[73] in general, no human being, because no psychism {?}. λόγος is characterized

---

71. Cf. Aristotle, *Ethica Nicomachea*. Recogn. F. Susemihl. Leipzig, 1882, bk. 6, 1140b20: ἕξις τοῦ ἀληθεύειν μετὰ λόγου ["capacity of disclosing the truth accompanied with logos"].

72. 97Bff.

73. Mullach, *Fragmenta*, Antisthenes, frag. 47, vol. 2, pp. 282–83; Aristotle, *Met.* Δ 29, 1024b32ff.: μηδὲν ἀξιῶν λέγεσθαι πλὴν τῷ οἰκείῳ λόγῳ ἓν ἐφ᾽ ἑνός ["he (Antisthenes) was wrong to think that only its own name can be said of a thing, one for each"].

111

more exactly in the course of this discussion, although not in its structure but, instead, as the basic comportment of the soul itself.

Now λόγος openly and explicitly becomes the theme, as a characteristic moment of ἀληθὴς δόξα. And λόγος—if our basic understanding of the dialogue is correct—is *ontological*, oriented again toward the general problem of Being, i.e., toward the question of μὴ ὄν, the ἕτερον, the πρός τι as such.

The discussion begins with a characterization of the πρῶτα {. . .} στοιχεῖα ["the first elements"] (201E1), the constituents of all beings (201D8ff.). That seems to be an extraneous consideration, even less connected to the theme than ψευδὴς δόξα, but only as long as we fail to realize that all these discussions are approaches to the problem of Being. ἀρχαί, στοιχεῖα.[74] Why these? In a certain sense, it has been established that λόγος concerns, in each case, a twofold: something *as* something. But now beings consist in elements; the latter constitute Being. Thus if there is something to be known, then, above all, it is these. Yet: αὐτὸ γὰρ καθ᾽ αὑτὸ ἕκαστον ὀνομάσαι μόνον (201E2f.), "something like that can only be addressed in itself," only be named;[75] προσειπεῖν δὲ οὐδὲν ἄλλο δυνατόν ["impossible to address it as anything else"] (201E3f.), αὐτό—"itself in itself," ἐκεῖνο ["that one"], ἕκαστον ["each"], μόνον ["single"], τοῦτο ["this"] (cf. 202A3f.), nothing other can be added, it cannot be addressed as "this," or "that," or even as a being or a nonbeing. περιτρέχοντα ["terms that run around loose"] (202A5) ἐνίας {. . .} διὰ πασῶν ὅπη ἂν τύχωσι πετομένας,[76] "arbitrarily flying among all," they stop everywhere, but in no particular place, in no actual determinate being.

ἀδύνατον {. . .} τῶν πρώτων ῥηθῆναι λόγῳ ["impossible for the elements to be expressed in *logos*"] (202A8f.), for ὀνομάτων γὰρ συμπλοκὴν εἶναι λόγου οὐσίαν ["the Being of *logos* consists precisely in the combination of names"] (202B4f.). That which is "put together," συγκείμενον (cf. 202B3ff.), out of the στοιχεῖον is so through combination, and λόγος emerges out of the corresponding combination of their appurtenant names.[77] στοιχεῖα are then ἄλογα, ἄγνωστα, αἰσθητά μόνον ["without *logos*, unknowable, merely perceived"] (cf. 202B6). Not interpretable, not comprehensible as something; they must purely and simply be accepted. But συλλαβαί ["syllables"] can be understood and expressed (203A, cf. 204A); consequently, a concept, not mere syllables! In this way, therefore, the ψυχὴ can ἀληθεύειν, γιγνώσκειν δὲ οὔ ["disclose the truth, but not know"] (cf.

---

74. Cf. above, pt. 1 {in the manuscript: "earlier introduction"}, §12e, p. 41.

75. See Mörchen transcription, no. 59, p. 211.

76. Cf. 197D8: dovecote.

77. Cf. Aristotle, *Met.* Z 4.

202C1f.), "have disclosed" the beings just as they are, and yet not have understanding and "knowledge" of them, not know them as such! Conviction about Being and about the matters at issue, but no knowledge which could be demonstrated on the basis of the things themselves.

But Socrates is not satisfied with this interpretation of knowledge (202D8ff.): "The elements should be unknowable," not, on the contrary, that which has the character of combination (what can be combined, σύναψις, σύνθεσις). To test this thesis, we will return to the phenomena which were brought forward to serve as a παράδειγμα: the elements and the combinations in writing—"letters" and "syllables" (202E6).

Question: are letters ἄνευ λόγου (ἄλογον) ["without *logos*"], whereas syllables {λόγον}[78] ἔχουσιν ["possess *logos*"] (cf. 203A3)? It appears to be so. Question: what is ΣΩ? σ and ω. What about Σ? It cannot be explained in the same way, since it is not a combination of this *and* that. "Something *as* something" in the background! The syllable itself is τὰ ἀμφότερα στοιχεῖα ["the two elements"] (203C4f.), or several of them, or μίαν τινὰ ἰδέαν γεγονυῖαν συντεθέντων αὐτῶν (203C5f.), "one visible thing arising out of the combination of both." Theatetus believes the syllable is a totality in the sense of a sum. Cannot whoever knows the syllable—and it is knowable—also {know}[79] both elements, the Σ and the Ω? But these are supposed to be unknowable, and yet whoever knows the συλλαβαί knows them as well. On the other hand, a syllable can be known only by way of knowledge of the letters. Therefore the thesis (element ἄλογον, combination λόγον ἔχον) is untenable.

Perhaps it is wrong, however, to take a syllable as a sum. Perhaps the totality has a different character, ἕν τι γεγονὸς εἶδος ["one *eidos* emerging from them"] (203E3f.), ἕτερον δὲ τῶν στοιχείων ["other than the letter-elements"] (203E4f.). If that {is correct},[80] then there are no parts here, for μέρη are parts only of sums. Or is there a different kind of totality (204E8f.), one that is autonomous, has its own proper content, is different from all its parts, and is something other than a part? Indeed. Thus wholeness is different than a sum? Yes.[81] But is not 6 a totality, an all? 6 is in fact nothing other than this sum! Number is a sum of parts. τὸ ὅλον {. . .} οὐκ ἔστιν ἐκ μερῶν ["the whole is not made up of parts"] (204E8). *Totum* ["whole"]—moments; *compositum* ["compound"]—pieces; formal totality—parts. Therefore if

78. Editor's interpolation.
79. Editor's interpolation.
80. Editor's interpolation.
81. See Mörchen transcription, no. 60, p. 211f.

a syllable is μία {. . .} ἰδέα ["one visible thing"] (205D5), ὅλον ["a whole"] (205D8), then it is as unknowable as a letter. Conversely, however, if the syllable is knowable, then so is the letter. And in fact it is so: in elementary school, we learn precisely by starting with the elements.[82]

§48. Clarification of the phenomenon of λόγος.

a) Attempt at determining the phenomenon of λόγος.

λόγος: "concept," "assertion" (cf. 206C4):[83]

1. *Expressing,* making an assertion, uttering: διανοίας ἐν φωνῇ ὥσπερ εἴδωλον ["like the image of thought in sound"] (208C5).

2. Showing of the τί ἐστιν, "*the whole* through the mediation of the element": διὰ στοιχείων τὸ ὅλον ["the whole through the elements"] (207C3f.), διὰ στοιχείου ὁδὸς ἐπὶ τὸ ὅλον ["a way to the whole through the element"] (208C6). Thus here correct opinion with enumeration, and yet no knowledge.

3. To be capable of σημεῖον εἰπεῖν ["to name a sign"] (208C7f.), whereby that which is to be shown distinguishes itself from all else. The *specific difference,* not human being in general, but also not properties which {. . .}[84] go together {?}, but, rather, on the basis of them (208D7ff.). About this I must have a true opinion; to which then the distinguishing indication is added? Yet if this is already knowledge, why should it still be connected with the distinguishing indication? Do not ἀληθὴς δόξα and λόγος coincide?

b) Summary: the question of knowledge and the function of λόγος in the problem of Being.

Summarizing: in the *Theatetus,* the problem of Being, μὴ ὄν, under the name of ἐπιστήμη, i.e., λόγος.

First definition:[85] knowledge is not without λόγος, for, otherwise, there would be no disclosure of beings at all, no understanding of Being.

Second definition: knowledge in relation to ψευδὴς δόξα is ἕτερον ἕτερον. λόγος is not tautological; otherness. ἀλλοδοξία: something in the place of. σύναψις: Connection of something with something. λόγος is the *basic activity of the soul;* therein σύναψις.

Third definition: knowledge is μετὰ λόγου. λόγος, συμπλοκή,

82. See supplement no. 11, p. 161.
83. See Mörchen transcription, no. 61, p. 212.
84. Passage illegible.
85. See Mörchen transcription, no. 62, p. 212f.

στοιχεῖον. There is always already the ὅλον and on its basis the particular.

λόγος: "showing," and therein ἀλήθεια. λόγος–οὐσία:[86] logic-Being. Ontology-concepts.

I. ψυχή: 1. understanding of Being in general, Dasein. 2. λόγος: interpretation. εἴδη–κοινωνία.

II. But under what presupposition is there διαλέγεσθαι, showing of the αὐτό, τοῦτο, and something like the διὰ πασῶν ["through all"]? Only if there is συμπλοκή. And how does the latter come about? Only in a totality. κοινωνία is to be included in the definition of Being itself.

Summary: shown in the *Sophist:*

κίνησις ["motion"]   — στάσις ["rest"][87]
ὄν ["Being"]: ταὐτό ["the   — ἕτερον ["the other"] (cf. 254D4ff.,
    same"]   256A7ff.)
κίνησις with στάσις ὄν (254D5)
ψυχή—ὄν: understanding of Being (cf. 248A11, 250B7)
κοινωνία—δύναμις παρουσίας, "possibility of co-presence," ἀγαθόν
    ["good"].

---

86. See Mörchen transcription, no. 62, p. 213.
87. Cf. *Sophist,* 255E11ff.; see Mörchen transcription, no. 62, p. 213; see also GA 19, p. 536ff.

4

Central concepts of Plato's philosophy in the context of the understanding of Being and the question of Being

§49. The Idea of the ἀγαθόν.

a) Being and the "for the sake of which" of understanding.

οὐσία and ἀγαθόν. How do we proceed from the principles and basic determinations of beings, from the Ideas as structures of Being, to the Idea of the ἀγαθόν,[88] from the logical to the ethical, from Being to the "ought"? οὐσία and ἀγαθόν.

Being, i.e., the Being of beings [*das Seiende-Sein*], is that which is understood purely and simply *for the sake of itself* and is the only thing that can be understood in such a way. *For the sake of itself*: the *end* of all understanding. If I say "for the sake of itself," that is still an assertion about it: end, πέρας, ἀγαθόν. In a naively ontic sense: something higher than Being itself, which, moreover, still is Being itself. Considered more closely, however, not an assertion about Being, but one that turns *away* from Being and is precisely not directed to Being itself but, instead, approaches it obliquely, in relation to how it is understood, what it is *for* the understanding and not as it is in itself. Even "Being" as principle is a derivative characterization.

At issue here is the Being of Dasein, the soul itself. At issue is *Being*, the "for the sake of which" of this being, that which it has "to be." The being to whose Being an understanding of Being pertains. Understanding of Being: the potentiality-for-being wherein Being is at issue. In the Greek sense: *that which is at issue,* the *for the sake of which,* itself as *a being,*

88. See Mörchen transcription, no. 63, p. 213.

116

the *good*. Being is τέλος, "end," the ἀγαθόν. It is a matter of the ἀγαθόν, because Being is understood as a being, an existing property, the good. More is said about the soul than the good, according to its sense, can bear. To restrict the ontological assertion to its proper limits.

To know, to see, is an *action, being out for.*

ἀγαθόν, πέρας, any seeing is already, and above all, related to the light. The understanding of Being is brought to completion in seeing. Being through the ἰδέα, "something seen"; Being through the ἀγαθόν, the "for the sake of which," the "end." The Idea of the good is Being in the proper sense and is a being in the proper sense.

b) Being and value.[89]

Being means, in the first place, presence. Beyond that, it is the "for the sake of which," the toward which, ἀγαθόν, ὠφέλεια, "utility." Being itself is *separated* and, as ὄν, equated with οὐσία.[90] Contributionality [*Beiträglichkeit*] is not itself understood ontologically but, instead, is coordinated to Being, because Being itself is restricted to *pure constancy*, bare *thingly presence*. Yet the thing "still" has, beyond this, a *toward-which*, a *value*, so called on the basis of an insufficient grasp of Being.

And in the moral realm? A fortiori in that realm. That is the issue! *Existence! Potentiality-for-being!*

§50. Summarizing retrospective.

a) Critical evaluation of Plato's treatment of the problem of Being.

What is ontologically decisive in Plato's work: ἰδέα and λόγος (ψυχή); δύναμις κοινωνίας τῶν γενῶν ["possibility of a communion of the genera"].[91] Not μέθεξις between the αἰσθητά and the εἴδη, but among the latter themselves.

κοινωνία τῶν εἰδῶν, *determinations of Being:*[92] 1. the formal determinations and the concrete ones not distinguished; 2. not said how these determinations of Being relate to the Idea of Being itself, Being the highest γένος; 3. not said whether in general one can make do with a neutral concept of Being.

Being is distinguished from beings. Proper way of apprehension: λόγος, and this possibility belongs to Dasein, an understanding of Being. Being *in* λόγος. λόγος: ἀλήθεια. λόγος: κατηγορεῖν, κατη-

89. See Mörchen transcription, no. 64, p. 213f.
90. Cf. *Theatetus*, 186C, versus 186A.
91. Cf. above, p. 115, n. 87.
92. See Mörchen transcription, no. 65, p. 214.

γορία. λόγος: σύν, "with," "together." Central problem—basic problem: λόγος—ψυχή—κίνησις.

Being: presence; on that basis, the more precise structure of Being: togetherness, co-presence, one-other, unity-otherness-multiplicity-sameness. *Being and relation*.

The structure of λόγος remains open, though it is predelineated: Being itself and its delimitation with regard to disclosedness; Being and possibility, δύναμις; Being and motion, κίνησις. Yet even what is acquired is *not at all a system*, finished and transparent, but is always under way, approached: obscurity. And precisely here resides what is genuinely productive, what points beyond and leads further on, exactly because we have here no system but, instead, *actual work in disclosing the phenomena*. That is why this work has never gone out of date. Not because it contains some finished, so-called eternal truth, but because it asks actual questions, which, as problems, do not lead mortal lives. To *pose a genuine problem* is decisive and demands actual investigative work. On the other hand, there is the sophistical solving of semblant problems. {This work will not be out of date}[93] as long as it is not unsuccessful in finding responses that grasp the radical intention and awaken a new one.

Thus no conclusion, but only *renewed impulses*.

b) Retrospective on pre-Aristotelian philosophy,
for the sake of a transition to Aristotle.

Before considering the highest level of pure scientific research, a look back.

Thales and Plato's *Sophist*.[94] Understanding of Being. Concept of Being and possibilities of conceptual interpretation. {Thales}:[95] explicit question of beings with respect to their Being; but grasped there on the basis of beings and as a being.

Parmenides: Being, but all beings are, so to speak, denied.

Plato: the Being of beings, λόγος, δύναμις κοινωνίας, *co-presence*. Being is *not* something simple and becomes accessible primarily in *logos*.

λόγος: The "logic" of beings, i.e., *founded* through *logos*; that is the primary guiding line. No ontology manifest. λόγος: whence the categories, etc.[96] The Aristotelian problems.[97]

---

93. Editor's interpolation.
94. See Mörchen transcription, no. 66, p. 214.
95. Editor's interpolation.
96. Cf. above, last paragraph beginning on p. 117.
97. See supplement no. 12, p. 161.

SECTION THREE
Aristotle's Philosophy

1

On the problem of the development and of the adequate reception of Aristotle's philosophy

§51. Biography and philosophical development of Aristotle.

a) Biographical data.

Born 384/3 in Stagira (Thrace). From his eighteenth year, 367/6 {in the Academy}.[1] Entered around the time of the composition of the *Theatetus*. Plato's student for twenty years, {up to}[2] 348/7. Upon Plato's death, Aristotle and Xenocrates went to stay with Hermias in Mysia. For three years Aristotle was the leader of the circle of Plato's students there. 343–336: at the Macedonian royal court as preceptor to the thirteen-year-old Alexander, the future "Great." 336: after Alexander assumed the throne, Aristotle returned to Athens. At the Lyceum (precinct sacred to Apollo Lyceus), led the school of the Peripatetics for twelve years. περίπατος, "promenade," along which the members of the school carried on their scientific discussions. With Alexander's death in 323, anti-Macedonian feeling broke free in Athens. Aristotle accused of impiety. Fled to Chalcis, died there in 322 at the age of sixty-three.

b) On the question of the development of Aristotle's philosophy.

Aristotle's philosophical development: the problem has been neglected for a long time, and not without reason, since the grounds for a deter-

---

1. Editor's interpolation.
2. Editor's interpolation.

mination are unstable. Chronology and character of the writings; studied in the nineteenth century. Character: published writings versus lecture notes. Only a very small part of the *Corpus Aristotelicum* was published by Aristotle. "You are not working in order to write books, but in order to make headway in the matters at issue." Today it is just the opposite. Typical is the remark of a famous theologian of the nineteenth century; in his letters he says he must now think of a topic for his next book. A book must be written; that comes first. Then one tries to find something to write about.

The developmental problem was taken up by Werner Jaeger.[3] The essential work is by H. Bonitz.[4] The schema of the development can be drawn out as follows: Platonic period: beginning; middle period: to Assos [in Mysia] and back, critique of Plato; mature period: Lyceum.[5] This schema and the questions it provoked have indeed advanced the problem, regardless of whether or not Jaeger's view is tenable.

There is a basic difficulty, one Jaeger himself does not see because of the narrowness of his philosophical interpretation: the writings on logic, on physics, and bk. Γ of the psychology are supposed to stem from the early period, but there the decisive problems are not merely posed in a tentative way but, instead, are already solved.[6] As long as this difficulty is not disposed of, or even faced, the reconstruction of Aristotle's development remains without a genuine foundation. The only way is that of an actual *philosophical* interpretation of Aristotle's investigations. But I am convinced that even that will not lead to a solution; the only possible standpoint which is scientific and objective is to *acknowledge the insolubility.*

Writings: *Organon, Rhetoric, Poetics, Physics, On the heavens, Coming to be and passing away, On the soul, Metaphysics, Nicomachean Ethics, Politics.*[7]

Aristotle is said to be the master builder;[8] coherent edifice, doctrinal system. Thomas. Pure fiction! Everything is open; basic problems.

3. W. Jaeger, *Aristoteles: Grundlegung einer Geschichte seiner Entwicklung.* Berlin, 1923 (henceforth, Jaeger, *Aristoteles*). Preliminary sketch in a more narrow framework in his *Studien;* see above, p. 26, n. 34.

4. H. Bonitz, *Aristotelische Studien.* Sitzungsberichte der philosophisch-historischen Classe der königlichen Akademie der Wissenschaften, 1862-1867. Reprinted, five parts in one volume: Hildesheim, 1969.

5. Jaeger, *Aristoteles,* see table of contents and pp. 9ff., 105ff., 331ff.

6. Ibid., pp. 37ff., 53ff., 45, 311, 355, 395.

7. *Aristotelis opera.* Ex recogn. I. Bekkeri, vols. 1-5. Academia Regia Borussica. Berlin, 1831ff.

8. Mörchen transcription: "Dogma: Aristotle, versus Plato, is to be characterized as a master builder. Confusing him with Thomas Aquinas. In Aristotle, even less of a doctrinal edifice than in Plato."

§52. On the reception of Aristotle's philosophy.[9]

Despite an Aristotelian tradition dominant since the time of Schleier-macher, the last decade has seen the slow emergence of a more fitting appreciation of Aristotle. Hegel, in his early, Frankfurt years, prior to his first projection of a system, was lastingly influenced by Aristotle. Schleiermacher, Hegel, Trendelenburg, Bonitz, Torstrik, Brentano: systematic, phenomenology.

Neo-Kantianism not only {interpreted}[10] Kant one-sidedly (as an epistemologist), but the same one-sidedness deformed the conception of Greek philosophy in general and led to a misinterpretation of Aris-totle. The distinction idealism-realism was transferred back to the Greeks. Aristotle would then represent naive, unscientific realism and, inasmuch as it was preceded by Plato, a decline. This conception was dominant and—in a less strict form—still is so today. In addition: the Middle Ages considered Aristotle "the philosopher," and that was all the more reason to see in him something obscure and superannu-ated. But neither the Middle Ages nor Neo-Kantianism should divert the correct interpretation of Aristotle.

In our preliminary remarks:[11] philosophical research, its genesis out of understanding in general. Proper task: understanding, showing of Being and of its grounds and constitution; critical versus positive knowledge.

We will now, in the concrete, follow the process of penetrating into Being, i.e., the exposition of the difference. Certainty of access to, and elaboration of, Being itself. Thereby a predelineation of science in the proper sense. The idea of this science and its problematics: what is to be questioned, how and on what path of disclosure, how taken up, which central problems posed, which way leads to a solution? The formation of philosophy as research: apex of ancient philosophy.

Outline:

1. Philosophical research in general. Problem of Being. *Met.* Γ 1 and 2, E, B.[12]

2. The fundamental directions taken by the questioning within the problematic of Being, four {such directions}[13] and δύναμις ["potenti-ality"], ἐνέργεια ["actuality"].[14] {. . .}.[15]

3. The point of departure for the ontological problematic. Motion.

9. See Mörchen transcription, no. 67, p. 214f.
10. Editor's interpolation.
11. Manuscript: "Introduction"; see above, §4 and §5, p. 5ff.
12. See below, chap. 2, p. 124ff.
13. Editor's interpolation.
14. See below, chap. 3, p. 130ff.
15. Text illegible.

Physics. *Phys.* A and Γ 1–3.[16] Taken positively: δύναμις, ἐνέργεια: thereby κίνησις possible {. . .}.[17]

4. Ontology of life. *De anima* B and Γ.[18] Thereby a possible foundation.

5. Ontology of Dasein, *Ethics,*[19] *Eth. Nic.*[20]

6. Philosophical research and concept formation. λόγος, demonstration and proof. *De interp., Anal. post.* B.

We will discuss only the main lines here, laying out the problems, no doctrinal edifice; but even the main lines will be presented only in their most characteristic traits. Looking toward the positive elaboration in the lecture course to be offered in the winter semester.[21]

16. See below, chap. 4, p. 142ff.

17. Text illegible.

18. See below, chap. 5, p. 153ff.

19. Cf. E. Arleth, *Die metaphysischen Grundlagen der aristotelischen Ethik.* Prague, 1903.

20. See below, chap. 5, §67, p. 157f.

21. Cf. *Geschichte der Philosophie von Thomas v. Aquin bis Kant.* Marburger Vorlesung Wintersemester 1926-27. GA 23.

2

The ontological problem and the idea of philosophical research

§53. The investigation into beings as beings, i.e.,
into Being, as the thematic domain of the
fundamental science for Aristotle.

There is predelineated in the essence of ontological questioning in general, and also, accordingly, in its historical development, a double concept,[22] i.e., a remarkable state of fluctuation. To understand and genuinely grasp beings *as* beings: on the one hand, *the particular being* that most appropriately satisfies the idea of Being. Which does not mean this idea becomes explicit. On the other hand, the *Being* of beings in general, attempt to determine Being. Yet without the ground and question of the most original problematic.

The double concept of the fundamental science:

1. science of *Being;*
2. science of *the highest and most proper being.*

What properly is: 1. the things that actually are; 2. what properly constitutes beings: Being.

Interpretation of *Met.* Γ and E (K and *Physics*).

Met. Γ 1:[23] ὡς φύσις τις ["(Being) in its own nature"] (cf. 1003a27) and the related ὑπάρχοντα ["determinations"] (1003a22). Ontic explanation of beings—ontological interpretation of Being. "If now even the questions posed by the ancients, who were investigating the elements, implicitly aimed at these basic determinations of Being as such,

22. See Mörchen transcription, no. 68, p. 215f.
23. 1003a21–32.

124

then the elements must not be, contrary to the opinion of these ancient thinkers, confinable to a determinate region of Being, but must be related to beings just insofar as they are beings" (1003a28ff.). This theme of research, of what is to be apprehended, is made up of "the first causes of beings as beings" (1003a31), *the first causes of Being*, that *from which Being as such is to be determined*. Here lies the catch, the double concept of a science of Being as both *ontic explanation* and *ontological interpretation*. Causes of beings: the theme is the Being of beings. Causes of Being: beings are the cause of Being. The problem can be discussed in a positive way only if we have a sufficient grasp of both concepts of the first science. We will begin with the first science as science of Being oriented toward ontological interpretation.

Being is the theme. This science obviously has more to say than simply: Being is Being. Yet the object is always Being. Just as geometry always deals with space, physics with material nature, and biology with organic nature, so the first science ever treats of *beings as such and in general, of beings just insofar as they are*, of Being. καὶ δὴ καὶ τὸ πάλαι τε καὶ νῦν καὶ ἀεὶ ζητούμενον καὶ ἀεὶ ἀπορούενον, τί τὸ ὄν ["what is always sought, and always leads to an impasse, already long ago and still now: what is Being"].[24]

The idea of this science is determined more precisely in Γ 2: the idea of the science of Being (1003a33–1004a9).

1. The unity of the object and of the thematic approach (Γ 2, 1003a33–b19).

2. To the object there corresponds an originally genuine kind of givenness, and indeed a direct one, αἴσθησις (1003b19–22).

3. The mode of self-pre-givenness (phenomenology, ontology).

4. ὄν and ἕν: co-originality (1003b22–1004a2).

5. Science of Being and sciences of concretely different regions of Being (1004a2–9).

Regarding 1: First of all, the unity of the thematic horizon: ἧ ὄν, "as being," with respect to Being, toward which everything is oriented. Being is the most universal.[25] Plato: κοινωνία τῶν γενῶν.[26] Are the γένη that to which the problematic of this science is ultimately reduced? The question is taken up in *Met.* B 3.[27] *Met.* B develops a series of problems, all of which serve to determine the object of this science. There we have what is decisive for the matter at issue and what is most important for understanding the new Aristotelian problematic over and against Plato.

---

24. *Met.* Z 1, 1028b2ff.
25. See supplement no. 13, p. 161f., and Mörchen transcription, no. 69, p. 216.
26. Cf. *Sophist*, 254B7f.
27. 998b14ff.

§54. The impossibility of determining
Being through genera.

The "origins,"[28] the basic determinations of Being, as well as Being itself, the ἀρχαὶ τῶν ὄντων, cannot be genera. The proof is carried out indirectly, from the impossibility of the opposite ὑπόθεσις. First of all, an example to clarify the concepts of genus, difference, species. Teaching example: *homo animal rationale* ["man is the rational animal"]. Genus: *animal* (includes the rational and the non-rational). Difference: *rationale*, divides the genus and determines it *as* something, as something that it itself, according to its idea, is not yet: living being as rational. And so the difference constitutes the species: *homo* (↔ beast) resides neither in *animal* nor in *ratio*, for God also possesses the latter. *Rationale* does not belong to *animalitas*, if *homo and* beast are not both *rationale*.

On the hypothesis that Being is a genus, then the species and differences, which differentiate Being in general into some definite mode of Being, should not be determined on the basis of Being, for differences introduce something that does *not* already lie in the genus. But if the difference, insofar as it differentiates, is supposed to be something at all, i.e., insofar as it is supposed to function as a difference, it must *be*. Assuming Being is a genus, then the difference and the species would necessarily possess the determinations of the genus itself.

We face here an either-or: either Being is a genus, but then it is a genus that by essence can have no differences and no species, for these would be utterly deprived of a connection to Being. Or there are differences and species, but then Being is necessarily not a genus. Now, since differences and species actually *are, valet consequentia:* ὄν is not a γένος. Being has no species and no differences. Then how is it articulated? How understand the *unity* of the general and the *multiplicity* of the "kinds" and modes of Being, the species and modalities? How are we to account here for the εἶδος and the διαφορά ["difference"]? As predicates, or as the being itself of which such a predication is made?

§55. The unity of analogy (of the πρὸς ἕν) as sense of the
unity of multiple beings in οὐσία.

Aristotle now provides the *positive* answer to the question of whether the ἀρχαί have the character of γένη, whether the ἀρχή of ὄν (i.e., οὐσία) = a γένος.

Met. Γ 2: "Beings are called beings in several senses" (1003a33). Therefore Being is understood in several senses as well. But the mani-

---

28. Related to *Met.* B 3, 998b14–28; see Mörchen transcription, no. 70, p. 216f.

foldness of the meaning of Being is not an utterly disparate one. It is not simply a matter of one and the same word used with completely different meanings, such as the cock [*Hahn*] of the chicken coop and of the water spigot: the same word, but the meaning is altogether different. Thus the expression "Being" is not equivocal, οὐχ ὁμωνύμως ["not merely homonymous"] (1003a34), *aequivoce*, but neither is it—since πολλαχῶς—συνωνύμως ["synonymous"], *univoce*, having the same meaning in every context.

What then are, positively, the meaning of Being and the mode of signification of this term? The meaning is not disparate, unrelated to some one thing; on the contrary, πρὸς ἕν καὶ μίαν τινὰ φύσιν ["related to one and the same specific nature"] (1003a33f.). Aristotle clothes his answer in two examples: τὸ ὑγιεινόν, the expression "healthy" has its meaning πρὸς ὑγίειαν; something is called "healthy" insofar as it has a *relation to* health. This relation can be of *various kinds,* while yet always remaining a relation to health:

ὑγιεινὸν τῷ φυλάττειν (1003a35), "healthy" inasmuch as it "maintains and preserves" health; e.g., walking is healthy.

ὑγιεινὸν τῷ ποιεῖν (1003a35f.), "healthy" inasmuch as it "produces" health. An organ is healthy.

ὑγιεινὸν τῷ σημεῖον εἶναι τῆς ὑγιείας (1003a36), "healthy" inasmuch as it "is a sign of health," a healthy complexion.

ὑγιεινὸν τὸ {. . .} δεκτικὸν αὐτῆς (1003a36f.), "healthy" inasmuch as it is something that is determined at all by health and illness. Only what *can* be ill can be healthy; not a stone, no more than a triangle. But indeed timber, an animal, a living being.

Taking a walk *is* healthy in a different sense of being healthy than a heart is healthy. "The heart is healthy" has a different sense than "healthy cheeks." Not because the latter differ from the heart as parts; here "are" does not mean that the cheeks themselves are not diseased but, rather, means "are a sign of." A comparable example to "healthy" is "medical" in relation to the practice of medicine. "Medical" is a performance, a comportment, something (such as an instrument) that pertains to this practice (cf. 1003b1–3).

Likewise, "is," wherever it is used, has significance in relation to "Being," μία ἀρχή—πρὸς ταύτην ["one principle–toward the same"] (cf. 1003b5f.), "in relation to Being" (1003b9), in each case proceeding from Being and returning back to it.[29] Beings *are* in different senses, and the difference results from the relation, different in each case, of the being to that which most properly is said to be.

τὰ μὲν {. . .} ὄντα λέγεται (1003b6) ["for beings are spoken of as":][30]

29. See Mörchen transcription, no. 71, p. 217f.
30. See Mörchen transcription, no. 71, p. 217ff.

1. ὅτι οὐσίαι (1003b6),[31] in themselves "things present-at-hand."
2. ὅτι πάθη οὐσίας (1003b7),[32] "states of what is present-at-hand."
3. ὅτι ὁδὸς εἰς οὐσίαν (1003b7), "a way toward being present-at-hand."
4. ὅτι φθοραί, στερήσεις (1003b7f.), "disappearances," "deprivations."
5. ὅτι ποιότητες (1003b8), "qualities."
6. ὅτι ἀποφάσεις (1003b9), "negations."

πρὸς μίαν λεγομένων φύσιν ["said in relation to one nature"] (1003b14). Cf. *Met.* K 3: τοῦ ὄντος ᾗ ὄν ["of beings as beings"],[33] εἶναι ["Being"],[34] πάθος ["affect"],[35] ἕξις ["comportment"],[36] διάθεσις ["disposition"],[37] κίνησις ["motion"].[38]

This relationship πρὸς ἕν ["to one"] is a mode of the καθ᾽ ἕν ["on one"],[39] *the unity of analogy,* ἐξ οὗ τὰ ἄλλα ἤρτηται, καὶ δι᾽ ὃ λέγονται (1003b17), something "on which the other modes of Being are dependent and through which those other modes are said to be." If this something is οὐσία ["presence-at-hand"], then on it depend the ἀρχαί. In each case is it a matter of a determinate οὐσία ["something present-at-hand"], or of οὐσία in general?

Regarding 2 and 3: to have constantly in view a more precise type of the primary access.[40] Mode of *pre*-givenness, *pre*-having. Here is a new science of Being as such. Explained in *Met.* K 3:[41] new concept of philosophy: ontology, thematic research into Being itself. Actually demonstrated, not just tentatively touched on. Delimitation over and against mathematics and physics:[42] mathematics abstracts and grasps simply: ἀφαίρεσις,[43] "taking away" something from something; this in various respects and yet *one* discipline.

ὄν ᾗ ὄν ["beings as beings"], Being itself already indicated. Being occurs in a multiplicity of *modes.* Unity: πρὸς ἕν, analogy. The analogical meaning of Being = question of Being in general. The problem of this analogy is the central problem for penetrating into Being in gen-

---

31. See supplements no. 14 and no. 15, p. 162.
32. See supplement no. 16, p. 162.
33. 1061a8.
34. 1061a10.
35. 1061a9; *Met.* Δ 21, 1022b15ff.
36. 1061a9; *Met.* Δ 20, 1022b4ff.
37. 1061a9; *Met.* Δ 19, 1022b1ff.
38. 1061a9; cf. *Phys.* Γ 1, 200b12ff.
39. Γ 2, 1003b15.
40. See Mörchen transcription, no. 71, p. 218.
41. 1061a28–b17.
42. See Mörchen transcription, no. 71, p. 218f.
43. Cf. *Met.* K 3, 1061a29.

eral. Where is the seat of this analogy? Whence derive the possibility of a relation of beings to beings and the possibility of various relations of that kind? λόγος–ὄν, something *as* something, together, one *with* the other. λόγος is the guideline, i.e., ὄν λεγόμενον, the possible mode of Being of what can be asserted.

κατηγορεῖν, κατηγορία. Being: its interpretation and the fixing of its modes. Category, λόγος–"assertion," analogy. ὄν ᾗ ὄν: how it *shows* itself in *logos* and is *encountered* in the mode of the "as something."[44]

ὄν of the categories: the first group within the first[45] sense of πολλαχῶς ["in many ways"].

44. See supplement no. 17, p. 162.
45. On the two different meanings of πολλαχῶς in Aristotle, see Mörchen transcription, no. 71, p. 219; cf. also M. Heidegger, *Vom Wesen der menschlichen Freiheit. Freiburger Vorlesung Sommersemester 1930.* GA 31. Frankfurt, 1982, p. 77.

3

The fundamental questioning
of the problematic of Being

§56. The essence of the "categories."

Terminologically, the expression κατηγορία[46] implies a relation to λόγος as *"showing."* Essentially, however, the categories signify *modes of Being.* How does it happen that modes of Being are designated with a term related to assertion? That should not make us wonder, for the question of Being is oriented toward λόγος, "showing." More precisely: λόγος is the showing of *beings;* in λόγος, beings are *accessible* and thereby also *Being.* Admittedly, thereby we clarify only the genesis of the relation with respect to the characters of Being. And yet it is not only terminologically, but also fundamentally, that ontology is oriented toward λόγος.

κατὰ πάντων γὰρ τὸ ὂν κατηγορεῖται,[47] "Being is asserted of all things." If a being is encountered, then Being, *inter alia,* is intended and understood. Being is the most general category. But that does not mean beings and Being are something subjectively thought; on the contrary, λέγειν signifies: to "show" beings in themselves. Categories are *modes of beings* with respect to their *Being,* not forms of subjective thought, which, moreover, they are not for Kant either. But a limit does indeed arise in another respect: there are beings and Being only insofar as they are accessible in assertion. Furthermore, in accord with the immediate meaning: only what is *present-at-hand,* things. Plotinus: the νοητά are over and against the αἰσθητά, but, even within the αἰσθητά, again only the present-at-hand things, *neutral presence-at-hand:* table, tree, mountain, sky.

46. See Mörchen transcription, no. 72, p. 219f.
47. *Met.* K 2, 1060b4f.

How does this {orientation toward *logos*}[48] appear, and how are the categories apprehensible in it? The categories give:

1. τὸ ὄν {. . .} κατὰ τὰ σχήματα τῶν κατηγοριῶν ["Being according to the configurations of the categories"].[49] The categories are σχήματα, "Gestalten," in which the modes of Being show themselves. How are they connected to λόγος?

2. τὰ κατὰ μηδεμίαν συμπλοκὴν λεγόμενα ["things said insofar as they are in no way combined"].[50]

3. καθ᾽ αὑτὰ δὲ εἶναι λέγεται ὅσαπερ σημαίνει τὰ σχήματα τῆς κατηγορίας· ὁσαχῶς γὰρ λέγεται, τοσαυταχῶς τὸ εἶναι σημαίνει ["Being in itself is said in as many ways as are signified by the Gestalten of the categories: in as many ways as it is said, that is how many ways Being is signified"].[51]

4. Τὸ δ᾽ ὑπάρχειν τόδε τῷδε καὶ τὰ ἀληθεύεσθαι τόδε κατὰ τοῦδε τοσαυταχῶς ληπτέον ὁσαχῶς αἱ κατηγορίαι διῄρηνται ["The attribution of this to that and the disclosing of this truth about that are to be taken in as many ways as there are different categories"].[52] Cf. *Met.* Δ 30: ὑπάρχειν καὶ ἀληθὲς εἰπεῖν ["is an attribute and is said truly"].[53]

5. τὰ πρὸς τὴν οὐσίαν λεγόμενα ["things said as related to presence"].[54] ὑποκείμενον—συμβεβηκότα ["substrate—things that supervene to it"]: ὑποκείμενον {. . .} ἐμφαίνεται ἐν ἑκάστῃ κατηγορίᾳ ["the substrate showing itself in each category"].[55]

6. διαιρέσεις ["divisions"], πτώσεις ["inflections"],[56] πρῶτα ["first things"], κοινά ["things in common"], γένη ["genera"].[57] Porphyry reports that the ancient commentaries named the book of the categories Περὶ τῶν γενῶν τοῦ ὄντος ["On the genera of beings"].[58] Stoics: term for the categories: τὰ γενικώτατα ["the highest genera"].[59]

Regarding 2: that which, according to its content, admits of "no compo-

48. Editor's interpolation; see Mörchen transcription, no. 72, p. 220ff.

49. *Met.* Θ 10, 1051a34f.

50. Cf. *Cat.* 4, 1b25; see supplement no. 18, p. 162f.

51. *Met.* Δ 7, 1017a22ff.

52. *Analytica priora* A 37, 49a6ff.

53. Cf. 1025a14f.

54. Cf. *Met.* Γ 2, 1003b9.

55. Cf. *Met.* Z 1, 1028a26ff.

56. *Met.* N 2, 1089a26.

57. Cf. *Phys.* Γ 1, 201a10; *De anima* 402a23. Cf. F. Brentano, *Von der mannigfachen Bedeutung des Seienden nach Aristoteles.* Freiburg, 1862, pp. 100–101.

58. *Porphyrii Isagoge et in Aristotelis Categorias commentarium.* Ed. A. Busse. *Commentaria in Aristotelem Graeca,* vol. 4, pt. 1. Berlin, 1887, p. 56, ll. 18–19.

59. Cf. *Stoicorum veterum fragmenta.* Ed. H. von Arnim. Leipzig, 1903ff., vol. 2: Chrysippus, pt. 2, §2, 329 and 334, p. 117; vol. 3: Diogenes Babylonius, pt. 1, *Logica,* 25, p. 214.

sition," ἐν οὐδεμιᾷ καταφάσει ["not in any affirmation"],[60] but which, for its part, makes possible intertwining in general, lets something be grasped *as* something; that which, *inter alia*, I have in view in assertion, that which is understood in a particular way. The stone is hard (quality). The tree is along the path (place). The resistance is too great (ποσόν ["quantity"]). The contents in view in an assertion about beings stemming from an understanding of Being. Contents not reducible to one another.

Regarding 3: beings in themselves with respect to their possible modes of Being. There are as many of these modes as there are modes of λέγειν, modes of the "showing" of something as something. The categories are therefore grounded in, and signify nothing other than, the *determinations of Being* that are *grasped in the "as something."* The supervenience of something, or, more precisely, the co-presence-at-hand of something with something, the possible mode of the co-being of something with something, and of each thing with that which, in the respective case, is called its ὑποκείμενον ["substrate"]. τὸ δ' ὂν τὸ μὲν τόδε τι, τὸ δὲ ποσόν, τὸ δὲ ποιόν τι σημαίνει ["'Being' signifies either the 'this,' the quantity, or the quality"].[61]

Regarding 5: πρὸς τὴν οὐσιαν λεγόμενα, "with respect to presence-at-hand, i.e., something present-at-hand in itself." οὐσία πρώτη ["primary presence"], full presence of the "this here." *The modes of the co-presence-at-hand of beings with* οὐσία *are expressed in the categories.* In every category, and according to the sense of that category, οὐσία also shows itself. If it was said earlier,[62] no "as that," no συμπλοκή, that does not mean the structure now grasped counts as an objection. What has a quality is something, what is related is something, related to place, to a time. Modes of co-presence-at-hand: something is this thing in itself and as this thing is qualified in such a way, related to such and such, etc.

Regarding 6: The categories are therefore, διαιρέσεις, that which can be selected out in this original "separating" of an οὐσία into determinations of Being. {πτώσεις:}[63] inflections, modes of co-presence-at-hand; {πρῶτα:}[64] the first, original, ontological characters of beings; {κοινά:}[65] what is common; {γένη:}[66] genera. Refers to the categories as modes, ways of being-with {. . .}[67] prior to {?} some general quality, the general for the respective determinate, concrete property, species in general for the various determinate species.

60. *Cat.* 4, 2 and 5f.; see supplement no. 18, p. 162.
61. *Met.* Z 4, 1030b11f.; κατηγορεῖν: categories: 10 (cf. *Topics* A 9, 103b21–23).
62. See above, num. par. 2, p. 131.
63. Editor's interpolation.
64. Editor's interpolation.
65. Editor's interpolation.
66. Editor's interpolation.
67. Passage illegible.

Summary: categories:

1. Modes of *co-presence-at-hand* with something present-at-hand in itself.

2. Therein the mode of Being of the possible being-with is determined.[68]

3. This mode of Being is in each case, *inter alia*, already understood in every concrete showing of a being as this or that. The "something as something" articulates Being-with; i.e., the mode of Being expressed in the category is the possible content of a *regard*. This regard is constitutive of the possibility of assertion. As red, as there with regard to ποιόν ["quality"], πού ["place"].[69]

4. The content of the regard is thus the guideline for the understanding of the Being of what is attributed to the being, what stands in the predicate of the sentence, and indeed κοινόν. The categories are therefore the *most general predicates*.

---

§57. Analogy (πρὸς ἕν) as the ontological meaning of the unity of the manifold modes of Being (categories).

What is decisive is the *ontological* meaning: *modes of co-presence-at-hand*, a) different among themselves, irreducible to one another, b) not under a highest genus, but also not a confused manifold; on the contrary, they are categories through the relatedness to οὐσία, which is 1. essential to all of them, 2. different in every case.

Being as presence-at-hand in general is *polysemic:* 1. present-at-hand in itself, 2. co-present-at-hand, together with, in the various modes.[70]

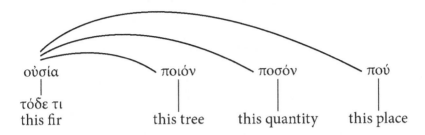

οὐσία	ποιόν	ποσόν	πού
τόδε τι			
this fir	this tree	this quantity	this place

just as {. . .}.[71]

---

68. See Mörchen transcription, no. 73, p. 222.
69. See supplement no. 19, p. 163.
70. See Mörchen transcription, no. 74, p. 222.
71. Passage illegible.

analogia attributionis ["analogy of attribution"]; *analogia proportionis* ["analogy of proportionality"].[72]

Analogia attributionis.[73] *nomen commune* ["a name in common"]. *ratio {. . .} eadem secundum terminum* ["the reason is the same according to one term"], it is always co-intended,[74] e.g., health or that which most properly is healthy; *primum analogatum* ["the primary term, which bears the analogy"], i.e., the being in the most proper sense, οὐσία; Being in general, i.e., the being in the most proper sense.

The "co-intended," that which is "co-" in general, in its possibilities: precisely expressed in the "categories," συμβεβηκός. The "co-" varies the "as such and such." Only the "co-" and purely on the basis of presence, or the "such and such" (in general) with?—*qualitas, quantitas.* Are these both then to be analyzed *temporally,* or can they be clarified as temporal only in a determinate ontological respect? Beings are essentially related to the being that *is* in the most proper sense.

diversa[75] *secundum habitudines* ["diverse according to their comportments (to the primary term)"], *identitas termini habitudinum* ["identity of the term of the comportments"], *diversitas habitudinum* ["diversity of the comportments"], i.e., *modalization* of Being. But a fundamental difficulty: here is an *ontological* meaning, or the basic meaning in general, the *meaning of Being in general.* In the examples, *ontic* meanings, a being (health), *qualitas.* But now *quality as such* is a mode, itself as such is πρὸς ἕν. Quality itself is an expression of a *habitudo* ["comportment, mode"] of Being. On the other hand, in the example it is a *terminus,* and indeed as a determinate quality, a "species." *Habitudo* is insufficient here: can also be κατά ["against"]; in ἀναλογία ["analogy"], however, what counts is the πρός τι ["relation to a one"].

The *relata* to the *terminus,* thus the categories, are the *analogata* ["the analogized things"]. The *primum analogatum* is οὐσια and at the same time the *nomen analogum* ["analogous name"]: εἶναι ["Being"]. εἶναι and οὐσία, Being in general and the most proper being, identical? Or else how do they go together? The One here in the proper sense and in the improper sense.

A further formulation of the concept of analogy: between νοητά and αἰσθητά. Not the same οὐσία for both.[76] δεῖ μέντοι τὸ ταὐτὰ

72. Mörchen transcription: "The structure of the universality of Being is the structure of analogy." See supplements no. 20, p. 163, and no. 21, p. 163f.

73. Cf. Th. Vio de Cajetan, *De nominum analogia.* Ed. M. de Maria. Rome, 1907. More precise bibliographical references and extensive (French) commentary in B. Pinchard, *Métaphysique et Sémantique suivi de Thomas de Vio-Cajetan, L'analogie des noms.* Paris, 1987 (henceforth, Cajetan), chap. 1, 3, p. 114.

74. Cajetan, chap. 2, 8, p. 115.

75. See Mörchen transcription, no. 74, p. 222.

76. Plotinus, *Enn.* 6, 1.1f.

ἀναλογίᾳ καὶ ὁμωνυμίᾳ λαμβάνειν ["yet it is necessary to take the same thing both analogously and homonymously"].[77]

Deus ist ens realissimum ["God is the most real being"],[78] *summum ens* ["supreme being"],[79] *ens infinitum* ["infinite being"] over and against *ens finitum creatum* ["finite, created being"].[80] Indeed Being, but not *univoce*. οὐσία: the most proper being, in the sense of infinite, which creates what is finite. The created is also substance, but *finita*, and, ontologically, of it once again an analogy holds.

The modes of Being, their multiplicity and the type of their unity and appurtenance. The first and original: πολλαχῶς. The second: the simple meaning of Being, to this meaning the Being of the categories is related. In what way?

Regarding the second: τὸ ὂν τὸ ἁπλῶς λεγόμενον ["Being as said simply"],[81] Being pure and simple, not this or that Being, not the Being of a definite being, not Being and this being, but *sheer Being*. The basic directions of questioning within the problematic of Being are first clarified on the basis of their connection with the Being of the categories, and thereby the concrete idea of the science of *Being in general* is determined. Then the question arises: how does the second concept of the science of Being, theology, relate to that?

From what has been said: presence-at-hand—a preeminent category. οὐσία: it expresses the original Being, and in relation to it there is co-presence-at-hand, modes. Presence-at-hand—co-presence-at-hand. "Co-"—λόγος—presence. To be sure, nine categories are founded in the first but, by essence, are given along with it. Being of the categories:[82] *present-at-hand* in itself, *co-present-at-hand;* καθ᾽ αὑτό ["in itself"], always, constantly, there of itself and in accord with its essence. What is to be present-at-hand as something *produced*. Being: *presence*,[83] and indeed of a multiplicity. *Co-presence* of something with something; i.e., in presence itself a reference from one to another. The totality of the peculiarities, meaningfulness, world (*inter alia*, especially in the phenomenon of οὐσία in general, παρουσία ["co-presence"]); i.e., a being is συγκείμενον ["something combined"]. Categories are conditions of possibility, basic modes of possible co-presence-at-hand.

Categories *applicable to* every being that is to be. *Supervenience*

77. Plotinus, *Enn.* 6, 3.1, ll. 6–7.

78. Cf. Kant, *Kritik der reinen Vernunft*, A 576/B 604.

79. Cf. Anselm of Canterbury, *Monologion* 16; Descartes, *Meditationes de prima philosophia. Oeuvres*, ed. Adam and Tannery (henceforth, *Meditationes*), 7 vols., Paris, 1904, vol. 4, 4; vol. 5, 11.

80. *Meditationes* 3, 22–24.

81. *Met.* E 2, 1026a33. See supplement no. 22, p. 164.

82. See supplements no. 23, p. 164f., and no. 24, p. 165.

83. See Mörchen transcription, no. 75, p. 222f.

[*Hinzugeratenheit*] is an *ontological* character that is not necessary to the most proper being and that also does not constitute the Being of the most proper being. The same holds for uncoveredness.

§58. Being in the sense of supervenience (συμβεβηκός).

Textual passages:

κατὰ συμβεβηκὸς εἶναι ["Being as supervenience"]: *Met.* E 2–3, K 8,[84] Δ 30. ὡς ἀληθὲς ὄν ["Being as truth"]: *Met.* E 4, K 8,[85] Θ 10; *De interpretatione; De anima* Γ 6.[86] Both {κατὰ συμβεβηκὸς εἶναι and ὡς ἀληθὲς ὄν}[87] are λοιπὸν γένος ["in some other genus"][88] versus δύναμις, ἐνέργεια, and κατηγορία.

ὂν κατὰ συμβεβηκός[89] – "supervenience," "what comes to something by the way." κατὰ συμβεβηκὸς εἶναι,[90] what comes to something in addition, occasionally, accidentally, not as τέλος ["proper end"]. Not nothing, but not Being in the proper sense either; very important for understanding the concept of Being in Aristotle and in Greek philosophy in general. From what is not Being in the proper sense, from what is apprehended that way, it becomes clear how Being in the proper sense is understood. ἐπίσταμαι signifies "understanding" in the broadest sense, to be involved with something in a understanding way, to deal with beings in an oriented way: e.g., house building. This orientation is related to something, to the thing one wants to produce, so that it will be ready-to-hand as a house in accord with what belongs to it as a work of craftsmanship. But what supervenes to this house, such as what in it pleases or displeases its inhabitants, or the fates and dispositions of those who use it, is a matter of indifference.[91]

1. On beings that are such and such by accident, οὐδεμία {. . .} περὶ αὐτὸ θεωρία ["they cannot be grasped in the theoretical attitude"],[92]

2. ὄνομά τι μόνον τὸ συμβεβηκός ["supervenience is merely a name"] (1026b13f.),

3. ἐγγύς τι τοῦ μὴ ὄντος ["close to nonbeing"] (1026b21),

4. (a) τίς ἡ φύσις αὐτοῦ ["what is the nature of the supervenient"], (b) καὶ διὰ τίν' αἰτίαν ἐστίν, and "on what grounds," how founded

---

84. 1064b15–1065a21.
85. 1065a21–26.
86. 430a26ff.
87. Editor's interpolation.
88. *Met.* E 4, 1028a1.
89. See Mörchen transcription, no. 76, p. 223.
90. *Met.* K 8, 1064b15f.
91. Cf. 1064b19ff.; see Mörchen transcription, no. 77, p. 223.
92. *Met.* E 2, 1026b3f.

(1026b25f.)? Regarding (b): 1. ἐξ ἀνάγκης (μὴ ἐνδεχόμενον ἄλλως) ["by necessity (cannot be otherwise)"]; αἰεί ["always"] (cf. 1026b28ff.). 2. ἐπὶ τὸ πολύ ["for the most part"] (1026b30). This is the ἀρχή for συμβεβηκός (1026b31). Regarding (a): 1. What is neither αἰεί, nor most of the time, but only occasionally (1026b32). 2. Such supervenience, occurring by chance and occasionally, is possible only if there is always already something present-at-hand in a constant or nearly constant way.

5. Examples.[93]

6. For this ὄν, there is no τέχνη (ἐπιστήμη), δύναμις ὡρισμένη [no "definite know-how (science) or capacity"] (1027a6f.). It is not a οἰκεῖον τέλος ["an end in the proper sense"];[94] it cannot be grasped in its possible determinateness and constancy. To what supervenes, there corresponds no definite understanding, no delimited comportment to which in each case the determinate being at issue would offer itself to be encountered in the appropriate manner. On the contrary, the essence of the συμβεβηκός is precisely to rise up παρά, "by" something, i.e., in very case *by the way* and *arbitrarily* (1027a16f.).

7. ἀρχή grasped more precisely: the ἀεί ["everlasting"] as ὕλη ["matter"] (1027a13): determinability in general, open to arbitrariness.

§59. Being in the sense of uncoveredness: ὄν ὡς ἀληθές (*Met.* E 4, K 8, Θ 10).

a) Conjunction and disjunction as ground of uncoveredness and coveredness.

Being as truth:[95] A is B. A is in fact; A is in *actuality*, not merely presumed to be. Concept of truth in general, judgmental truth, conformity.

Met. E 4: the text of this chapter is uneven. Noticed very early. Jaeger has found in this an occasion to excise various parts. Lines 1027b25-27 seem to be later interpolations, since there a concept of truth is discussed that could not have been foreseen at the start.[96]

Uncoveredness—dissembling (falsity, not to be such as, to be other than). Here the only questions are: what sort of modification of Being in general is this? And how is it connected to the Being of the categories?

Uncoveredness and coveredness stand together, grounded in conjunction and disjunction. λόγος, something *as* something; apart and together within the unitary steadfastness of the pre-given being. Uncovering,

---

93. See Mörchen transcription, no. 77, p. 223f.

94. *Met.* K 8, 1064b23.

95. See supplement no. 25, p. 165; see Mörchen transcription, no. 78, p. 224.

96. Jaeger, *Studien*, pp. 23-28, esp. 27; Jaeger, *Aristoteles*, p. 217.

showing, letting be seen, means: (disclosing in itself) *showing in the mode of attribution* with respect to what is present-at-hand together, or *showing in the mode of denial* with respect to what is not gathered together. To dissemble and cover over is the corresponding opposite: showing in the mode of attribution with respect to what is *not* gathered together, {or}[97] showing in the mode of denial with respect to what *is* present-at-hand together. "The board is black": attribution of "black" to "board" and thereby showing what is present-at-hand together. "The window is not closed": denying closedness to the window and thereby showing that the two are not gathered together. The window is in fact not closed, but it is said, "The window is closed": here attribution of closedness to the window in view of what is not actually gathered together, and thereby covering over the being as it is, giving it out to be something it is not. Saying of the black board, "It is not black": denying blackness to the board in view of something actually present-at-hand together. Or, something as something ("is black") which it is not: not "not black," but "black."

Uncovering—covering over:[98] an attribution and speaking about something *as* something. That gives expression to the *intending of something as something:* ἅμα καὶ {. . .} χωρίς:[99] "at the same time," "in unity," the being itself that is to be shown; or "separated," "apart," disjoined. But this ὥστε μὴ τὸ ἐφεξῆς (1027b24), "not as one after the other," not at first the whole in its unity and then separated, but, rather, ἀλλ᾽ ἕν τι γίγνεσθαι (1027b25) "such that a unity comes to be," i.e., the whole itself in and through the separation, and precisely throughout the separation as a unitary whole and as the being itself in the "how" of its Being. ἄλλος λόγος ["another *logos*"]: *Met.* Z 12; *De anima* Γ 6ff.

To intend, to run through perceptually, not simply to look at, but to penetrate it through and through with the look, διανοεῖσθαι. Conjunction and disjunction are carried out in διάνοια. Something *as* something, a structure that is "not in the things" themselves, οὐκ ἐν τοῖς πράγμασι (1027b30f.), but a structure of the *understanding* and *disclosing,* of *uncoveredness and coveredness,* constituted through and in the comportment to the uncovered thing itself. Uncoveredness does not pertain to beings in themselves; they can be without uncoveredness and coveredness. These latter *are* only insofar as there is διάνοια.

Uncoveredness is not only impossible without the Being of that which shows, but also without the Being of the beings to be shown.

ἕτερον ὂν τῶν κυρίως ["other than Being in the most proper sense"] (1027b31), there is "another" Being in uncoveredness, other than the "proper Being" of the categories.

---

97. Editor's interpolation.
98. See Mörchen transcription, no. 79, p. 224f.
99. *Met.* E 4, 1027b24.

b) Grounds for excluding both Being as supervenience and Being as uncoveredness from the fundamental consideration of Being.

Both[100] modes of Being, ὂν κατὰ συμβεβηκός and ὂν ὡς ἀληθές, are ἀφετέον ["to be dismissed"] (1027b33f.). συμβενβηκός is ἀόριστον (1027b34), "undetermined," unstable, nothing that can be possessed and shown as always there. ἀληθές is διανοίας τι πάθος (1028a1), a "state" of the soul. ἀμφότερα {. . .} οὐκ ἔξω δηλοῦσιν οὐσάν τινα φύσιν τοῦ ὄντος (1028a1ff.), "both modes of Being do not reveal a type of Being that would stand on its own outside of Being in the proper sense." Both modes of Being are *not unfounded*. ἔξω: "outside" of every essential relation to Being in the proper sense. ἔξω does not mean outside of consciousness. That does hold in a certain way for Being as truth, although even this is not related to "consciousness." But ἔξω is different {?} for the two types of Being, and συμβεβηκός is unquestionably a dependent being.

τὸ ἔξω ὄν ["Being on its own, outside"][101] is unfounded Being, not grounded essentially on another; χωριστόν ["separate"] (1065a24) is what is autonomous and constant, autonomous constancy.

c) The mode of the founding of Being qua supervenience and of Being qua uncoveredness in the Being of the categories.

How are both modes founded in ὂν τῶν κατηγοριῶν ["the Being of the categories"]? This latter is κυρίως ὄν ["Being in the most proper, ruling sense"];[102] then how is ὂν ὡς ἀληθές supposed to be κυριώτατον ["most proper, most lordly"]?[103]

συμβεβηκός—ἀληθές (how are these founded?) and κατηγορία. The categories are the possible modes of possible co-present-at-hand beings. Supervenience is a kind of Being grounded on the Being of the categories or, more precisely, on the idea of Being that lies at the foundation of the articulation {?} of the categories: what is in itself present-at-hand and co-present-at-hand. Supervenient positing is formally a mode of co-presence-at-hand, specifically such that it characterizes beings which do not necessarily and constantly belong among beings in the proper sense and fall to the level of nonbeings. Ontological συμβεβηκός: this mode of Being does not fully correspond to the idea of Being in the proper sense (perpetual constancy). Ontic συμβεβηκός, in its ontological meaning, never corresponds; it is not a being in the

100. See Mörchen transcription, no. 80, p. 225f.
101. *Met.* K 8, 1065a24.
102. Cf. *Met.* E 4, 1027b31.
103. Cf. *Met.* Θ 10, 1051b1: κυριώτατα ὄν ["Being in the highest sense"]; see Mörchen transcription, no. 81, p. 225f.

proper sense. Because it is founded and, furthermore, is not a being in proper sense, {supervenience is}[104] not included in the basic thematic of the science of Being. Such a being is not the possible object of a *dianoia*, and thus, for the Greeks, even its Being deserves no further discussion. Nevertheless, its consideration, carried out in *dianoia*, does belong to a comprehensive theory of Being in general.

ὂν ὡς ἀληθές[105] -κατηγορία, λόγος-"to uncover," διανοεῖν–νοεῖν. Even this is not καθ᾽ αὑτό, Being in itself, but only something encountered and *uncovered*. Yet even this mode of Being is not merely founded on what is in itself, but as such {?} it is understandable only out of λόγος, though in a different respect. At the same time this mode of Being, versus what is κατὰ συμβεβηκός, is not nothing; on the contrary, just the reverse: it brings to completion Being in itself. It characterizes beings in their presence in the proper sense. {Beings are}[106] present not only in general but are uncovered as such and accessible in their presence, placed in the utter {?} present.

---

§60. Being as potentiality and actuality: ὂν δυνάμει–ἐνεργείᾳ (*Met.* Θ).[107]

κίνησις—μεταβολή. Retrospective in Aristotle, *Phys.* A; δύναμις from δύνασθαι ["to be powerful"]. δύναμις (δυνατόν ["able, strong"]).

1. ἀρχὴ κινήσεως ἢ μεταβολῆς ἡ ἐν ἑτέρῳ ἢ ᾗ ἕτερον.[108] Potentiality is the *"point of departure of a motion,* a change, in another as the moved or inasmuch as this latter is other."* Handcraft is the potentiality, the ability, of a craftsman effected in another as the work (the shoe) or inasmuch as it is other. Healing, a doctor; the moved is the one who is ill. The doctor can heal himself, but then he is the object of his practice not qua doctor, but qua one who is ill.

2. δυνατὸν (δύναμις)[109] πάσχειν (cf. 1019a21f.), "the potentiality to *undergo* something" from another, or inasmuch as it is other.

3. δύναμις for something; not simply to act in some way or other, but καλῶς {. . .} ἢ κατὰ προαίρεσιν ["well and as anticipated"] (1019a26f.). To be able [*können*] in an emphatic sense, to be an adept [*Könner*]. "He *can* run," said of a sprinter. "He *can* play" = he plays well.

---

104. Editor's interpolation.

105. See Mörchen transcription, no. 81, p. 226.

106. Editor's interpolation.

107. Cf. *Met.* Δ 12: δύναμις (1019a15ff.); *Phys.* Γ 1-3, E; see Bröcker transcription, no. 1, p. 232f.

108. *Met.* Δ 12, 1019a15f.

109. In the manuscript, δυνατόν is crossed out, and δύναμις is written over it.

4. ἕξεις καθ᾽ ἃς ἀπαθῆ (1019a26f.), "the ability to be insensitive" to change and deterioration. Power to resist, viability. A thing is sometimes destroyed not insofar as it has an ability, but insofar as it lacks it, i.e., on account of the absence of something.

Corresponding to δύναμις, the δυνατόν, "capable of" (1019a33); likewise, ἀδυναμία (1019b15f.), "inability"; ἀδύνατον (1019b18), "not capable of." The term "impossible," on the other hand, is employed with a meaning unrelated to δύναμις and ἀδυναμία. ἀδύνατον μὲν οὗ τὸ ἐναντίον ἐξ ἀνάγκης ἀληθές (1019b23f.), "impossible: that whose opposite is necessarily true." κατὰ μεταφορὰν δὲ ἡ ἐν τῇ γεωμετρίᾳ λέγεται δύναμις ["it is only by metaphor that in mathematics we speak of powers"] (1019b33f.). The preceding meanings, however, πάντα λέγεται πρὸς τὴν πρώτην ["are all said with reference to the primary sense"] (1019b35f.), analogy, κύριος ὅρος ["the ruling sense"] (1020a4).

From this *ontic*[110] concept of δύναμις, there must be distinguished: δυνάμει (δύναμις), not an extant ability, but a *character of Being,* and indeed first visible in the moving thing, just as δύναμις (in the ontic sense) is related to μεταβολή.

---

110. See Bröcker transcription, no. 1, p. 232f.; Mörchen transcription: "ἐντελέχεια is used identically with ἐνέργεια."

4

The problem of motion and the ontological meaning of that problem. Origin, sense, and function of δύναμις and ἐνέργεια

{Outline of this chapter:}[111]

A. Analysis of motion (§61).
B. The ontological meaning of this analysis.

   1. The new characters of Being, δύναμις, ἐνέργεια (§62).
   2. The interpretation of beings as a whole (§63).

      i. *Ontically,* motion is recognized as a fact;
      ii. but *motion as such* is a problem;
      iii. if *solved,* then motion thereby becomes a *universal character of Being.*
      iv. *Fundamental determination of Being* and radical interpretation of οὐσία become possible.

φύσις, world.[112] κίνησις is not merely one state among others, but is an *essential determination.* Therefore *motion as a mode of Being is fundamental.* World, beings pure and simple, wherein each and every being is. Motion is ontologically central, even as something ontic. On the basis of motion: the ontological analysis is not a mere expansion and supplementation of what has preceded; on the contrary, it is a fundamental and more radical apprehension of these beings, the φύσει ὄντα

---

111. Editor's interpolation.
112. See Bröcker transcription, no. 2, p. 233.

["beings of nature"], and, as such, is a pan-dynamics {?} of *Being in general*. From motion and its ontological characters, *all* beings, even the unmoved (cf. δυνάμει, ἐνεργείᾳ), *inter alia:* "temporality," χρόνος, κίνησις, ἐντελέχεια ["completeness"]. Hegel: transition, becoming.

§61. The analysis of motion.[113]

Motion, *Phys.* Δ 1–3: κινούμενα φύσει ὄντα ["natural, moving beings"]. Changing from–to, "one after the other," phenomenon of succession: ἐφεξῆς;[114] συνεχές (200b18), "continuous succession." ἄπειρον (cf. 200b19), "unlimited," no boundaries or interruptions in the transition, εἰς ἄπειρον διαιρετὲν συνεχές ["what is divisible without limit is continuous"] (200b20). τόπος ["place"]; κενόν ["void"]; χρόνος ["time"] (cf. 200b21).

κίνησις is not παρὰ τὰ πράγματα ["beside the things"] (200b32f.), is not a γένος; on the contrary, in each case only as a *determination of Being*, characteristic of a being which is such and such, and indeed it applies to οὐσία, but this κατὰ ποσόν, ποιόν, τόπον ["with respect to quantity, quality, place"] (cf. 200b34). κοινὸν {. . .} οὐδὲν {. . .} λαβεῖν ["something common to them cannot be found"] (200b34f.).

ἕκαστον γένος ["each genus"] is to be differentiated into δυνάμει, ἐνεργείᾳ[115] (cf. 201a10). Doubled: μορφή—στέρησις ["form—deprivation"] in the "this here" (cf. 201a4f.).

Definition of κίνησις (201a10f.).

Analysis of motion: ready-to-hand [*zuhanden*], present-at-hand [*vorhanden*]; worked by hand [*unterhanden*]: in the case of production, what is produced in the production is apprehended in being *worked by hand*.

The motion imparted to the wood is its *being worked by hand*, {it is the motion}[116] of preparedness as such. Not the wood as present-at-hand, but the wood in its potentiality-for-Being. As this "preparedness for," the wood is *present* in its *preparedness*. This mode of Being, *movedness*, holds for everything moving or at rest, for the φύσει ὄντα. At the same time, a *higher* presence resides therein, *insistence* on that which it can be and is. The self-moving: that which does not, so to speak, simply allow its presence to remain fixed in itself, like something present-at-hand at rest, but, on the contrary, is insistent, explicitly thrusts itself forward in its presence, forms this insistent presence of motion. In the phenome-

---

113. See Bröcker transcription, no. 3, p. 233ff.
114. *Phys.* Γ 1, 200b16.
115. Prantl's reading: ἐντελεχείᾳ for ἐνεργείᾳ.
116. Editor's interpolation.

non of transition, there resides this fluctuation of higher presence and absence within something present-at-hand.

κίνησις is ἀτελής ["incomplete"] (cf. 201a6). It is indeed readiness-to-hand, but the one of mere preparedness. The readiness-to-hand of what has been finished: ἔργον ["the product"]. Thus what is finished has no more motion. Readiness-to-hand and yet motion, but no incompletion. Ontic concept of an ἐνέργεια versus ontic concept of a κίνησις. Presence of what is not yet finished as such. The latter: ἐνέργεια τοῦ δυνάμει {. . .} ᾗ τοιοῦτον ["the actuality of the potential as such"] (201a10f.); the former: ἐνέργεια *pure and simple*. ἐνέργεια τελεία ["complete actuality"]. Presence and yet already finished, what is by essence {?} already complete, finished, and yet in the process of being carried out. To bring itself into the present.

The "for the sake of which" in what is moving is itself nothing other than moved*ness*. Is the readiness-to-hand of movedness as movedness here the {?} purest {?} Being? Being: *having been produced;* Being: *producing;* Being: *pure making as such*.

---

§62. The ontological meaning of the analysis of κίνησις. The ontological sense of δύναμις and ἐνέργεια.

This "potential," the ready-to-hand, can be present in a more insistent sense in immediate use.

οὐσία: that which is autonomously and constantly present-at-hand. Now according to two basic possibilities: δύναμις, ἐνέργεια, "act-ual-ity" [»*Wirk-lich-keit*«].[117] Both are ἀνάλογα ["analogs"].

This is the articulation: δύναμις–ἐνέργεια on the basis of the structure of beings as things produced, composed. Consideration of what constitutes presence, namely, form; this latter as ἐνέργεια. ὕλη and δύναμις.

δυνάμει–ἐνεργείᾳ. 1. What does this determination mean as a character of *Being*? 2. How does it go together with the other determinations, above all with οὐσία?

Regarding 1:

a) Potentiality, ability, in an *ontic* sense, δυνατόν.[118]
b) Ontological sense of potentiality as a character of Being: δυνάμει ὄν:[119]

---

117. See supplement no. 26, p. 165f.; see Bröcker transcription, no. 4, p. 235f.
118. *Met. Δ* 12.
119. *Met. Θ* 6.

α) Founded, later as ἐνέργεια;
β) ἐνέργεια itself, fundamental presence, reference, "world."

Motion is a determination of the Being of beings, of moving beings. What does motion mean *ontologically? Readiness-to-hand of what is prepared in its preparedness.* ἀτελές–ἐντελέχεια ["incomplete-complete"].

Ontologically and fundamentally δυνάμει ὄν–ἐνεργείᾳ ὄν: preparedness–readiness-to-hand. At the same time, levels of Being. Motion–activity.

Levels of Being: ἐνέργεια and οὐσία. This {ἐνέργεια}[120] as radical interpretation of οὐσία. δύναμις, ἐνέργεια are at the same time *basic possibilities* of οὐσία. Present-at-hand–ready-to-hand.

δυνάμει ὄν–ἐνεργείᾳ ὄν, potentiality and actuality. Misunderstood as mere possibility, pure possibility; i.e., understood negatively: nothing stands in the way for the thing to be. On the contrary: this "potentiality" as a mode of presence, *suitability, preparedness for,* availability for, but *in view of a "toward-which,"* a *"not yet,"* στέρησις ["deprivation"],[121] but not nothing, not nonbeing; instead, presence-at-hand. Actuality, presence-at-hand, as *being-in-act.* Actuality is a mode of Being, with whose help motion can be grasped ontologically. Conversely, there {belong}[122] to this mode ζωή ["life"], act, working, doing, as ontological characters.

The "potential" is not un-actual in the sense of something not at all present-at-hand, but is un-actual as *not now being actualized.* The actuality of what is at rest is to be understood on the basis of motion. The other way makes everything unclear.

Potentiality understood *negatively:* non-contradiction, potentiality-for-Being in general. Understood *positively: definite ability to be something, suitability as such.* Potentiality: suitability, but suitability-for, readiness, preparedness; it lacks only the carrying out of the transformation; *fully prepared.* When something present-at-hand in such a way is ready-to-hand with respect to this mode of Being, then it is in *motion.*

Preparedness {to become}[123] a table. When it, as this prepared thing, is ready-to-hand as present in its preparedness, then it is in motion. The *preparedness of what is present-at-hand:* this present-at-hand thing present *with respect to* its preparedness, *as* prepared. When does it, *in and of itself,* become ready-to-hand in its preparedness? When and how does it *show itself in itself in its preparedness?* Not when I simply observe it. For then all I can say is that it is something which can become a table. The preparedness is manifest in itself when the wood is being worked on and as long

120. Editor's interpolation.
121. Cf. *Phys.* Γ 2, 201b34.
122. Editor's interpolation.
123. Crossed out in the manuscript.

as it is *in hand*, i.e., during the whole time in which it is being worked up into something. As long as it is worked on, this *becoming, changing*, is then the *presence of the present-at-hand in its preparedness* and with respect to its preparedness: κίνησις. To be taken up and worked on, i.e., the Being of the being, that which is *disclosed through being manipulated*, the act of being taken in hand, *readiness-to-hand*.

Readiness-to-hand of preparedness as such; *temporality* of preparedness; temporality of readiness-to-hand; temporality of the ready-to-hand as preparedness as such. Modality of preparedness for the readiness-to-hand as something that is in hand {?}.

Readiness-to-hand, preparedness: both are modes of presence, *the particulars*. Even what is prepared is present, ready-to-hand, but not necessarily in its preparedness. Wood is lying about. When is something, from itself, ready-to-hand in its preparedness? When it is *in hand*, i.e., in the *motion of handwork*.[124]

δύναμις–ἐντελέχεια.[125] "Preparedness"–"availability";"readiness-to-hand."

ἡ οὐσία, εἶδος, ἐνέργεια,[126] readiness-to-hand. When taken in such a way, then it is understood in its Being, *without reference to something other, purely on the basis of itself,* and only ἐνέργεια, the τέλος *not still outstanding:*[127] νοῦς–ζωή. Ancient {?} and proper {?} idea of presence. *Life* has a τέλος, an ἐντελέχεια. Life as the *most proper presence-at-hand: presence out of itself* and *constantly complete,* and yet *not at rest,* not simply lying there immobile. Movedness and presence, ἐντελέχεια. οἶον ζωή τις ["a kind of life"],[128] in "life": a kind of Being of a higher mode. But, as presence, maintaining itself constant, autonomous and constant in full, finished presence.

ἐντελέχεια:

1. not only present in general,
2. not only moveable, ἀτελής ["incomplete"], ἀόριστον ["indefinite"],
3. but out of itself, according to its essence, only in act. ἐνέργεια τελεία ["complete actuality"], finished and yet *not stopping in its insistent presence;* on the contrary, Being resides precisely therein; πέρας ["limit"] and yet no stopping. I have seen,[129] and I see in the same way now. I have been happy and am now happy in precisely the same way. I have lived and live that way now.

124. See supplement no. 27, p. 166.
125. Cf. *Phys.* Γ 1, 201a10f.
126. *Met.* Θ 8, 1050b2.
127. See Bröcker transcription, no. 4, p. 236f.
128. *Phys.* Θ 1, 250b14.
129. See Bröcker transcription, no. 4, p. 236f.

§63. Interpretation of beings as a whole (B 2).

1. Movedness: essential determination of the φύσει ὄντα.
2. "Motion" must be constant, eternal[130] (the idea or the moving thing?).

{Outline:}[131]
Thesis: by necessity there is always motion.

1. On the basis of the very idea of motion. } Connection
2. On the basis of time: }

   a) Time is eternal in virtue of the essence of time, namely, the now.
   b) Time within motion requires: if time always is, then a fortiori so is motion.

3. If motion always is, then there is always something moved.
4. That which is always moved: how must it be in itself, and what must be its kind of motion?
5. What is necessarily co-posited in this κίνησις κύκλῳ ["circular motion"]? What is co-present-at-hand with it? This is the πρῶτον κινοῦν ["first mover"], but not ἀκίνητον ["unmoved"], in itself there is still a τέλος.
6. πρῶτον κινοῦν ἀκίνητον ["first, unmoved mover"].
7. How is this first mover itself the most proper being? How is it connected to the idea of Being?

a) Proofs for the eternity of motion.

{Regarding 1: On the basis of the very idea of motion:}[132] εἶναι {. . .} κίνησιν πάντες φασὶν οἱ περὶ φύσεώς τι λέγοντες ["all who have held forth on nature say that there is motion"].[133] Motion always is, there is always something moved, for coming-to-be and passing-away are possible only if κίνησις *is*. δυνάμει ὄν is a ὑπάρχειν ["presupposition"]. ἀναγκαῖον ἄρα ἀπάρχειν τὰ πράγματα τὰ δυνάμενα κινεῖσθαι καθ᾽ ἑκάστην κίνησιν ["each kind of motion necessarily presupposes the things with the potential for such motion"] (251a10f.). There is also κίνησις even if all there is is something at rest, ἡ γὰρ ἠρέμησις στέρησις τῆς κινήσεως ["for rest is merely the deprivation of motion"] (251a26f.). Thus the very essence of motion implies that motion always already was

---

130. See Bröcker transcription, no. 5, p. 237.
131. Editor's interpolation.
132. Editor's interpolation.
133. *Phys.* Θ 1, 250b15ff.; see Bröcker transcription, no. 6, p. 237f.

and must always be, for δυνάμει ὄν is something at rest, which has come to rest out of motion.

{Regarding 2: On the basis of time, b):}[134] Motion: μεταβολὴ ἐκ τινος (δυνάμει) εἴς τι ["change from something (in potentiality) to something"].[135] Prior to the motion, something unmoved. τὸ πρότε-ρον καὶ ὕστερον πῶς ἔσται χρόνου μὴ ὄντος; ἢ χρόνος μὴ οὔσης κινήσεως; ["Could there be the before and the after if there were no time? Could there be time if there were no motion?"][136] — "There is no 'earlier' or 'later' without time, and no time without motion." But time is eternal, and so motion is eternal as well.

{Regarding 2: On the basis of time, a):}[137] Is time eternal? The es-sence of time: the now. The now is the now that just was and the now that is not yet. ἀρχὴ τοῦ ἐσομένου, τελευτὴ τοῦ παρελθόντος ["the beginning of the future, the end of the past"] (cf. 251b21f.). οὐδὲν γὰρ ἔστι λαβεῖν ἐν τῷ χρόνῳ ["for there is nothing else to be found in time (except the now)"] (251b24).[138]

b) Attempt at an ontological clarification of eternal motion: the divine, unmoved, first mover as pure ἐνέργεια.

Regarding 4: καὶ ἔστι τι αἰεὶ κινούμενον κίνησιν ἄπαυστον, αὕτη δ᾽ ἡ κύκλῳ· καὶ τοῦτο οὐ λόγῳ μόνον ἀλλ᾽ ἔργῳ δῆλον ["There is something eternally moving with a motion that never ceases, and that is motion in a circle: which is evident not only in logos but also in fact"].[139] ἡ κύκλῳ τινι φορά ["the primary, circular motion"] (cf. 1072b9) is that of the πρῶτος οὐρανός ["first heaven"] (1072a23). κίνησις ὁμαλής,[140] "uniform motion," constant. This encompasses all other motions, that of the planets and other erratic things. ὅθεν ἡ ἀρχὴ τῆς κινήσεως ["whence the beginning of motion"].[141] Thus the circular motion of the first heaven is the first cause of all motion.

Regarding 5: But eternal, genuine motion is thereby still not onto-logically clarified in an exhaustive way. For κίνησις is ἀτελής. βαδίζειν εἰς τέλος ["proceeding toward the end"]. Every κινητὸν {. . .} εἰς τὸ αὑτοῦ εἶδος {. . .} φέρεσθαι ["everything that moves is carried toward its own eidos"].[142] Also for local motion and for bodies

134. Editor's interpolation.
135. Cf. *Phys.* E 1, 225a1; see Bröcker transcription, no. 6, p. 238f.
136. *Phys.* Θ 1, 251b10ff.
137. Editor's interpolation.
138. See supplement no. 28, p. 166.
139. *Met.* Λ 7, 1072a21f.; see supplement no. 29, p. 166f.; see Bröcker transcrip-tion, no. 7, p. 239.
140. *Phys.* E 4, 228b17.
141. *Met.* A, 984a27.
142. *De caelo* Δ 3, 310a33ff.

moved in that way, there is οἰκεῖος τόπος ["its own proper place"] (πῦρ ["fire"] is always ἄνω ["up"]), πάντα γὰρ παύεται κινούμενα, ὅταν ἔλθῃ εἰς τὸν οἰκεῖον τόπον ["for all things cease to move whenever they come to their proper place"].[143] The point of departure of motion is στέρησις: that toward which the motion is proceeding has not yet been reached. As the motion itself progresses, the στέρησις disappears. ἅπασαι γὰρ ἐξ ἀντικειμένων εἰς ἀντικείμενά εἰσιν αἱ κινήσεις καὶ μεταβολαί ["for all motions and changes are from an opposite to an opposite"].[144] οὐ πᾶσα φορὰ ἐν ἐναντίοις ["not every locomotion has an opposite"],[145] and yet πάσης κινήσεως τέλος:[146] every κίνησις has a τέλος. Eternal motion must indeed have an οἰκεῖον τόπον and a τέλος and yet may never stop.

Regarding 6: But what by essence moves in a circle has always the same place. It returns back to the place from which it started, and so constantly; every place on its path is both starting point and end. τοῦ δὲ κύκλῳ σώματος ὁ αὐτὸς τόπος ὅθεν ἤρξατο καὶ εἰς ὃν τελευτᾷ ["with a body moving in a circle, the same place is both that from which it begins and at which it ends"].[147] The uniformity of circular motion, which is constant but neither approaches nor distances itself from its τέλος, requires, according to its own essence, a τέλος to which it maintains a uniform relation[148] and which therefore is itself uniform, unchanging, and ἀεί ["eternal"]: πρῶτον κινοῦν ἀκίνητον ["the first, unmoved mover"].[149] δεῖ δὲ οὐδὲ τὸ κινούμενον πρὸς ἐκεῖνο ἔκειν μεταβολήν, ἵνα ὁμοία ᾖ ἡ κίνησις ["it is necessary that what is moved does not at all change in relation to the mover, in order for the motion to be uniform"].[150] In this πρῶτον ["first (mover)"], every possibility, every "not yet," must be excluded. δεῖ ἄρα εἶναι ἀρχὴν τοιαύτην ἧς ἡ οὐσία ἐνέργεια ["it is necessary that there be such a principle, whose very Being is actuality"].[151] No ἀτελής, no κίνησις, but, instead, pure ἐνέργεια, pure energy, i.e., *pure, autonomous, constant presence based on nothing but itself.* To the Being and essence of this being, there belongs act as such. No τέλος or ἔργον outside of itself.[152] κινεῖ δὲ ὡς ἐρώμενον ["it moves in the manner of something loved"] (1072b3), ὡς ὀρεκτόν ["in the manner of something desired"] (cf. 1072a26).

143. *De caelo* A 9, 279b1f.

144. *Phys.* Θ 7, 261a32f.

145. Cf. *De caelo* A 3, 270a18ff.

146. Cf. *Met.* B 4, 999b10f.

147. *De caelo* A 9, 279b2f.

148. See Bröcker transcription, no. 7, p. 239f.

149. *Phys.* Θ 6, 258b12.

150. *Phys.* Θ 10, 267b5f.

151. *Met.* Λ 6, 1071b19f.

152. See supplement no. 30, p. 167.

Regarding 7: νόησις νοήσεως ["knowing knowing"] (1074b34),[153] "absolute spirit," "knowing that knows itself." Not meant as spirit-person, but only in the context of an *ontological clarification of eternal motion* itself, and here νόησις, ζωή, has no further relevant meaning. What is proper to this πρῶτον is: 1. no relation to the world, 2. nor to human beings. 3. Above all, what has no place here is the concept of creation, governing, providence, or the like. 4. In addition, νόησις νοήσεως is not self-intuition in the sense of the contemplation of the archetypes of things, according to which all things are created, i.e., the Platonic-Plotinian-Augustinian notion of contemplation.

θεῖον ["the divine"][154] and θειότατον ["the most divine"] have nothing to do with religiosity; on the contrary, it simply means τιμιώτατον ὄν ["the most eminent being"] (cf. 1064b5), Being in the proper sense, a *neutral, ontological* concept. θεολογία ["theology"] (cf. 1064b3) is the science of that which is *most properly a being;* πρώτη φιλοσοφία ["first philosophy"] (E 1, 1026a24) is the science of *Being.*

Recapitulation

πρῶτον κινοῦν ["first mover"] is itself not κίνησις ["motion], not ἀτελής ["incomplete"]. Thus *pure* ἐνέργεια. Moreover, its comportment is such that it has its τέλος in itself, in what it already is, not in an ἔργον. ζωή—νοεῖν. No external ἔργον or τέλος; also has no mathematical object, but only itself: νόησις νοήσεως.

θεῖον as ontic foundation of all motion, but not ever {?} as primal ground of all Being in the sense of an ἀρχή and certainly not a creator; {instead},[155] the ultimate τέλος of the eternal motion of Being. It is a matter of making *ontologically* and *ontically* comprehensible that which is in motion, but not by tracing back its origin to some genesis, creator, or explanation; on the contrary, ἀεί, what is *most properly in motion.*

---

§64. The connection of δύναμις and ἐνέργεια to οὐσία; the problem of the double concept of ontology as fundamental science.[156]

δύναμις–ἐνέργεια, "preparedness for" and "actuality": two basic modes of Being, i.e., of presence-at-hand, of οὐσία with the four ontological determinations that comprise a radical grasp of οὐσία. The most proper

---

153. See Bröcker transcription, no. 7, p. 240f.
154. *Met.* Λ 8, 1074b3.
155. Editor's interpolation.
156. See Bröcker transcription, no. 8, p. 241; see Mörchen transcription, no. 82, p. 227.

character of οὐσία is ἐντελέχεια, which is "prior," πρότερον,[157] than every other mode of Being; i.e., there must be something present-at-hand in the first place, in order for modifications to be possible.

Insofar as δύναμις and ἐνέργεια determine οὐσία as such, which is the primary category and to which the others are related *analogously*, then δύναμις and ἐνέργεια also extend, as modifications, to all the remaining categories. In this way, everything is led back to οὐσία as the basic phenomenon, specifically such that ἐνέργεια is the *highest kind of presence-at-hand*.

The being that genuinely is in this highest sense of Being is the πρῶτον κινοῦν ἀκίνητον, the ὂν θειότατον ["most divine being"].[158] The science of this most proper being, of the being that is everything a being can be, is θεολογία. The science of beings, of what they are as beings, the science of Being, is πρώτη φιλοσοφία.[159] καθόλου πασῶν κοινή ["universally common to all"] (1026a27), [this science is about] that which determines every being as a being, and at the same time [it is] about Being. This *fundamental science* deals with that which properly is, with that which is the most proper being, with the highest being and with Being, with what properly belongs to a being.

Problem: 1. fundamental ontology: one particular being is by necessity exemplary and thus becomes the theme, though with a view to understanding Being in the sense of a concept of Being. 2. Being of the categories: ὄν ["a being"], ἕν ["one"], ἀγαθόν ["good"], ἕτερον ["other"], ἐναντίον ["opposite"], μὴ ὄν ["nonbeing"]. Formal ontology.

The double concept of the fundamental science is not a confusion or a conjunction of two different approaches that have nothing to do with each other; on the contrary, it always proceeds from a necessity lying in the content of the problem. Aristotle did not master this problem, nor did he even formulate it as such, which is why it later fell into complete oblivion.

1. Motion as movedness. Ontological meaning of motion.

2. This character of Being, which imposes itself on the moved and on its mode of Being, is grasped universally. δυνάμει is, taken positively, a mode of presence; δύναμις καὶ ἐνέργεια {?} are modes of presence; ἐνέργεια is a mode of presence. ἐντελέχεια: motion and yet not only that, but also what is contained in it.

3. ἐνέργεια is πρότερον,[160] ontically–ontologically. Guideline. Highest presence, autonomous, constant. In and of itself: i. present (moveable); ii. constant; iii. but not in motion.

4. What properly is ἐνεργείᾳ ὄν with respect to the whole of Being?

157. *Met.* Θ 8, 1050b3f.

158. Cf. *Met.* Λ 9, 1074b26.

159. *Met.* E 1, 1026a24; cf. above, p. 150.

160. See above, n. 157.

οὐρανός ["the heavens"]. How is motion in general possible? The ontological—is it itself ontic? And so back to ἐνέργεια? This also taken ontically?

What is here the purely ontological problematic was, to be sure, not fully mastered. It would appear later in completely different contexts, whereby this ontology was taken up into that of God and man. Decisively in the philosophical anthropology of the modern age.

5

Ontology of life and of Dasein

We are attempting to characterize how, on the basis of a radically apprehended ontological problematic, two preeminent regions of beings are determined in their ontological structure. From the presentation of the origin of two fundamental determinations of Being, namely, δύναμις and ἐνέργεια, it already became clear that ζωή thereby receives an exemplary significance. Indeed, this is precisely the first-ever phenomenological grasp of life, and it led to the interpretation of motion and made possible the radicalization of ontology. How does this ontology now react back on the explication of the structure of a living being in general? Here again it must be emphasized that many things have become common to us today which Aristotle had to wrest from the phenomena over and against extant dogmatic theories about them and also in the face of an insufficient conceptual framework.

---

§65. The treatise Περὶ ψυχῆς as primary source for accessing Aristotle's ontology of life.

Aristotle laid out the first fundamental traits of an ontology of life in his treatise Περὶ ψυχῆς ["On the soul"]. It is completely misleading to see therein a psychology or to use such a title for it.

a) The Aristotelian treatise *De anima:* outline.[161]

Three books:

Bk. A: exhibition of the problem of an ontologically categorial determination of life. Critical retrospective on the opinions of the earlier philosophers.

---

161. See Mörchen transcription, no. 83, p. 227f.

Bk. B: Positive conceptual determination of the soul and exhibition of the levels of life; in particular, perception.
Chap. 1: General laying of the foundation.
Chaps. 5–6: αἴσθησις.
Chaps. 7–11: αἰσθήσεις.
Chap. 12: *collegit:* αἰσθήσεις, the possible forms of αἴσθησις in general.

Bk. Γ: chaps. 1 and 2 belong to bk. B; description and theory of νοεῖν, fundamental perspective.
Chaps. 1–2: on αἴσθησις.
Chap. 3: φαντασία ["imagination"].
Chaps. 4–8: νοῦς ["understanding"], διάνοια ["thought"].
Chaps. 9–13: νοῦς, ὄρεξις ["desire"], and the life of lower creatures.

Uneven in working out the themes. Most unitary, clear, and concrete is bk. B, least is bk. Γ, even though it is in the latter that the most important problems are articulated in a positive way.

Parva naturalia: περὶ αἰσθήσεως καὶ αἰστητῶν ["On perception and things perceived"] (436a1–499b3), περὶ μνήμης καὶ ἀναμνήσεως ["On memory and recall"] (449b3–453b11), περὶ ὕπνου καὶ ἐγρηγόρσεως ["On sleep and waking"] (453b11–458a32), περὶ ζωῆς καὶ θανάτου ["On life and death"] (467b10–470b5). περὶ ζῴων κινήσεως ["On the motion of animals"] (698a1–704b3),[162] περὶ ζῴων πορείας ["On the ambulation of animals"] (704a4–714b23).

b) The character of Aristotle's treatise, *On the soul.*

{ψυχὴ} ἔστι γὰρ οἷον ἀρχὴ τῶν ζῴων,[163] "the soul is something like the ground of Being of a living being." Not an isolated power; not reducible to the principles of material, lifeless nature; not the sum or the result of bodily processes, but also not separable for itself. Yet it is precisely Aristotle who set in motion the theory of the soul as a substance, which was often opposed later, until it was treated exhaustively in Kant's first *Critique,* in the section on the paralogisms of pure reason.[164] But what if all of that rested on a fundamental misunderstanding of the sense and intention of the Aristotelian theory of the soul? There it is so little a matter of the soul as a substance, in the sense of physical breath, housed for itself somewhere in the body and at death vanishing into the heavens, that it was precisely Aristotle who first placed the problem of the soul on its genuine ground. τὸ δὲ ζῆν τοῖς ζῴοι τὸ εἶναί ἐστιν ["with regard to living things, their life is precisely their Being"],[165] the soul is not a thing

---

162. Jaeger, *Studien*, pp. 153–154.
163. *De anima* A 1, 402a6f.
164. *Kritik der reinen Vernunft*, A 341–405/B 399–432.
165. *De anima* B 4, 415b13.

(the psychical) beside the bodily (the physical); on the contrary, it is the very way of Being of a determinate corporeal being, one which, on the basis of this Being, differentiates itself, as something living, from what is lifeless. The lifeless stands on this side of the opposition between life and death. Death is not lifeless; on the contrary, it is what is deprived of life and so is a determination of a living being, just as rest is a determination of motion. The positive outcome of Aristotle's analyses shows that his theory of the ψυχή is aiming at an *ontology of life.*

§66. Analysis of ζωή.

Articulation:

1. ἄψυχον–ἔμψυχον ["unsouled–ensouled"][166] (ζῆν ["life"], εἶναι ["Being"], general philosophical characters).

2. ζῆν (ψυχή): κρίνειν–κινεῖν ["distinguishing–moving"] (oriented comportment in a world).

3. possibilities of κρίνειν and κινεῖν: αἴσθησις–ἐπιθυμία ["perception–appetite"] (413b23f.). νοῦς–ὄρεξις ["understanding–desire"] (433a13), (προαίρεσις ["anticipation"]: cf. 406b25). χρόνος ["time"] (cf. 433b7)–ὀρεκτόν ["the desired"] (433b11)–κινητικόν ["setting in motion"] (cf. 433a13).

4. ψυχή is the Being of a living being: comportment toward; assignment to; in the mode of disclosure. Not something co-present-at-hand, juxtaposed; instead, belongs to life itself as that from which, against which, and in which life is lived. νοῦς is τὰ πάντα ["all things"] (cf. 431b21).

5. ἐντελέχεια. ψυχή: i. οὐσία (412a21); ii. ἐντελέχεια {?} (412a21); iii. ἐντελέχεια ἡ πρώτη ["first actuality"] (412a27); iv. ἐντελέχεια σώματος φυσικοῦ ὀργανικοῦ ["actuality of a natural body with organs"] (cf. 412a27ff.).

Regarding 1:[167] bk. B, chap. 2: ἄψυχον–ἔμψυχον: διωφίσθαι {. . .} τῷ ζῆν [(what has soul) "differentiates itself by manifesting life"] (413a21f.). Everything is living, we say, in which is found: perception of something, self-motion, self-maintenance, nutrition, growth, and decline. Therefore also φυόμενα (413a25), plants, as living: they manifest growth, aging, and decay; they move in opposite directions at the same time. (Physical bodies at the same time {?} in each case in only one direction.) Plants move not only upward and downward, but also πάντοσε, "in all directions" (413a29). A plant is θρεπτικόν (413b5), it "takes in nourishment," grows and decays, all while remaining fixed in

166. Cf. *De anima* B 2, 413a21ff.
167. See Mörchen transcription, no. 84, p. 228.

one place. The animal, on the contrary, is distinguished through αἴσθησις; even if something does not move, does not change its place, but does perceive, then it is an animal. αἴσθησις is primarily the sense of touch, grasping. Where there is perception of something, self-orientation in a world, there is λύπη τε καὶ ἡδονή ["pain and pleasure"] (413b23), feeling oneself *attuned* in such and such a way, feeling well and ill, and thus also being on the lookout for: ὄρεξις (cf. 413b23).

Regarding 2:[168] *basic determinations* of what is alive: κρίνειν, κινεῖν. Something is alive that *can* exhibit these, that is determined by this *potentiality-for-Being* as such. αἰσθητικόν (417a6); sleep (cf. 417a11). κίνησις as movedness of life.

κρίνειν: αἴσθησις–νοῦς–λόγος; ἄλογον ["without *logos*"]–λόγον ἔχον ["possessing *logos*"] (cf. 432a30f.). αἴσθησις is in-between, neither one nor the other (cf. 432a30f.). αἴσθησις:[169] since it discloses the world, though indeed not in speech and assertion, not in showing and making the disclosure intelligible. Fundamental concept of sensibility: *letting a world be given and encountered by disclosing it.*

As to method: how are these possibilities to be grasped? αἰσθητικόν (425a17)–πρότερον {. . .} αἰσθάνεσθαι ["first of all, perceiving"] (415a18)–ἔτι πρότερα τὰ ἀντικείμενα ["even prior to that, the respective objects"] (415a20), "reduction."

Bk. B, chap. 6: αἴσθησις: 1) ἰδία ["its proper objects"] (cf. 418a10), 2) κοινή ["objects in common"] (cf. 418a10), 3) κατὰ συμβεβηκός ["accidental objects"] (418a9).

ὄψις ["sight"] (B 7, 418a26); ἀκοή ["hearing"] (cf. B 8, 419b4); ὀσμή, "smell," (cf. B 9, 421a7); γεῦσις, "taste," (B 10, 422a29); ἀφή ["touch"] (cf. B 11, 422b17).

Regarding 3:[170] phenomenal givenness of life (bk. Γ, chaps. 9–10). κίνησις is πορευτικὴ κίνησις (cf. 432b14), "to move oneself toward," "to betake oneself to," have dealings with. ἐνεκά τινος ["for the sake of something"] (cf. 432b15), μετὰ φαντασίας ἢ ὀρέξεως ["along with imagination or desire"] (432b16), ὀρεγόμενον ἢ φεῦγον ["grasping for or fleeing"] (432b17), διώκοντος ἢ φεύγοντος ["pursuing or fleeing"] (cf. 432b28f.); question of κινοῦν, ἀρχή.

κινητικά are ἄμφω ["both"] (433a13): νοῦς[171] (φαντασία) καὶ ὄρεξις (cf. 433a9f.) ["producing motion are both: understanding (imagination) and desire"]; ὄρεξις καὶ διάνοια πρακτική ["desire and practical thought"] (433a18). ὀρεκτὸν γὰρ κινεῖ ["for, what is desired moves

---

168. See the articulation on p. 155 above.

169. See Mörchen transcription, no. 84, p. 228f.

170. See the articulation on p. 155 above; see Mörchen transcription, no. 84, p. 229.

171. See the articulation on p. 155 above; see Mörchen transcription, no. 84, p. 229.

us"] (433a18f.), ὄρεξις pre-gives this ἐρεκτόν, which is not accessible as such. διὰ τοῦτο ἡ διάνοια κινεῖ ["through that (the desired), thought produces motion"] (433a19). The ὀρεκτόν is ἀρχὴ τῆς διανοίας ["the desired is the beginning of thought"] (cf. 433a19f.). τὸ ὀρεκτικόν is τὸ κινοῦν ["the desired is the mover"], and indeed ἕν {. . .} τι ["some one thing"] (433a21), κοινὸν {. . .} εἶδος ["one common *eidos*"] (433a22) — προαίρεσις ["anticipation"] (cf. 406b25); not on the contrary νοῦς {. . .} θεωρητικός ["theoretical understanding"] (432b26f.).

ὄρεξις {. . .} ἐναντίαι ἀλλήλαις ["desires may be opposed to one another"] (433b5); πλείω τὰ κινοῦντα ["many things move us"] (433b13).

Regarding 5:[172] ἐντελέχεια: ὡς ἐπιστήμη, {. . .} ὡς τὸ θεωρεῖν ["actuality: as (latent) knowledge or as (active) disclosive looking"] (412a10f.). Waking: θεωρεῖν ["disclosing"], sleeping: ἔχειν καὶ μὴ ἐνεργεῖν, ἐπιστήμη προτέρα ["possessing knowledge but not actualizing it; the former is prior to the latter"] (cf. 412a25f.).

οὐσίαι ["things that are present"] are first of all σώματα ["bodies"] (412a11f.); these latter are living and lifeless. ἔχει ζωήν ["having life"] (412a13): γένεσις ["coming to be by birth"] and κίνησις δι' αὑτοῦ ["self-moving"] (cf. 412a14) = σῶμα φυσικόν ["natural body"] (412a15): ἀρχή and τέλος in oneself, to be in and of oneself, to grow, to preserve oneself and, in and of oneself, to perish; οὐσία, Being for a determinate σῶμα (412a16f.), i.e., δυνάμει ζωὴν ἔχοντος ["potentially having life"] (412a20f.), preparedness in oneself to be such and such on one's own basis. The soul is the *presence of this potentiality-for-Being in its Being.* "Earlier" means: that which makes possible, organizes this potentiality-for-Being.

1. ἡ ψυχή ἐστιν ἐντελέχεια ἡ πρώτη σώματος φυσικοῦ δυνάμει ζωὴν ἔχοντος ["the soul is the first actuality of a natural body potentially having life"] (412a27f.). Actuality, autonomy of an independent, bodily being which is determined by its preparedness for life.

2. ἐντελέχεια ἡ πρώτη σώματος φυσικοῦ ὀργανικοῦ ["the first actuality of a natural body with organs"] (412b5f.), actuality, autonomy: mode of Being that {determines}[173] something present-at-hand.

---

§67. Ontology of Dasein.

Essence of life.[174] Life and Dasein, λόγον ἔχον:[175] to *disclose* the world and oneself explicitly *as* these beings and as such and such, to make

172. See the articulation on p. 155 above.
173. Editor's interpolation.
174. See Mörchen transcription, no. 85, p. 229f.
175. Cf. *Nic. Eth.* 1, 7, 1098a3f.

them accessible, understand them from various perspectives, comprehend them, ground them. Disclosure of the ground.

λόγος–νοῦς–ὄρεξις–προαίρεσις ["*logos*-understanding-desire-anticipation"];[176] ἕξεις τοῦ ἀληθεύειν: ποίησις–πρᾶξις ["capacities for disclosing the truth: making–doing"] (cf. 1140a2); πρακτική τις, ζωὴ πρακτική τις τοῦ λόγον ἔχοντος ["something practical, the practical life of that which possesses *logos*"] (cf. 1098a3f.); the τέλος is not παρά ["beside, outside"]. ἴδιον ἔργον ["in itself is the product"], action is the Being of the being itself. The τέλος resides in the very Being of Dasein. καθ᾽ αὐτὸ τέλειον ["in itself is the end"] (cf. 1097a33) — τελειότατον ["the highest end"] (1097a30); αὐταρκες, "self-sufficient" (1097b8). ψυχῆς ἐνέργειά τις κατ᾽ ἀρετὴν τελείαν ["a certain activity of the soul in accord with complete excellence"] (1102a5f.), with respect to the possibility of Being that is highest according to its ontological meaning: genuine Being lies therein. Being is everlasting constancy. θεωρεῖν ["contemplation"] is without χρῆσις ["use"], no ἔργον ["product"] (cf. 1178b3f.); its object is ἀεὶ ὄν ["eternal Being"].[177]

---

176. See above, p. 155ff.
177. See Mörchen transcription, no. 86, p. 230f.

Appendices

1. Cause. (Supplement to p. 27.)

Beings, all beings. Beings: overwhelming and, at first, "world," nature in the broadest sense, φύσις.

Beings are. *On what does it depend that beings are rather than are not? Whence these beings at all,* the things, the states of affairs? Whence arises the cause of these states of affairs [*die Ur-sache dieser Sachen*]? Whence the cause, out of what, consisting in what? Beings out of beings, how did they come into being, how were beings made, how was Being produced? What makes a being a being: 1. Which being brings beings forth? 2. What pertains to Being in general? 3. Which being, and how understood, is ontologically exemplary?

Whence, out of what, on what ground, which cause, why thus and not otherwise, why at all, and by what means? Formally and in general ἀρχαί– αἴτιον: to what are beings *obliged*?

Cause: 1. the causal agency itself, 2. the mode of causality and the sense of causation in general.

Question of the why.

2. (Crossed out, supplement to p. 84.)

In order for Dasein to encounter beings, what is necessary is: a) pre-givenness of the world in general; b) an understanding of Being, truth, even if not explicit; c) a determinate mode of encountering in each case, and d) a διαλέγεσθαι, a "speaking all the way through," (e.g., to take in the εἰκασία, the immediate "appearance"). A level of truth is thereby characterized: truth in the sense of the uncoveredness of encountered beings. Shadows on the wall.

3. (Supplement to p. 85.)

Plato: *"illumination"*
"Idea"—"sight"
Seeing
Brightness (light)
Illumination

4. (Supplement to p. 94.)

Questions:

Being and motion	Time
Being and ἀγαθόν	Care
Being and truth	Disclosedness, discourse, dialectic
(soul)	
Being and relation	

5. (Supplement to p. 96f.)

2. κίνησις–εἶναι, κίνησις–ἀγαθόν.

Relation and relativity: 6 is greater than 4: 1½. 6 is less than 12: ½. 6 is greater and smaller at the same time, ½ = 1½. Can something be other than it is, without changing? To be other while remaining constant and self-same. What does "to be" mean here? "To be" and "to become"; self-sameness and otherness (change).

6. (Supplement to p. 102.)

Theatetus: what is knowledge? At the foundation lies the question of Being. In knowledge: the disclosing of the one who grasps beings, understanding of Being. Perception does not give anything like that. *Knowledge is not perception.* Knowledge is opinion, to be of a certain view, to have a conviction.

7. Different version of a passage in §42b. (Crossed out, supplement to p. 104.)

δόξα. We do say that one δοξάζειν is ψευδῆ, the other δοξάζειν is ἀληθῆ, ὡς φύσει οὕτως ἐχόντων ["true, as holding in this way by nature"],[1] just as if that pertained to our own Being. Opposed is the sophistical thesis: οὐκ ἔστιν {. . .} ψεύδεσθαι ["there is no false speaking"] (194A9f.) Either we know or do not know (as a fact; leaving aside learning and forgetting) *what* an opinion is about, *what* it relates to: one who has an opinion has it about something he knows or does not know. One who is of a false opinion about something: a) has the opinion about something he knows. He does not take this for this, but for something else, whereby he knows that this is not this but is something else which he does not know, thus continually knowing both and yet not knowing both, or b) has the opinion about something he does not know, takes it for something else he does not know, such that someone who knows neither Socrates nor Theatetus can mistake Socrates for Theatetus or Theatetus for Socrates.

In general: with regard to what one knows, one is not of the opinion that one does not know it. With regard to what one does not know, one is not of the opinion that one knows it.

8. (Supplement to p. 105.)

To clarify λόγος on the basis of the κοινωνία, μὴ ὄν of the δόξα: φαντασία.[2]

1. Plato, *Theatetus*, 187E6f.
2. Cf. *Sophist*, 260C9ff.

Ψευδὴς {. . .} δόξα ἔστι τἀναντία τοῖς οὖσι δοξάζουσα ["false opinion amounts to maintaining the opposite of that which is"].[3] μὴ ὄν: a) nothing, b) ἕτερον.

9. First version of a passage in §45. (Supplement to p. 107.)

3. Before taking the discussion further, he runs through the genuine phenomena once again. Reference to the phenomenon of illusion: Socrates is known to me, someone else meets me on the street, and I take him for Socrates, ᾠήθην εἶναι Σωκράτη ["suppose him to be Socrates"] (191B4f.). The *interpreted* is what we know. It is because of Socrates that we do not know. We take what we know for what we do not know, i.e., Socrates for the unknown, who becomes, through the mistake, the known. That is impossible. Thesis counter to the phenomena.

10. ψευδῆ δοξάζειν. (Supplement to p. 110.)

Question: to take something for something which it is not, which is other than it; something *for* something and, specifically, for something it is not.
1. ψευδῆ δοξάζειν = μὴ ὄν δοξάζειν = οὐδὲν δοξάζειν.
a) ἐν ταῖς αἰσθήσεσιν [(not) "in the perceptions"] (195C8).
b)[4]
2. ψευδῆ δοξάζειν = ἑτεροδοξεῖν, ἐν ταῖς διανοίαις [(not) "in the thoughts"] (195D1).
3. ψευδῆ δοξάζειν, cf. 1. What we know cannot make us not know, cannot make us be mistaken. But this phenomenon is a fact: I know Socrates, and in virtue of this knowledge I take someone in the distance for Socrates. Hence precisely this knowledge about, this *familiarity,* is the condition of possibility of *dissimulation:* taking something encountered *as* something (Socrates) it is *not.* ἐν τῇ συνάψει αἰσθήσεως πρὸς διάνοιαν ["in the conjoining of perceptions to thought"] (195D1f.).

11. (Supplement to p. 114.)

If the syllable itself is μία ἰδέα ["one Idea"], εἶδος,[5] and is not composed of parts, then it is as unknowable as a letter. But if the syllable is knowable, then so are letters; and in fact learning does proceed from the elements, the letters. The same for other elements and composites.

12. Brief recapitulation. (Supplement to p. 118.)

Ontological problem in the *Sophist:* basic distinction: formal-concrete determinations of Being, but not arbitrary ones, soul—constancy. Thales—Plato. The Aristotelian problems.

13. (Supplement to p. 125.)

Met. Γ 2, 1003a33-1004a9: ὄν ᾗ ὄν, "[beings] with respect to their Being." How is this "in respect to" possible, toward what is it directed? What is Being?

---

3. *Sophist*, 240D6f.
4. Left blank in the manuscript.
5. Cf. *Theatetus*, 205D4f.; ἰδέα interpolated by the editor.

Being is the general; geometry: space; physics: material nature; biology: organic nature.

14. ὄν—οὐσία. (Supplement to p. 128.)

ὄν,[6] "beings," and εἶναι, "Being"; *ens* (*esse*) ["a being (Being)"]. οὐσία: *Being* in the proper sense, presence-at-hand, *and* the *being* in the proper sense, that which is present-at-hand. A singular thing present-at-hand; subsequently τί, "whatness."[7] The τί, "whatness," belongs to presence-at-hand; the founding does not proceed in the opposite direction. Indeed {?} presence-at-hand (to be grasped formally and methodologically in the "essence").

15. οὐσία. (Supplement to p. 128.)

1. Being as presence-at-hand;
2. that which is present-at-hand;
3. that which is most properly present-at-hand (ἀεί, ἀκίνητον, χωριστόν ["eternal, immobile, separate"]). This precisely in its presence-at-hand. Theology is also ontology; the intention is toward *Being*, but what is emphasized is Being with respect to the particular most proper *being*, instead of a universal clarification of Being in general. Never both together, problem of *fundamental ontology*.

16. (Supplement to p. 128.)

Squinting is a mode of crookedness, but one in which the eye is necessarily co-intended. Relation to crookedness, purely as such. Thus ontology treats of *Being as such* and not Being insofar as it is the *Being of a determinate being qua determinate*.

17. (Supplement to p. 129.)

Idea of the science of Being: unity of the topic; where and how is Being accessible in general.

The remaining points; fourfold division: κίνησις, ψυχή, ἦθος–λόγος ["motion, soul, comportment-*logos*"], λόγος–κατηγορία.

Categories: "forms of thought," crammed down onto the content; a framework by which order is imposed. Most general concepts? Universality?

18. (Supplement to p. 131f.)

κατηγορεῖν is used by Plato in the sense of "assertion" and not in the technical sense it has for Aristotle. Aristotle also uses the word in its pre-philosophical {meaning},[8] but then not as a *terminus technicus*.

κατὰ πάντων γὰρ τὸ ὂν κατηγορεῖται ["Being is predicated of all things"].[9] Categories are τὰ κατὰ μηδεμίαν συμπλοκὴν λεγόμενα,[10] what is asserted purely and simply in itself, "with reference to no συμπλοκή," what,

---

6. Cf. *Met.* Δ 7.
7. Cf. *Met.* Δ 8, 1017b21f.
8. Editor's interpolation.
9. *Met.* K 2, 1060b4f.
10. Cf. *Cat.* 4, 1b25.

according to its content, allows no συμπλοκή. Not as something else. ἐν οὐδεμιᾷ καταφάσει,[11] but, precisely, for that reason, said "within every composition." Not to be translated "what is said outside of the composition"; on the contrary, "what is *within them all*"!

19. (Supplement to p. 133.)

Categories are not "what-concepts" [*»reale Begriffe«*]; on the contrary, a grid on which all concepts that determine the "what" are plotted![12] It is not the things themselves in their actual constitution that are inscribed therein, nor is it already fixed and determined generic concepts (γένη!), but, instead, the *condition of possibility of genera at all*. Are quality and quantity issues? No; instead, the *structures of something at issue in general!*

Meaning of the most general predicates? κατηγορίαι τοῦ ὄντος, the categories are not primarily related to assertions and the elements of assertions, but to ὄν.[13] Of course; but how? ὄν—λεγόμενον—δηλούμενον ["Being— what is said—what is manifested"]. Modes of Being in general: τὸ δ᾽ ὂν τὸ μὲν τόδε τι, τὸ δὲ ποσόν, τὸ δὲ ποιόν τι σημαίνει.[14] For beings are *uncovered* in λόγος. As such, they are the foundation for possible aspects, which are the guidelines for the concrete understanding of the possible "as what." Beings are accessible in λόγος. That is why the characters of Being are κατηγορίαι. Thereby a particular conception of the problem of Being in general is showing its colors, something we will not understand if we use categories.

20. Analogy: proportionality. (Supplement to p. 134.)

Proportional to one relation is another. Sight: body—understanding: soul. From the proportional relations and on the basis of a proportionality between the related terms, sight-understanding, and specifically two terms as x, y with reference to two known things and their relation.

In relation = proportional to another. To be proportional = to be such as, and to become intelligible on the basis of the "as." To be named, not directly, with respect to the "what," but with respect to the *"such as."*

21. (Supplement to p. 134.)

1. *analogia proportionis.* As subjects {?}, so also quality, the individual thing in relation to this qualification; sameness of the "relations," i.e., in all categories as categories the essence with respect to the "fact." But in each case the *relata* are concretely different. The reality formally the same: γένη in this respect, but not their unity.

11. *Cat.* 4, 2a5f.

12. Ch. A. Brandis, *Handbuch der Geschichte der Griechisch-Römischen Philosophie. Aristoteles und seine akademischen Zeitgenossen.* Zweiten Theils zweiter Abtheilung erste Hälfte. Berlin, 1853, p. 394ff.

13. Ibid., p. 376: "The fact that his point of departure is the question of the most general determinations of concepts is shown by the expression he chose, which designates, in its most general meaning, each and every determination of Being as well as of thinking, and not mere predicates."

14. *Met.* Z 4, 1030b11f.

2. *analogia attributionis*. The *analogata* are the categories. They correspond among themselves with respect to their relation to the same term. This belongs to them by essence, formal mode of the possible "as what," ontologically!

a) Wherein lies the difference? How does λέγειν itself come to be modalized? To what extent and why not genus and διαφορά ["difference"]?

b) How is there "unity"?

c) Basic phenomenon: α) something as something, or β) something qua οὐσία, or γ) neither of these. To be together, σύνθεσις, κοινωνία: is this articulated through λόγος, since the γένη were related to the unity of λόγος (λεγόμενον)? ὄν—λόγος.

22. (Supplement to p. 135.)

τὸ ὂν ἁπλῶς: ἁπλῶς ὄν ["Being pure and simple"],[15] χωριστόν ["separate"]. ἁπλῶς ὂν κατὰ πλείους λέγεται ["Being pure and simple is spoken of in many ways"].[16] τὸ ὂν τὸ ἁπλῶς λεγόμενον ["Being as said simply"],[17] four-fold. τὸ ποιόν, {. . .} τὸ ποσόν {. . .} οὐδ᾽ ὄντα ὡς ἁπλῶς εἰπεῖν ταῦτα ["quality, quantity are not spoken of as beings pure and simple"].[18] Not so with regard to οὐσία. τὸ πρώτως ὂν καὶ οὐ τὶ ὂν ἀλλ᾽ ὂν πλῶς ἡ οὐσία ἂν εἴη ["Being in the primary sense, Being pure and simple and not in relation to something else, is presence"].[19]

23. Categories (Aristotle) 1. (Supplement to p. 135.)

What are categories? No definition. Formal characters of beings. {. . .}[20] Determinations of Being, γένη, "stems," to which the concrete characters of Being are reducible; and indeed beings are here taken as primarily experienced in λόγος. What is the connection of these categories, the γένη, among themselves? That is different from the question: to what extent can they be characterized as unitary? In virtue of the *analogia proportionis*.

The connection of the γένη on the basis of the idea of Being itself; this latter is not a genus. Then how is there a possible articulation of the connection of the *relata* among themselves, or with respect to one and the same thing? In their essence as κατηγορίαι there is predelineated the "as what," founded essentially in the "something."

The γένη themselves are not in a genus and the γένη-character is not the one and essential moment of the categorial structure.[21] (This is something the categories have in common with every "concept" grasped in the Greek manner!) The γένη are *modes of the meaning-function of the Being* of beings, as these beings are accessible in λόγος. What gives these modes their γένη-character is only the grasping of them as something.

15. Cf. *Met.* E 1, 1025b9f.
16. *Met.* K 8, 1064b15.
17. *Met.* E 2, 1026a33.
18. *Met.* Λ 1, 1069a21f.
19. *Met.* Z 1, 1028a30f.
20. Passage illegible.
21. Cf. *Anal. post.* B 13, 96b21–25.

Categories = "ontological kinds,"[22] kinds of Being! And Being? The modalization of presence! Principle of modalization on the basis of the idea of Being itself. Temporality. Cf. Kant: schematism![23] How are the kinds to be acquired? Being—δύναμις παρουσίας. Presence of many things (plurality?), formal multiplicity, accessible in the "something as something." Categories are the (highest) concepts of the modes of Being, and as such they are γένη. Modes of the togetherness of multiplicities as beings, presences.

24. Categories (Aristotle) 2. (Supplement to p. 135.)

Modes of togetherness, *temporal* determination and variation of the "with," of the ontological correlate of the "as." All the συμβεβηκότα have a with-character, which is distributed into those modes. This character is not itself a "genus," however; on the contrary, it modalizes itself directly—in each case as a "with." Modes of togetherness in what is properly present. Togetherness is founded on *primordial presence*. This latter is not juxtaposed; instead, it modalizes itself. *Temporal* possibility of this modalization!

25. (Supplement to p. 137.)

Understanding as disclosing the world, "the particulars," something as something. World: possibility of encountering innerworldly beings in their (formal) multiplicity. Origin of the question: τί ἐστιν; ["What is it?"]. Its possible exposition, existentially-ontologically, leads to the manifold modes of the "as what." ὁσαχῶς γὰρ λέγεται ["for (Being) is said in as many ways"],[24] manifoldness of the "as what" in the "what," or also in the "as" per se? Something "as," or is this anticipation indeed {?} more original and is it, above all, a determinate development aimed at grasping the essence—pure presentification of the origin; and does this latter have, as does "genus," an *ontological sense*?

A is B, A as B. Is the Being of A and that of B understood on the basis of the "is"—more precisely, on the basis of the present assertion—or here does this "is" raise up the intended Being? λόγος in rigorously articulated beings. And how does λόγος articulate beings in their Being?

Beings—Being. Assertion as the primary mode of access to beings, in the specific Greek sense. The categories are the possible characters of Being, the possible, guiding aspects of interpretation. Categories: to be of such a quality, to be so many, to be in relation. The categories are not properties of beings, but *possibilities of Being*.

26. (Supplement to p. 144.)

οὐσία: 1. autonomous constancy, presence-at-hand; 2. such a particular being itself, the respective "this."

δυνάμει–ἐνεργείᾳ, "preparedness"–"actuality" (currently in hand). Tree: something present-at-hand in a wide sense. As this, it is prepared to become wood, beams, boards. Wood: prepared to become a table. Table: game table,

22. H. Maier, *Die Syllogistik des Aristoteles*. Tübingen, 1. Teil, 1896, 2. Teil, 1900, 2. Teil, 2. Hälfte: Die Entstehung der aristotelischen Logik, pp. 303-304.

23. Kant, *Kritik der reinen Vernunft*, A 137ff./B 176ff.

24. *Met.* Δ 7, 1017a23f.; cf. *Anal. post.* A 22, 83b11-31.

dining table, work table. In its actuality (readiness-to-hand), the prepared-ness has been consummated, and, at the same time, this actuality has its own preparedness to become something else.

Actuality of Being: Being of the potentiality-for-Being, motion, presence of the preparedness. Most things that are actually present-at-hand are at rest. Thus κίνησις allows things to be grasped ontologically. Actuality: presence of what is prepared as prepared, κίνησις ἀτελής, but in such a way that it is fulfilled in its preparedness, or in the "toward-which" of its preparedness, and precisely without stopping.

ἐντελέχεια: presence of the potentiality-for-Being in its potentiality, such that it is precisely itself in this Being, not to be at its end, to stop, but precisely *to be in the proper sense.*

27. (Supplement to p. 146.)

Potentiality,[25] *suitability* for, *peculiarity,* preparedness; what comes later. To be in hand, to be worked on. Readiness-to-hand: constancy of circumstances; utter readiness-to-hand. Motion and activity. Motion.

Connection with the categories: founded modes. Explication of the basic modes of οὐσία itself: δυνάμει ὄν, ἐνεργείᾳ ὄν, Being in the proper sense, thus also analogously.

Truth—νοῦς—νόησις νοήσεως.[26]

28. (Supplement to p. 148.)

A tentative determination of Aristotle's analysis of time: the now, νῦν, is a "limit," ὁρίζει[27]—πέρας (cf. 220a21). The now is a "point," στιγμή (cf. 220a10). The now is the absolute "this," τόδε τι (cf. 219b30). To be sure, Aristotle does not make these identifications, but he does see here determinate nexuses of founding.

29. (Crossed out, supplement to p. 148.)

ᾗ γὰρ ἕν τι καὶ ταὐτόν, καὶ ᾗ καθόλου τι ὑπάρχει, ταύτῃ πάντα γνωρίζομεν ["for we know all things inasmuch as there is something one and the same which underlies things universally"].[28] Unity, constancy, as the Being of what is changeable, the αἰσθητά. Condition of the possibility of its knowability.

What is moved. Motion, this is ἀεί, since in time. Time "is" eternal. Therefore that which founds it qua κινήσεως ἀριθμός ["the numbered of motion"], hence κινούμενον ["the moved"], is οὐρανός ["the heavens"]. καὶ ἔστι τι αἰεὶ κινούμενον κίνησιν ἄπαυστον, αὕτη δ᾽ ἡ κύκλῳ· καὶ τοῦτο οὐ λόγῳ μόνον ἀλλ᾽ ἔργῳ δῆλον {. . .} πρῶτος οὐρανός ["There is something eternally moving with a motion that never ceases, and that is motion in a circle: which is evident not only in *logos* but also in fact . . . the first heaven"].[29]

The ontological interpretation of circular motion leads to the first mover.

25. *Met.* Δ 12.
26. *Met.* Λ 9, 1074b34.
27. Cf. *Phys.* Δ 12, 219a22.
28. *Met.* Β 4, 999a28f.
29. *Met.* Λ 7, 1072a21.

Autonomous constancy: autonomy from, constancy for, always already finished. The finishedness refers to Being itself; insofar as completeness is present, the thing is what it is. No τέλος outside of itself.

30. Motion. (Supplement to p. 149.)

Basic phenomenon of the Being of *physis*. Rest is only a limit-case of motion. Thus what is moved amounts to a change in Being. Motion as such is *ontological*, a mode of Being. Of what kind? ἐνέργεια. But indeed ἀτελής. τέλος and πέρας are likewise basic concepts of Being. τέλος: in itself in its own Being; unity is not determined through something else, but is present as stepping forth utterly from itself.

κίνησις in the proper sense, eternal motion of Being; the τέλος is then necessarily an *eternally unmoved mover*. This mover is ἀεὶ ὄν and always complete, pure ἐνέργεια, ζωή and indeed νοεῖν, νόησις νοήσεως:[30] even the latter is meant only as an exemplar of the *ontological* idea of ἐνέργεια in the purest sense, not God as spirit, father, person. Has no knowledge of the world and no ideas that would be archetypes of created things.

---

30. Cf. *Met.* Λ 7, 1072b25ff. and 1074b34.

EXCERPTS FROM THE MÖRCHEN TRANSCRIPTION

1. (Relates to p. 18.)

The scientifically most ideal way for an introduction to ancient philosophy would be to begin by introducing Aristotle and then working backwards and forwards. On a practical level, that way is impossible for us. Middle way: follow the indications given to us by Aristotle.

Aristotle understood the Greeks better than did the pedants of the nineteenth century, who held that Aristotle did not understand Plato.

First book of his *Metaphysics* (*Met.* A): introduction to his philosophy. Articulated into ten chapters. Chaps. 1-2: origin of the theoretical attitude and genesis of science as such; determination of the object of scientific questioning, namely, the whence and the why, the ἀρχή and the αἰτία. Chaps. 3-10: development of the problematic of scientific philosophy up to his time. He shows how, in the course of the development of philosophy, there arose various possibilities of asking about the ἀρχή and the αἰτία. Theory of the four causes.

2. (Relates to p. 18.)

Interpretation of the first book of Aristotle's *Metaphysics* (*Met.* A). Aristotle will be cited according to the edition of the Berlin Academy of sciences (Academia Regia Borussica),[31] in five vols. Vols. 1 and 2, paginated as one vol., contain the Greek works; vol. 3: Latin translations; 4: scholia; 5: index by Bonitz and fragments.

The *Metaphysics* is a collection of individual treatises. It is wrong to constrain Aristotle's *Metaphysics* to a unitary problematic.[32] The title *Metaphysics*, μετὰ τὰ φυσικά: those treatises which, in the order of the writings, come after the ones dealing with the things of nature; it is an editorial-technical title (Andronicus of Rhodes, ca. 70 BC). Those who were collecting the writings saw that here were a number of works whose theme was different from those of the texts on physics and the like. The editors saw that at issue here was Being, not beings. The word "metaphysics" did not at first refer to any specific content; it received such a meaning only later: collection of writings which, according to their factual theme, deal with what lies behind beings, or beyond beings. In contrast, the writings on nature deal with "what is accessible to humans," πρότερον πρὸς ἡμᾶς, versus what is πρότερον τῇ φύσει (cf. Aristotle, *Anal. post.* A 2, 71b34), "what resides in every being," i.e., its Being. The concept of the content of metaphysics acquired a double sense in the Middle Ages and in the modern period, down to our own times. According to Aristotle, the science of Being is πρώτη φιλοσοφία. But he also recognizes a first science which he calls ἐπιστήμη θεολογική: it deals with a specific being, the ground of the world: νοῦς, "spirit," God. Thus metaphysics deals with Being and also with one specific being. The science of theology is therefore not[33] to be excluded from the science of Being. In this way, metaphysics possesses, even today, a double meaning: within scientific philoso-

31. See above, p. 11: Aristotle.

32. H. Bonitz, *Aristotelis Metaphysica.* Vol. 2: Commentarius. Berlin, 1849; W. Jaeger, see above p. 121, n. 3.

33. [Reading *ist nicht auszuschließen* for *ist auszuschließen* ("is to be excluded"). —Trans.]

phy, metaphysics is taken to be (in part) ontology, science of Being, whereas the common understanding is that "metaphysics" is something occult, which reverts back to the meaning as "theology." The fact that both meanings exist together in Aristotle is grounded in the problematic of ancient philosophy in general. Aristotle did not fail here; on the contrary, he had to take philosophy to this limit.

3. (Relates to p. 19ff.)

Met. A 1, 980a21ff.: determination of apprehension, knowledge, understanding, experience, and similar concepts. Aristotle was the first to accomplish this. σοφία, ἐπιστήμη, φρόνησις, τέχνη are concepts that are still unclarified in Plato. They are all encompassed by the term "understanding"—not in the specifically theoretical sense, but in a practical sense: e.g., "everyone understands his own business," "knows" his own trade; "to understand" [*verstehen*] is literally ἐπίστασθαι, "to have mastery [*vorstehen*] over something." Only gradually did these expressions acquire a specifically theoretical cast.

Aristotle interprets the process of understanding. He shows how, out of the nature of humans, the various possibilities of understanding arise in genetic connection. That requires a glance at the being whose mode of Being is determined by understanding or knowledge. This being which, insofar as it is, *eo ipso* understands, we call life or, in a narrower sense, human Dasein. Understanding belongs to the mode of Being of human Dasein, and in a certain way it also belongs to the mode of Being of animals. To say that something is understood means that it is *manifest* in its being such and such; it is no longer concealed. In understanding, there resides something like truth, ἀλήθεια: that which is unconcealed, not covered over, but, on the contrary, uncovered. Insofar as understanding belongs to a being, insofar as it is alive at all, that being is disclosive; with its Being, as one characterized by understanding, other beings are uncovered in their Being. Everything that is alive, to the extent that it exists, has a *world*, which does not hold for what is not alive. Every living being is oriented to something, pursues it, avoids it, etc. To be sure, that may happen indeterminately. Thus we can comprehend protozoa and other forms of life only indirectly, in analogy with ourselves. By the very fact that a living being discloses a world, the Being of this being is also disclosed to it. It knows about itself, even if only in the dullest way and in the broadest sense. Along with the disclosure of the world, it is disclosed to itself. Indeed this already goes essentially beyond Aristotle, but it is necessary for understanding him.

Levels: 1. αἴσθησις, 2. μνήμη, 3. ἐμπειρία, 4. τέχνη, 5. ἐπιστήμη, 6. σοφία: highest level of knowledge.

Aristotle's course of thought: characteristic of it is the first sentence: "To the essence of humans there belongs the urge to insightful understanding" (980a21). εἰδέναι (mostly translated as "know") = insightful understanding, seeing for oneself into what something is. The evidence for this claim is the predilection humans have for perception, an urge to see and to hear (αἴσθησις). This predilection is called "curiosity" [*Neugier*, "craving for the new"]. Not the narrow psychological concept of perception; it refers, rather, to the experiencing in general of whatever there is. This craving [*Gier*] is alive in humans, even if it has no practical purpose; it is a craving to see *just for the sake of seeing.* For the most part, curiosity satisfies itself in seeing, "through the eyes" (908a23f.). Seeing is the sense in which the Greeks primarily lived; ὄμμα τῆς ψυχῆς ["eye of the soul"] (cf. Plato, *Republic* bk. 7, 533D2): the understanding that belongs to everything alive. Seeing has the priority over all other modes of orientation, in that it "most of all makes us familiar with what is happening around us and manifests many differences" (cf. 980a26f.). In seeing, we experience at once motion, number, the form of things. Vision makes accessible to us a multiplicity of determinations of beings. What Aristotle does not yet mention is that seeing is a distance sense, in contrast to touch; and so is hearing. Seeing and hearing have a wider sphere of objects.

"Things that live (τὰ ζῷα) are such that when they receive their Being they already have αἴσθησις, they already perceive" (980a27f.). If there is something alive, there is also already αἴσθησις. Through this αἴσθησις, "memory," "retention," μνήμη, arises in many living beings. Difference between αἴσθησις and μνήμη: what is characteristic of αἴσθησις is that the beings which are disclosed are there in the present along with the respective living thing. If the living thing were determined by αἴσθησις alone, then its world would extend only as far as it sees, feels, etc., at any given moment. The living thing would be restricted to the sphere of what is immediately present-at-hand. By possessing μνήμη, however, the living thing becomes in a certain sense free, no longer bound to the beings currently given in perception. In this way, the living being dominates wider portions of the world, which become and remain available to it. Thereby synopsis and comparison are possible. Its being-in-the-world no longer requires ever new perceptions; on the contrary, when it finds itself in the same position within the world-nexus, it already knows how matters are arranged. The living beings that have μνήμη are φρονιμώτερα, "more prudent"; they do not live simply in the instant but, instead, in a whole which they dominate. As φρονιμώτερα, they are also μαθητικώτερα (μάθησις: "learning"; μάθημα: "what can be learned"), they are "more teachable," more accessible. They thereby increase the store of what they understand and know. There are living beings that do have φρόνησις over and above αἴσθησις, yet they are not teachable: namely, ones that do not hear, bees for example. Only living things endowed with hearing can learn, for something can be imparted to them which they themselves have not perceived and grasped. Hearing is a distance sense and makes possible a peculiar sort of communication. "The most proper mode of αἴσθησις is hearing"—a completely un-Greek assertion, which shows that Aristotle has a deeper understanding of the connection between discourse and hearing.

In the sphere of animality there also belong for Aristotle, without any reservations, human beings. They are distinctive in that they possess, beyond teachability and prudence, the possibility of τέχνη and λογισμός. τέχνη is not the same as "art," inasmuch as art alludes to the practical. τέχνη is not "manipulation"; on the contrary, it is "knowledge," "know-how that directs a manual operation." τέχνη is therefore the proper expression for medicine, i.e., a theoretical science, not an acting and doing. This kind of knowledge is denied non-human forms of life. Along with τέχνη, λογισμός is also named. Humans speak, possess λόγος, can bring what is experienced to the level of the concept. λογίζεσθαι: "to speak all the way through," within oneself about something, "make it transparent," "clarify" it. Because humans possess these two higher possibilities, they can take what is available through μνήμη and develop it to a higher level: ἐμπειρία, "experience." This term must not be understood in the modern sense as an epistemological concept (experience [*Erfahrung*] versus thought); instead, the opposite of ἐμπειρία is unproficiency [*Unerfahrenheit*]; ἐμπειρία = "proficiency in something." How does experience arise out of the capacity to retain? Experience arises out of a multiplicity of memories, through seeing again and again; thereby a determinate connection is produced in the understanding. In mere perception, I see only an individual thing. Experience relates to a connection: when so and so appears, then my behavior must be such and such.

Connection of μνήμη with ἐμπειρία. In μνήμη, a multiplicity of perceived things is available. If now the act of retaining is repeated and if, in retention, a determinate connection among beings becomes known, then proficiency arises. That consists in know-how within certain limits. It means to know that if so and so, then such and such follows: *if-then:* that is the structure of what we call experience. The experienced ones have ὑπόληψις, "knowledge in advance" about a determinate connection with which they have to do. If certain symptoms appear, then such and such means are to be applied. Yet the one with experience is held fast within the sphere of the if-then. τέχνη can develop out of ἐμπειρία. If ἐμπειρία does not entirely give itself over to acting on the current case but at the same time looks for that which shows itself from case to case, then there arises the possibility of seeing that, in every case, such and such is taking place, that ultimately the being is standing in an intrinsic connection and not in a mere succession, and that this connection has the character of a *because-therefore*. For example, this physiological condition requires that chemical intervention. In order for such seeing to arise, what is required is an understanding of the causal connection. The gaze must penetrate through to that which is present in every case. Then the understanding is not a mere noticing [*Kenntnis*], but an apprehension [*Erkennen*]. The one who understands knows not only the "that" but also the "why." He does not merely notice the sequence of events, but he comprehends [*begreift*] the being just as it shows itself, he has a λόγος, a "concept" [*»Begriff«*]. Thereby, τέχνη is already genuine understanding, and it comes close to scientific knowledge. The εἶδος is disclosed, the substantive connection is seen.

For the goals of practical intervention, ἐμπειρία is indeed more sure than is τέχνη. There can be a good diagnostician who nevertheless is poor at helping the sick. That is because ἐμπειρία is always directed to the current individual case, whereas scientific comprehension is directed at the universal that shows itself in every case. With regard to the practical goal, ἐμπειρία is a higher level. With regard to genuine understanding, however, τέχνη is the higher level: the one who possesses τέχνη is a μᾶλλον σοφός ["wiser person"]. The meaning of ἐπιστήμη and σοφία is the disclosure of Being. Within the domain of practical activity, the supervisors have more understanding than the manual laborers. The supervisor sees the why and is able to direct the individual workers. He is equipped with more genuine understanding and is able to instruct others. Instruction consists in indicating the grounding connections. Thus an intention toward the universal lies in genuine understanding. Accordingly, λόγος has a priority over αἴσθησις, since perceptions never give information concerning why something is the way it shows itself. Pure gazing at beings themselves, apart from practical interest, is the distinctive mark of the sciences. So-called σοφία, "genuine understanding," aims at the first causes and origins of things and of beings in general.

4. (Relates to p. 22ff.)

Of what sort are these causes, the ones that become thematic in such research? That is the question of *Met.* A 2 (982a4ff.). Aristotle does not deduce the idea of science from an invented concept; on the contrary, he attends to what natural Dasein already means by it. Aristotle seeks to raise to a concept that which is already familiar to pre-theoretical consciousness. Thus in chap. 2 as well, Aristotle seeks illumination from the natural understanding of Dasein. ὑπολαμβάνομεν ["we suppose"] that the one with genuine understanding πάντα ἐπίσταται—i.e., the scientific person counts, for those who are excluded from this possibility, as someone who "knows everything."

πάντα ἐπίσταται (cf. 982a8): 1. determination of σοφία. 2. δυνάμενος γνῶναι τὰ χαλεπά (cf. 982a10): capacity to see even what is difficult to see. 3. σοφία is ἀκριβεστάτη, the most rigorous knowledge, and at the same time it is best able to teach, μάλιστα διδασκαλική (cf. 982a13). 4. ἑαυτῆς ἕνεκεν (982a15), it is pursued for its own sake, solely for the sake of research into beings just as they are and why they are as they are. 5. ἀρχικωτάτη (cf. 982a16f.): the knowledge that rules over all other knowledge.

Aristotle now attempts to interpret these five moments in their philosophical meaning. 1. Not all-knowing in the sense everyday consciousness would give this term; on the contrary, the σοφός knows everything because he knows the most general, that which pertains to every being. Therefore he precisely does not need to know each and every individual thing. 2. For the same reason, he also understands what is most difficult: the universal is that which is most removed from the common understanding. 3. This science of the universal is consequently the most rigorous science, because the determinations that belong to beings as a whole become ever fewer in number as the distance from mere appearances increases. There the whole becomes more surveyable, and the conceptual interpretation more clear. Geometry is more rigorous than arithmetic,[34] because the latter has a more extensive content. Everything and anything can be counted, but not everything is in space. A geometrical assertion is therefore already restricted to a determinate realm of beings. 4. What understanding aims at does not allow, according to its very content, any other relation to itself except pure contemplation. Thus this content requires that understanding be pursued simply for the sake of understanding. 5. This science rules all the other ones.

5. (Relates to p. 24.)

There is nothing of jealously or affectivity in the essence of the gods. As is jealousy, so also love and every affect are excluded from the divine essence, which is pure contemplation. On the other hand, affectivity is by essence di-

---

34. [Reading *Die Geometrie ist strenger als die Arithmetik,* instead of the reverse in the text. —Trans.]

rected toward something which is not yet possessed. But then the essence of the gods would be incomplete. (People later appealed to this passage as evidence for the conception of the divine as pure love; which is something Aristotle will hardly say.) The gods are not jealous. Therefore, humans should indeed strive for genuine understanding.

6. (Relates to p. 25.)

Met. A 3, 983a26ff.: 1. οὐσία = τὸ τί ἦν εἶναι: the "Being in beings, what the being always already was. What always already was, prior to every individual being, is the ἰδέα or οὐσία, the essential ground of beings, the *causa formalis*. *Forma* = εἶδος; εἶδος here = ἰδέα = οὐσία. 2. ὕλη, the "material." The production of a table not only requires the idea of the table but also requires the material, an "out of which," the *causa materialis*. 3. ὅθεν ἡ ἀρχὴ τῆς κινήσεως, the "start of the motion." To produce a table it is necessary that someone takes the initiative and actually brings it forth; an impetus must come from somewhere: *causa efficiens*. 4. τέλος = οὗ ἕνεκα: producing a table also requires a view toward something, toward a table for a specific use: a predelineation of how the table is supposed to look concretely. When the τέλος is reached, then the being is actual as a being, *causa finalis* (*finis* = τέλος).

7. (Relates to p. 25.)

In his interpretation of the ancient philosophers, Aristotle uses the concept of ἀρχή as a guideline, although they themselves did not yet have such a concept. Is that unhistorical? It is in a certain sense, but in another sense it is a genuinely historical procedure: provided history means to appropriate the past. The successors understand the predecessors better than they themselves did. It is not a matter of correcting their errors but, instead, of thinking their intentions through to the end. Only in this way is history alive, but unless history is taken in this living sense Aristotle was in fact "unhistorical."

8. (Relates to p. 26f.)

Met. Δ. This book intrudes like a foreign body at this point of the *Metaphysics*. Every one of its chapters deals with a basic concept and does so according to a specific method; the book is a "catalog of concepts." Aristotle refers to this book under the title, περὶ τῶν πολλαχῶς, "Concerning those concepts that have a manifold meaning," and specifically it is a matter of basic concepts. Every word has a meaning, through which it is related to some matter at issue. But the meaning can expand, so that the word relates to several matters. The concept is a determination of the meaning of a word that has arisen from, and been stamped by, scientific research itself. Aristotle recognizes nexuses in beings which are basic determinations of beings and of Being. The term λόγος also means "concept." Aristotle's *On the categories* (*Cat.* 1, 1a1-15): three kinds of meaning: 1. ὄνομα as ὁμώνυμον, *aequivocum*, is determined in such a way that *one* word means different things. E.g., ζῷον is, on the one hand, a being, a "living being," an actually occurring thing. But the vocable ζῷον, the written word, has nothing to do with the being it signifies. 2. συνώνυμον, *univocum* (not to be confused with the grammatical concept of "synonym"), the same word and the same meaning: e.g., the same word ζῷον used both for a wild animal and for a human being. 3. παρώνυμον, derived from another word, such as γραμματικός from γραμματική, designates a derived meaning. Aristotle exhibits the differences in the meaning of the basic concepts alone, and he does so methodologically, not arbitrarily: he ascends from the common to the philosophical meaning of the words.

The theme of the first chapter of book Δ is the different meanings of ἀρχή. This concept itself was not yet employed in the earlier philosophy of nature. Of course, the ἀρχή was already investigated there, but not explicitly.

9. (Relates to p. 27.)

That does not mean these principles are known at first. On the contrary, they are far from the common understanding. πάντα γὰρ τὰ αἴτια ἀρχαί (*Met.* Δ 1, 1013a17), all causes have the formal structure of a principle. Cause refers back to ἀρχή. Common meaning of ἀρχή: τὸ πρῶτον εἶναι ὅθεν ἢ ἔστιν ἢ γίγνεται ἢ γιγνώσκεταί τι (cf. 1013a18f.), what is first regarding the Being, the coming to be, or the coming to be known of something. For the retrospective consideration, these principles are the ultimate, and to them all Being, coming to be, and knowledge are led back. *Met.* Δ 17, in parentheses: the ἀρχή is πέρας τι (1022a12), a limit, a limit-concept. In *Met.* Δ 2, Aristotle treats of the αἰτίαι themselves and enumerates the four causes we discussed above (corresponds almost word for word with *Phys.* B 3, 194b16ff.).

10. (Relates to p. 28ff.)

The theme of the earlier philosophy was φύσις. Περὶ φύσεως is the most common title. Cf. Plato, *Phaedo* 96A8: ἱστορία ("findings") περὶ φύσεως. Aristotle sometimes calls his predecessors φυσιολόγοι (cf. 986b14), those philosophers who attempt to expound the λόγος of φύσις, who determine φύσις in a conceptual discussion. That is different from the even earlier consideration of the world in the theogonies and cosmogonies. There the coming to be of the world was narrated in a story: the lineage of the stages the cosmos has traversed. The physiologues, on the contrary, asked about the Being of beings, although they did not understand themselves as doing so.

φύσις: the beings that produce themselves from themselves and are constantly present-at-hand, out of themselves, prior to all human or divine involvement. Idea of beings that are always already present-at-hand in themselves. Way of disclosure in the philosophy of nature versus the mythological explanation of the world: seeing beings that are purely and simply present-at-hand in themselves. φύσις: the ever-constant versus the becoming. Yet φύσις is even conceived as the latter, although neither conception touches the heart of the matter. The emphasis lies on the "being always already on its own basis." This concept of Being is then accepted in the philosophical tradition as self-evident. Aristotle also names the research of the older philosophers φιλοσοφήσαντες περὶ τῆς ἀληθείας (983b2f.). That does not refer to making truth itself the theme in the sense of working out a logic or a theory of knowledge; on the contrary, it refers to truth in the Greek sense of the uncon-cealedness, the uncoveredness, of beings themselves. Research into truth moves within the sphere of beings, with a view to uncovering their Being.

Aristotle begins his historical survey by indicating that, among the four named causes and perspectives for considering beings, it was ὕλη that first came into view in philosophy. The ancient philosophers carried out their investigations by taking the material cause as their guideline. They asked for that "from which" beings are, and they understood the "from which," the ἀρχή, as ἐν ὕλης εἴδει (983b7f.). They asked: in what do beings consist? They believed that by answering this question they would disclose what beings are.

Which cause had to come into view at the beginning of philosophy? The "cause" is the being that lies at the foundation of all beings. A certain understanding of Being and of beings must thereby already guide the inquiry. Which being has a character that allows it to function as a cause? Inasmuch as, for the ancient thinkers, what counted as Being in the proper sense was *that* being which *always* is, the question turned to what, in change and succession, constantly remains: that must be what satisfies the idea of cause. In this mode of questioning, the concept of cause, the concept of Being, is still obscure. The investigative regard aims at a being which is to be encountered in all beings. In what does that being consist? The whole of the world was understood as something produced out of something. In a produced thing, that which maintains itself throughout as constantly present-at-hand is, in a statue, for example, the bronze.

Thales: ὕδωρ, "moisture," is that being which is constant, always already present-at-hand, and lying at the foundation of everything that is and changes. The first cause is the ὕλη, the "material." Anaximenes: ἀήρ, "breath." Heraclitus: πῦρ, "fire." Empedocles: γῆ, earth; although he grasps all the previously mentioned four elements together. Anaximander: his questioning is further advanced. If beings are conceived to be in constant change, but such that something unchanging lies at their foundation, then this that is unchanging must be infinite—in order for the change to be infinite. The ἀπειρία is the basic principle that lies at the foundation of all beings. In this sense, the ὁμοιομερῆ, the "elements whose parts are alike," are limitless; σύγκρισις and διάκρισις. These theories seem very primitive. But what is decisive is the principle that is investigated and the progress of the research. In order to find correctly the genuine cause of beings, the basic determinations of beings themselves *must* be disclosed and grasped in advance.

11. (Relates to p. 29f.)

There is indeed a present-at-hand material, a cause, which is involved in change. But a second factor comes to light: in the whole of the universe a τὸ εὖ ἔχειν shows itself, for change is not arbitrary, becoming has an order, the world is a κόσμος. A κόσμος is determined by τάξις. This good arrangement manifests, in the events and Being of the world, determinate directions of processes as well as ordered connections. The directionality requires a determination, the ordered connections require a guiding hand. Both are possible only through deliberation, reflection. Accordingly, there must be reflection lying at the foundation, i.e., sense, reason [*Vernunft*], νοῦς. The factual occurrence of the εὖ and the καλῶς constrains us to acknowledge sense in beings. The person who went beyond the first two causes and disclosed the presence of sense appears like a sane man among the mad (cf. 984b17f.). For he took the facts of the εὖ and the καλῶς, just as they offer themselves, and did not assign just any arbitrary cause.

It was Anaxagoras who discovered this νοῦς. Thereby a further cause was certainly brought to light, but the ancient thinkers up to Aristotle did not grasp the causal character of this cause. They indeed saw beyond the first two causes, but they missed the causal character of reason [*Vernunft*] and sense by conceiving of νοῦς as an impetus; thus the causes relapsed back into *two*. Anaxagoras himself did not manage to clarify the world with his principle but, instead, let νοῦς function arbitrarily, like a deus ex machina. Now, inasmuch as the consideration bearing on the first cause had already yielded four elements, so the *causa efficiens* also became manifold. Since the world is not only καλῶς, but also αἰσχρόν, since ἀταξία is right beside τάξις and is even predominant, then a cause had to be sought for that as well. φιλία and νεῖκος were the causes that were supposed to explain the attraction and repulsion of the elements and their mixing. Yet these causes remained obscure and conceptually indeterminate. Basically, the first two causes were still not surpassed.

12. (Relates to p. 31.)

Leucippus and Democritus: their causes had a higher generality. The "plenum" and the "void" are causes, τὸ πλῆρες and τὸ κενόν, density and rareness, ὄν and μὴ ὄν: thus even nonbeing *is*! They themselves still did not understand this thesis; Plato was the first to do so. They still grasped the universe in terms of ὕλη. They said: the world is *composed* out of these two factors. Democritus displayed the highest scientific interpretation of the world in his conceptual proofs. The world-manifold changes in three directions: ῥυσμός, διαθιγή, and τροπή (cf. 985b15f.), "(ordered) relation," "contact," "turning." Thereby three basic categories in which the plenum and the void are apprehended: σχῆμα, "configuration," according to which the things are distributed in their relations; τάξις, "order," the way they are in contact with one another; θέσις, "position," the way they turn to one another (985b16f.). Aristotle designates these as "differences," διαφοραί (cf. 985b13). Such an explanation of the world is oriented toward spatial separation, which is why Democritus has mostly been interpreted as a materialist. But that misses his positive significance, which lies not in his view of matter as akin to the earlier elements, but in his predelineation of the basic concepts of the science of nature in Plato and in the moderns.

Aristotle says these thinkers themselves did not deal with motion. They dealt only with what remains constant and with what causes motion. Aristotle was the first to make motion itself a problem.

13. (Relates to p. 32.)

The fourth cause has not appeared up to this point: the τί, the "essential ground." It is the most difficult to see. Yet Parmenides already had it in view, and then the so-called Pythagoreans and Plato. The question of the essential ground is not about the "out of which" or the impetus or the end, but is about what determines beings themselves as beings, determines them just as they are. It is the question of Being.

14. (Relates to p. 32.)

Principles of mathematics are here posited as principles of beings themselves as well. These thinkers believed they saw, in the universe, that numbers themselves contain many similarities with things which are and become. Numerical relations reside in harmonies. The whole world consists in numbers. Numerical relations and the presentation of numbers were more narrow than they are for us. Numbers were presented through ὄγκοι:

$$\begin{array}{cl} \cdot & 1 \\ \cdot\ \cdot & 2 \\ \cdot\ \cdot\ \cdot & 3 \\ \cdot\ \cdot\ \cdot\ \cdot & 4 \end{array}$$

The sequence of natural numbers, 1, 2, 3, etc., is always presented as a triangle. Peculiar connection between the number 10 and the number 4. 4 is the sacred number; $1 + 2 + 3 + 4 = 10$. The Greeks did not think purely arithmetically, but always in the mode of spatial presentation and configuration. By way of this spatial configuration, the spatial itself is grasped as number. Number becomes λόγος, "concept"; number makes beings conceivable and determinable.

15. (Relates to p. 34.)

For example, they said the double is a principle of the world. Insofar as the double shows itself first of all in the number 2, they identified the double with twoness; but 4 and 6, for instance, can also be grasped as doubles. Thus these thinkers were unpracticed in disengaging the concept as such.

16. (Relates to p. 34f.)

That which, in a preeminent seeing, is seen by extraction out of the respective individual cases is the Idea. The ἰδέα is 1. παρά, "beside" what is sensuously perceived, 2. λέγεται κατά, the things of sense "are spoken of with respect to" the Idea. The bravery of a brave person is of a different mode of Being than bravery in general. But *what* bravery is is something by which the brave person himself is determined.

$$\left.\begin{array}{l} \pi\alpha\varrho\acute{\alpha} \\ \\ \kappa\alpha\tau\acute{\alpha} \end{array}\right\} \ \mu\acute{\epsilon}\theta\epsilon\xi\iota\varsigma, \text{ "participation"}$$

Through participation in the Ideas, the sensory thing is determined in its being such and such. The multiple sensory things not only have the same name, but also are the same. This sameness of the essence expresses itself in the Idea. The Pythagoreans used the term μίμησις, "imitation," instead of μέθεξις. But Plato and the Pythagoreans never said what imitation and participation mean; they left it to others to investigate the connection. The question is still not resolved today. Every Platonism still distinguishes today between the ideal and the real, and yet the connection between the two remains unclarified. The fact that this connection is unresolved must make philosophy wonder. Was not the entire approach perhaps too hasty?

The outline of the Platonic theory of Being and beings is still not complete thereby. Between αἰσθητά and ἰδέα, Plato inserts the μεταξύ (987b16), number, the mathematical. Numbers have a peculiar relation to the things between which they stand. They are, like the Ideas, ἀΐδια, "eternal," and ἀκίνητα, "outside of all motion." With the αἰσθητά they have multiplicity in common, whereas every Idea is always *one;* the highest determination of the Ideas is the ἕν. Plotinus made the Idea of the ἕν the point of departure for a new problematic.

The Pythagoreans characterized the sensuous as the ἄπειρον, the "indeterminate," which receives its determinateness, its Being, through number. Plato sees in the sensuous the dyad of the great and small; μέγα-μικρόν (cf. 987b20), the "Great-Small." Numbers are determined by the participation of the Great and Small in the Idea of unity. Plato concurs with the Pythagoreans that the ἕν is not a sensuous being among others and, furthermore, that numbers must be drawn into the explanation of beings.

Plato's σκέψις ἐν τοῖς λόγοις (cf. 987b31f.) is his "investigation into the utterances" about beings. He looks into that which is genuinely meant in any utterance, e.g., one about a brave man. Aristotle identifies this procedure with διαλεκτική, "dialectics."

Plato teaches two causes: 1. Ideas, or numbers, 2. the μέγα-μικρόν, the indeterminate, which has the character of ὕλη, out of which beings are constructed. (Ideas = essential ground.) Plato also distributes good and evil to these two causes. The ἕν is good; ὕλη is evil.

17. (Relates to p. 37.)

Aristotle sees (*Met.* A 9, 992b18ff.) a fundamental lack in Plato inasmuch as it is impossible to investigate the causes of beings appropriately without having first taken up the problem of what is to be understood by Being. The discovery that Being is spoken of in a manifold way is attributable to Aristotle. It is decisive for his determination of philosophy itself. Aristotle recognizes four different meanings of Being. He enumerates them in *Met.* E 2, 1026a33f.:

1. ὂν τῶν κατηγοριῶν, the "Being of the categories";

2. ὂν κατὰ συμβεβηκός, the Being which refers to that being which in the essential determination of a being can supervene and in each case has already supervened;

3. ὂν ὡς ἀληθές, "Being in the sense of truth";

4. ὂν δυνάμει καὶ ἐνεργείᾳ, "Being in the sense of possibility and actuality."

18. (Relates to p. 38.)

Why are precisely these four causes posited as fundamental ones? Which being played here, in a certain sense, an exemplary role? What does the basis of causes and reasons consist in? Why is there a why, a reason? Every individual science presupposes that it is founded and claims that a foundation is posited. The Greeks did not raise these questions.

Only Ideas, the general beyond everything that changes, can be grasped scientifically, for they are the only possible objects of fixed and constant knowledge.

Plato leaves the connection between Ideas and beings obscure. μέθεξις, too, is something, and, as such, must be characterized as a being, as a mode of Being. Here lies a basic difficulty of Platonism. This question of the connection between the individual thing and the essence is also a burning issue in today's phenomenology.

Parmenides is concerned with determining the whole world. He apprehends the ἕν as a pure category. Thereby he advances a step in the domain of the categorial itself (Aristotle, *Phys.* A 3, 186a4ff.). The One of Parmenides is (essentially over and against the One of Thales and the like) unity pure and simple.

The question of the four causes contains manifold difficulties. 1. to be demonstrated: whether and why these four causes are the only ones. 2. to be demonstrated: which region of Being corresponds, as original, to the respective individual cause, in which region of Being each cause is at home, and how far each can be transferred over to another region. In that way, space is the ὕλη of geometrical objects. 3. Systematic investigation of the universal domain of beings themselves. 4. Question of Being in general; question of what in general Being signifies for each being. 5. Question of how Being is to be conceived with regard to the various ontological realms. But there is a question that is even more a matter of principle, the question of the meaning of foundation itself. On what does it depend that there is something like a foundation? This question seems to involve a vicious circle. In terms of formal argumentation, that is correct. But the question is whether proof is to be understood as deduction, or whether at issue here is a mode of proof in the sense of the showing of something which is simply given, but which is indeed hidden to us in its givenness.

19. (Relates to p. 38.)

The problem of foundation is known in modern philosophy under the title of the principle of sufficient reason (Leibniz, *Monadologie*[35]). Up to Leibniz, the problem of foundation remained unclarified; foundation and cause were not distinguished. It was thus among the Greeks and in scholasticism.[36]Descartes, influenced by the latter, said quite scholastically: *Nulla res existit de qua non possit quaeri quaenam sit causa cur existat* ["Nothing exists of which it cannot be asked: what is the cause why it exists?"].[37] No being escapes this question. Even God himself, whose Being is understood as *ens realissimum* ["most real being"],[38] is subject to the question of the *causa*. Of course, this *ens realissimum* is dependent on no other being, for that is the meaning of substance. But infinity itself is the cause, the foundation of our knowledge that God needs no cause in order to exist. The idea of an infinite being essentially excludes causation by an other. In the concept of the most perfect being, the concept of Being is necessarily co-thought. Otherwise, the infinite would lack something, so that it would not be infinite. Problem of the *causa sui* ["cause of itself"] in speculative theology.

Leibniz, *Monadologie* (1714): our rational knowledge rests on two principles: 1. on that of contradiction, in virtue of which we designate everything as false that is contradictory, 2. on that of sufficient reason: no fact is true and existent, no utterance correct, without there being a sufficient reason why it is so and not otherwise, even if these reasons might in most cases be unknown to us.[39] Wolff

35. See above, p. 38, n. 62.

36. For the scholastic posing of the question, cf. F. Suarez, *Disputationes metaphysicae* (see above, p. 19), disp. 12, secs. 1–3.

37. Descartes (see above, p. 135, n. 79), *Secundae responsiones. Axiomata sive Communes notiones* 1, p. 164.

38. See above, p. 135, n. 78.

39. See above, p. 38, axioms 31 and 32.

articulated this principle more sharply: *Principium dicitur id, quod in se continet causam alterius* ["what is called a principle is that which contains in itself the cause of something else"].[40] Three principles: 1. *principium fiendi* ["principle of becoming"], 2. *principium essendi* ["principle of being"] (cf. Wolff, §874, p. 648), 3. *principium cognoscendi* ["principle of being known"] (§876, p. 649). 1) *ratio actualitatis alterius* ["reason for another's actuality"] (cf. §874, p. 648), *actualitas* = ἐνέργεια, "actuality." 2) *ratio possibilitatis alterius* ["reason for another's possibility"] (cf. §874, p. 648), recurrence of the concept of δύναμις, "possibility."

Aristotle determined the concept of ἀρχή according to the same division of principles. Kant formulates the principle of sufficient reason quite differently. In Leibniz, an ontological principle: the ground that something is; for Kant the principle relates not to beings, but to the motives for believing in a truth: foundation = ground for accepting something as true; that which justifies taking a pre-given truth as true; principle of certitude.[41] Every true proposition requires a ground, on the basis of which the truth is affirmed as a truth.[42] Furthermore, the principle of consequentiality, in a formal-logical sense: "If the sufficient reason is true, then so is its consequence also true {. . .}, if the consequence is false, then so is the sufficient reason also false."[43] *A ratione ad rationatum; a negatione rationati ad negationem rationis valet consequentia* ["the reasoned follows from reason; the negation of reason follows from the negation of the reasoned"].[44]

In Hegel, the problem is of crucial importance, because he identifies cause and foundation once again.

20. (Relates to p. 42.)

Brief, introductory, systematic orientation: beings are given first of all. They are seen before Being is understood or conceived. A naive consideration never goes beyond the domain of beings. Nevertheless, insofar as beings are experienced as beings, an understanding of Being is present. The task of philosophy is to make transparent this dim understanding of Being and raise it to the level of the concept.

First step: from beings to Being and its concept. Understanding (knowledge) itself is co-present to the gaze of philosophical reflection. Only with the increasing disclosure of λόγος does the possibility of grasping the λόγος (concept) of Being also increase. λόγος: every assertion is an "addressing" of something as something. Philosophical assertion: to address beings with re-

40. Wolff (see above, p. 38, n. 67), §866, p. 645: instead of *"causam,"* Wolff has *"rationem* [reason]."

41. *Kritik der reinen Vernunft*, A 820ff./B 848ff.

42. Kant, "Eine neue Beleuchtung der ersten Prinzipien der metaphysischen Erkenntnis." In *Kleinere Schriften zur Logik und Metaphysik.* 2nd ed., Erste Abt.: *Die Schriften von 1755-65.* Leipzig, 1905; Zweiter Abschn.: *Über das Prinzip des bestimmenden, gewöhnlich zureichend genannten Grundes,* p. 12ff.

43. *Handschriftlicher Nachlaß,* vol. 3: *Logik. Kant's gessamelte Schriften.* Ed. Königl. Preuß. Akad. d. Wiss. 3rd. Abt., vol. 16. Berlin and Leipzig, 1924, §364, p. 718.

44. Ibid., no. 3218, p. 717.

gard to their Being. With the question of λόγος, there is posed the question of what every being always is as a being, i.e., the question of Being.

This decisive step is accomplished in the philosophy of Parmenides.

21. (Relates to p. 44.)

Regarding 1: the Greeks conceived of the earth as a disk. Yet Anaximander discovered that the disk also has a heaven beneath it and so is held in suspension. Regarding 2: the basic thesis is: water = moisture as a whole. Questionable whether this is to be understood physiologically or, instead, meteorologically. Either one observes the various states of aggregation and gives a meteorological explanation; or physiologically: all seeds are alive, and moisture is the principle of life. This latter seems to agree with the third thesis. Even if water is taken to be all that is, one must not conclude that such a view is materialism, since matter and spirit have not yet been separated: hylozoism. This designation is misunderstood if the two principles in the unity are thought of as already separate in themselves.

In positing his principle, Thales is asking about something constant over and against change; question of constancy and stability in general. For that question, the distinction between the constant and the changing must be fixed theoretically in advance.

22. (Relates to p. 44.)

Anaximander (born ca. 611 BC) is the genuinely philosophical thinker among the Milesian philosophers of nature. He posits the ἄπειρον as the ἀρχή. He reaches that conclusion by following this train of thought: beings are moving in constant change and opposition, there must be at the foundation a being which makes this change possible, which in a certain sense is inexhaustible, and which guarantees ever new oppositions in spatial and temporal extension; but then it must precede all oppositions and cannot be a determinate being such as water (cf. Thales). 1. This ἀρχή has to be something that has no determination in the sense of a member of an opposition; it must be indeterminate. 2. It has to be beyond all opposition and be inexhaustible. Aristotle, *Phys.* Γ 4, 203b18ff.: ground for positing the ἄπειρον: "Only if all becoming arises out of something indeterminate and infinite can it be guaranteed that coming to be and passing away will not themselves pass away."

Anaximander conceives the whole of the world in such a way that around the known world there are, at the same time, innumerable other worlds in all directions. The ἄπειρον embraces these countless worlds. Anaximander also calls these worlds θεοί, but that has no religious meaning: θεοί are not objects of adoration; the θεός is simply the highest and most proper being. Naive cosmology. But the fact that Anaximander, in the ἄπειρον, seeks to penetrate beyond every determinate being shows his philosophical instinct. Precisely the fact that he makes the ἀρχή indeterminate demonstrates his philosophical understanding. Aristotle has especially high respect for Anaximander; as, e.g., in *Met.* Λ 2. Aristotle sees in the idea of the ἄπειρον, the indeterminate, the idea of potentiality as well. What can actually be is only what has such potential. Anaximander himself, however, proceeds without the concept of potentiality.

23. (Relates to p. 46.)

The Milesian philosophy was also aware of oppositions but did not thematize oppositionality as such and make it a problem. An opposition is not a simple difference; it is a very determinate one: the opposing members have a relation to each other, an antagonism. Day and night, cold and heat are not arbitrary differences such as stone and triangle, sun and tree. The discovery of oppositionality signifies the apprehension of a new kind of difference and thus also a deeper penetration into the structure of Being itself. All the oppositions that come into consideration are oriented toward human Dasein. Everything in the world is opposition. That is more than saying everything in the world changes and differentiates itself.

1. Parmenides emphasizes the negativity in oppositionality. Every opposed being possesses no Being. What has Being is only the One, which is prior to all oppositions.

2. Heraclitus emphasizes the connection in oppositionality. The One is indeed not the other, but it is also the other. The antagonistic is precisely that which is. Oppositionality is the true world and constitutes the Being of beings.

24. (Relates to p. 48.)

Heraclitus. The tradition places Heraclitus in close connection with the Milesians, so that Parmenides would have known him. Reinhardt has advanced the thesis that Parmenides is not polemicizing against Heraclitus, but vice versa.[45] Reinhardt's arguments, in terms of content, have much to recommend them, even if they are not conclusive philologically. Nevertheless, we will begin with Heraclitus, for the sake of an easier understanding.

Heraclitus is by reputation ὁ σκοτεινός, "the obscure." The Stoics transformed his philosophy into a philosophy of nature. Influence on Philo and gnosticism. The fragments of Heraclitus came to light at the time of the Church Fathers and therefore were interpreted in manifold ways. Aristotle's characterization of Heraclitus was already erroneous when he wrote that in contrast to Thales (water) and Anaximenes (air), Heraclitus posited fire. For Heraclitus's philosophy is not a philosophy of nature in the sense of the Milesians, i.e., not a cosmological theory, as if he wanted to explain the present configuration of the world on the basis of fire. Fire has a symbolic meaning for him. πάντα ῥεῖ: that is only one side for Heraclitus; it does not mean everything is merely transition and change. On the contrary, it signifies persistence within change, μέτρον in μεταβάλλειν. What he intends is precisely sameness within change. The basic principle is not fire, but λόγος, "world-reason" [»Weltvernunft«]. For the first time, λόγος becomes the principle of philosophy, even if ambiguously.

25. (Relates to p. 49f.)

1. Question of oppositionality and unity;
2. λόγος as principle of beings;
3. disclosure and determination of the soul, the spiritual.

45. See above, p. 48, n. 31.

Περὶ φύσεως: it is uncertain whether this title comes from Heraclitus him-self. Only fragments have survived.[46]

Frag. 108: "Of all the discourses I have heard, none have recognized that there is (*a single*) reason [*Vernunft*] beyond all things." The previous interpre-tation of the world adhered to beings. But Being lies beyond every being and is no longer a being. First thrust toward the idea of transcendence: Being lies beyond all beings. Frag. 67: "God is day and night, winter and summer, war and peace, plenty and famine; God changes as does fire . . ." God is the unity of all these oppositions, but, precisely as such, he transforms himself. Insofar as this One is, it is its opposites. Heraclitus introduces an analogy, since the conceptual interpretation is insufficient. Every time a different incense is thrown into the fire, the fragrance changes, and the fire is never the same. Frag. 78: the world-reason [*Weltvernunft*], as divine, is delimited against human reason [*Vernunft*]. "The human mode of Being (ἦθος) lacks insight, whereas the divine mode possesses it." A human indeed has λόγος but does not see the oppositions as a whole and in their unity. Humans cannot under-stand the whole as such. Frag. 102: "With God, everything is beautiful, good, and just; humans, however, take one thing as just and another as unjust." Human reflection is one-sided. Frag. 56: a principle is not a being among oth-ers: "Humans allow themselves to be fooled in their knowledge of visible things, just as did the wise Homer . . ." Unity has a non-sensory character; a principle is not to be found anywhere within experienceable beings.

How does Heraclitus now characterize oppositionality itself? The entire op-positionality of the world is taken as the ground of the questioning. Frag. 61: "Seawater is the purest and the foulest, vital for fish and mortal for humans." Always other, depending on the use, and yet the same. Frag. 62 demonstrates the identical point; not a mere picture of the changes in the appearances of the world but, instead, presupposes a reflection on oppositionality itself. Frag. 126: everything becomes its opposite. Frag. 111: "Illness makes health pleasant . . ." Opposites are not cut off from each other; on the contrary, each opposed mem-ber has an intrinsic connection to the other. If oppositionality constitutes Being, then the opposed beings must obviously be in harmony: frag. 88. Frag. 54: "Invisible harmony is higher than visible harmony." Appearances are not what makes it possible to see beings and to understand Being. Frag. 51: humans "do not understand how the One holds itself together by way of counter-striv-ing." Here again an image: "Counter-striving unity as in the case of a bow or lyre." A bow is a bow precisely in that its ends strive against each other and are held together by the string. Frag. 103: The ends of an opposition run into each other, as in a circle: ξυνὸν γὰρ ἀρχὴ καὶ πέρας ["for the beginning and the end are in common"]. Frag. 90: "A mutual conversion takes place between the all and fire, as well as between fire and the all, just as gold converts to com-modities and commodities to gold." Frag. 30: "No god or mortal has created this state of the world; it always was, is, and always will be eternally living fire, in measure flaming up and in measure dying out." The μέτρον, "measure," rule, is what is essential, not the transformation. This rule is the lawfulness of the world itself: namely, reason [*Vernunft*].

46. H. Diels, see above, p. 49, n. 37; 126 genuine fragments, without context.

Fire is the symbol of eternal change. The true essence of beings is pastness, presentness, and future. Sextus Empiricus: according to Heraclitus, the essence of time would be something bodily, namely, fire.[47] Constant change, what is self-opposed and yet one, is nothing other than time itself. Insofar as time is now, it is constantly not yet and no longer.

26. (Relates to p. 50.)

How is all this connected to the λόγος? Frag. 50: "You have not heeded me, but the λόγος, if you say understanding is manifest in the recognition that the One is all things." What is essential is that the λόγος itself says: ἕν πάντα. The One, constancy, is at the same time everything, the oppositions. Insight amounts to ruling everything through everything (frag. 41).

λόγος means, in the first place, "discourse," "word," the basic function of which is δηλοῦν, "divulging." Discourse makes manifest. λόγος: 1. λεγόμενον, "what is divulged in the word," the beings themselves; 2. λέγειν, the "divulging" itself. Heraclitus employs the concept λόγος in a double sense and does not separate the two meanings. 3. ὑποκείμενον: λόγος divulges that which makes beings beings, their concept, their ground, that which founds them (Kant): λόγος = ratio as "foundation." Ratio, but also reason [Vernunft]: 4. νοῦς, ratio as "reason" [»Vernunft«]. 5. Especially in trigonometry: λόγος addresses a being as being such and such. λόγος divulges a being with respect to its relation to another being: λόγος = "relation," "proportion," "ratio," e.g., the relations among the sides of a triangle. In Aristotle, 1 and 2 are refined further: ὁρισμός, "concept," "definition."

Only where there is λόγος is there unconcealedness, ἀλήθεια. Where λόγος is wanting, λανθάνει ["concealing"]. Frag. 2: Heraclitus's essential characterization of λόγος: "It is a duty to follow the common λόγος. Nevertheless, although λόγος is common to everyone, most people live as if they had a λόγος all their own." λόγος is what divulges, shows beings as they are in themselves. What is manifest in λόγος is obliging, binding, on everyone. Frag. 114: "If one wishes to speak of beings with νοῦς, then one must arm oneself with λόγος as a city arms itself with law, and all human laws take their nourishment from actuality." Absolute objectivity of pure λόγος itself, over and against human points of view. Frag. 29: "To be sure, most stand there like cattle." Heraclitus is the first philosopher known to have withdrawn from public life.

27. (Relates to p. 50.)

Frag. 115: "The soul itself possesses λόγος and indeed as something that is self-increasing." Frag. 116: "It is given to all humans to know themselves and to have insight." Reference of knowledge back to the knower himself. Here for the first time the soul itself comes into the domain of philosophical investigation. To be sure: "You can never measure the limits of the soul . . ." (frag. 45).—Being is understood as transcendent with regard to beings. λόγος claims to be absolutely binding over every isolated opinion.

Hegel places special stress on Heraclitus. Hegel does not posit a particular being as a principle but, instead, the dialectical itself, unity in opposition, the

---

47. *Adversus mathematicos;* see above, p. 50, n. 39.

movement of oppositions and their surmounting. Hegel already placed Heraclitus *after* Parmenides and sees in Heraclitus the first genuinely philosophical speculations: the necessary advance of Heraclitus lies in his progressing from Being as the first immediate thought to becoming as the second.[48]

28. (Relates to p. 54.)

Being is grasped even if not all beings are there before the gaze. This Being itself, which is held fast in reason [*Vernunft*], cannot be torn apart. For Being is something common to all beings and lies beyond the differences of beings. Every being, insofar as it is determined by Being, is a whole. The unity and wholeness of beings transcend all oppositions. Beings and Being are here at issue in expressions such as absence and presence: that is the way of the Greek conception of Being. Determination of beings with respect to time: only what is present, the present itself, *is* in a unique sense. Unity, wholeness, and presence are the three determinations (of Being) for Parmenides.

28a. (Relates to p. 57.)

Parmenides did not grasp the phenomenon of time purely as such; on the contrary, for him it was a being. Thus time had already been long ago identified with that by which it is measured, the sky, the sun. Plato: time is the heavenly sphere. Thereby we can perhaps understand why Parmenides says: "Being is a well-rounded sphere" (frag. 8, v. 43).

Parmenides does not emphasize or understand time per se as foundational. His sharpest determination of Being with the help of temporal characters: that it never was and never will be but, on the contrary, is constantly now. The same result is then expressed from its negative side: Being is unbreakable, without degree, unmoved. On this basis, Parmenides can formulate more pointedly his earlier statement, that Being and the thought of Being are the same (frag. 8, v. 34ff.): "The apprehension and that on account of which the apprehended exists are the same; for you will never encounter an apprehension without the being in which the apprehending and thinking are expressed." Every apprehension is an apprehension of beings. Therefore apprehension itself is a mode of Being. Because Being is one and unique, apprehension and Being are identical. Phenomenology first recognized the phenomenon that every apprehension is an "apprehension of . . ." Primordial structure of life and Dasein. Apprehension is not the only being that, according to its structure, is essentially related to another being; the same applies to willing, wanting, questioning, etc. Essential relatedness of all comportments of life and Dasein to beings. In this regard Plato again acquires, over and against sophistry, a sharper concept of λόγος when he says: λόγος is λόγος τινός, "speaking about . . ." Parmenides: apprehension is itself a mode of Being.

Comparison with a well-rounded sphere which is equally expansive from the middle in all directions. It is no accident that the sphere is introduced as a symbol of Being. Time is in view in the analysis of Being, and the naive understanding of time is oriented toward the course of the sun and toward the celestial sphere.

48. See above, p. 51, n. 44.

29. (Relates to p. 58.)

How is that connected to the second part of Parmenides' poem (which is even more fragmentary)? For philosophical understanding, only frag. 19 is important: δόξα versus ἀλήθεια. "Therefore, according to appearances, this arose . . ." The world of appearances changes, grows and passes away, and humans seek to bring fixity to this change by giving names to its individual stages. But the names say nothing, for what they aim at is already not any more and will not be any more. Accordingly, there is no relying on words. One must turn back to the things themselves that are to be grasped, and the only thing graspable is that which persists, Being.

Such power of reflection on Being and such certainty in linguistic formulation were never attained previously. The result established: Being is unity, uniqueness, wholeness, fixedness, unchanging presence. All these determinations have a positive meaning.

(Addendum on Parmenides: the Being of apprehension is interpreted in terms of the apprehended being, and it is so in the entire subsequent philosophy. Repercussion of the ontological character of the world onto the ontological character of life, spirit, etc.)

The subsequent theory of Being consists only in a negative exhibition of consequences. Thus Zeno of Elea: he tried to show the opponents of Parmenides that if the opposite of Parmenides' theses were valid, the result would be contradictions and absurdity.

30. (Relates to p. 59.)

Regarding 1 (Diels, 19 A 24):[49] with respect to spatial magnitudes, two assumptions are possible: a) the elements of what is spatial are non-spatial. But then how could something like space and spatial formations arise out of an agglomeration of what is non-spatial? It follows that the assumption is false. b) The elements of a spatial formation are spatial themselves; in Greek terms: every one of them is already at a place in space. Everything that is is in space, and space itself, if it exists, must also be in space. This consequence, too, is impossible: infinite series of spaces, contained one inside the other, and, at the same time, unknowable, inasmuch as knowledge, in the Greek view, always involves a delimitation. Both assumptions lead to absurdity. Thus beings as a whole, spatial things, cannot be determined by multiplicity; therefore Being is one, undifferentiated, whole.

Regarding 2 (Diels, 19 B 1):[50] the same with respect to magnitude-relations in general. The consequence is either no magnitude at all or infinite magnitude. No number arises out of mere nullities. But if number consists in units, magnitudes, points, then between any two points there is always another point, and so on to infinity. Therefore number is infinitely divisible and so scientifically undeterminable. And what is not determinable in knowledge *is* not.

Regarding 3: with respect to motion, two assumptions are possible. It can break down either into immobile elements, ultimate points at rest, or into elements that already in themselves possess motion and change. In the for-

49. See above, p. 59, n. 72.
50. See above, p. 59, n. 73.

mer case, it cannot be seen how something like motion could arise out of an agglomeration of rest, of positions. To every now there corresponds a here, where the moving thing is situated. The combination of heres will never yield motion. In the latter case, the extension traversed in any motion from A to B is still an extension and contains an infinity of extensions that would have to be traversed before any place could be reached. The moving body can, as a matter of principle, never make any progress; and there is no question of slow and fast, and so the slowest can never be overtaken by the fastest.

31. (Relates to p. 61f.)

4. χρόνος, "time": the half of a time can be equal to the whole. Let there be three series of points:

a.　　. . . .
b.　　. . . .)
c.　　　(. . . .

When the configuration of the motion appears in this way:

a.　　. . . .
b.　　. . . .
c.　　. . . .

then the time for *c* in relation to *b* is the same as *a*, since in order for these three series of points to align, *b* must traverse the whole of *c*, though at the same time it traverses only half of *a*.

$$t^c = \frac{t^a}{2}, t^c = t^a$$
$$\overline{\phantom{t^c = \frac{t^a}{2}, t^c = t^a}}$$
$$t^a = \frac{t^a}{2}$$

That is the problem of the continuum. Parmenides characterizes Being in its unity as συνεχές, such that in it no spatial or temporal points can be distinguished. Among all the points of two line segments of different length, there exists a univocal coordination.

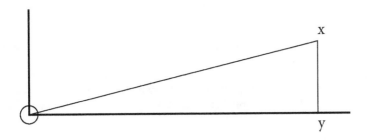

With regard to the continuum of both line segments, the infinite delimitation makes no difference. Or again, on the periphery of a circle there are infinitely many points having no curvature. How can a circle arise out of them? How can the partitioned become a whole? Thus the continuum, the whole, can never be put together out of parts.

The arguments seem at first to relate to various phenomena: racecourse, space in general, time. But the crux is that which lies at the foundation of all these, namely, the continuum. The problem does not reside in time (at least according to this conception of time), but in the continuum. Thus it becomes necessary to conceive the continuum as something primordially original; it receives the characters Parmenides attributed to Being. The problem recurs in the nineteenth century (B. Bolzano; G. Cantor; B. Russell; H. Weyl).[51]

The phenomenon of the continuum is *prior* to the mathematical domain. The continuum precedes every possible finite calculation. Being differentiates itself fundamentally from beings. If the continuum lies beyond every finite and infinite determination, then Being is transcendent in relation to beings. All determinations of Being, if they are genuine, are transcendental.

Still a difficulty: it is in relation to time that Parmenides grasps the characters of Being. But it has just been shown that time in itself, like space, traces back to the continuum. Thus, how can one interpret Being in relation to time, if time refers back to the continuum? Yet time is always understood here in the sense of the vulgar (and, for the Greeks, also theoretical) understanding of time; Aristotle understands it in the same sense. When we say Parmenides achieves his grasp of the characters of Being in relation to time, we are referring to a more original understanding of time, not as a succession of nows.

In all these arguments, the difficulty resides not in time as time or in space as space, but in the character of the continuum. Thus the gaze was freed for the phenomenon of continuity; Zeno thereby led beyond Parmenides.

32. (Relates to p. 62.)

Melissus of Samos. He also stands within the same problematic. He diverges from Parmenides inasmuch as he attempts to fill out the concept of Being by appealing to concrete natural science. A good number of fragments were handed down in Simplicius's *Commentary on Aristotle's Physics* (ed. H. Diels).[52] Especially important are frags. 7 and 8: the concept of Being (i.e., the concept of unity) is brought into relation with characters of beings such as dense and rare, full and empty. No limit can be imposed on Being; therefore Being not as a sphere delimited in itself, but as an infinitely homogeneous mass without lacuna. Frag. 7: "The void is nothing." Being cannot move; there is no place to which it can withdraw. If it withdrew, it would have to do so into the void. But there is no such thing as the void. Thus Being has no possibility of motion. A thing must be full if it is not empty. But if it is full, it does not move. Thereby a relation is established with the then-contemporaneous philosophy of nature, which has nothing more to do with Milesian philosophy. Ontologically, something positive is indeed disclosed here, while failing, however, in regard to the disclosure of beings.

51. See above, p. 62.
52. See above, §6b, p. 12.

The orientation of the ancients, and in general also that of the moderns, toward Being in the sense of constancy should undergo revision.

Frag. 8: Multiplicity is illusory and deceptive; if it existed, change would be impossible. "If there were many things, i.e., if multiplicity and change were attributable to Being, then the multiple and changeable would have to be in the manner of the One." If change and motion were grasped scientifically, then they would have to be grasped as the One. It is thus in Descartes: all aspects are reduced to a single denominator. All properties of a thing are merely accidental determinations and are reducible to quantitative modifications of beings. *Extensio* is the property that determines Being.[53] If all beings are reducible to modifications of quantitative extension, then beings are never graspable in their Being, unless unity (and not merely in the formal sense) is maintained. The problem is then how the various levels are connected among themselves. That is still unresolved today.

33. (Relates to p. 64ff.)

First approach toward an apprehension of Being, and yet at the same time a relapse to beings. The later philosophy of nature (Empedocles, Anaxagoras, Leucippus, Democritus) adheres to the thesis of Parmenides and yet attempts to determine beings in such a way that they might be objects of scientific knowledge. The question is whether beings, as given in sense experience, do not indeed exhibit structures that are connected to Being. The proper mode of grasping the world is not αἴσθησις but, instead, λόγος. Thus Parmenides' thesis is maintained; at the same time an intention to σῴζειν τὰ φαινόμενα (Plato). Their rights are to be restored to the supposed nonbeings. At the same time, a methodological reflection on the understanding that makes the phenomena accessible. Empedocles: sharper gaze into the peculiarity of perception. Frag. 4: "The individual senses have their own particular rights. . . . Consider every individual thing carefully with each sense . . ." Every αἴσθησις has its proper evidence, and claims to knowledge are to be judged according to the evidence.

An ideal of knowledge ought not to be set up a priori. With every mode of knowledge there should also be delimited those beings made available in that mode. Anaxagoras, frag. 21: "On account of the weakness of the senses, we are unable with their help to grasp beings themselves, beings in their unconcealedness." Aristotle, *De generatione et corruptione,* introductory part: consideration of the earlier philosophy with respect to the uncovering of the elements (A 8, 324b25ff.).

Heraclitus posits oppositionality as that which properly is; Parmenides denies it. Neither achieves a scientific grasp of beings. Question: is there a way to grasp the change and succession of beings scientifically and yet in accord with the questioning of Parmenides?

Now a more precise understanding of the principle of sufficient reason. Leucippus, frag. 2: "Nothing arises by chance; on the contrary, everything comes from definite foundations and by force of necessity." A way to grasp beings, i.e., to ask whether change and succession can be "founded" in Being,

---

53. Cf. Descartes, *Principia Philosophiae.* Tome VIII. Paris 1905, II, 1 and 4.

whether something constant is to be substituted for succession. αἰτιολογία:[54] it is in λόγος that the αἴτιον will be apprehended. Democritus said he would be prepared to renounce the throne of Persia for some αἰτιολογία. Foundation of beings in Being.

The immediately given beings must be grasped in a more penetrating way than they were previously. They are not to be dismissed as sheer semblance but, instead, grasped in their structure itself. More precise determination of change as such. Change and succession are not identified with Being (nor are they distinguished from it merely in a formal way), but something is to be placed at their foundation: στοιχεῖα, "elements" (first of all, Plato, *Theatetus* 201E1). Change is not some free-floating thing next to Being; on the contrary, it has its own determination as something constant in the sense of continual blending and separating. Nothing arises or passes away. Otherwise, utter nullity would always be threatening. Empedocles, frag. 8: "I want to announce something else to you. There is no arising for any thing and no passing away to mortal death, there is only blending; passing away is simply a term used by the common understanding." Arising is called φύσις. Change is not understood as growth in the sense of a cosmogony; on the contrary, all things always are, but they constantly exchange their possibilities. Anaxagoras, frag. 17: "Incorrect way of speaking by the Greeks with regard to coming to be and passing away. Everything blends and separates out of already *present-at-hand* beings." Change is not opposed to Being; instead, change exists on the basis of what is present-at-hand. Aristotle: "Motion is impossible if there is no ὑποκείμενον" (cf. *Physics* A 7, 190a34ff.). Blending and separating are moments that show the ultimate structure within the whole of Being, such that τάξις, σχῆμα, and θέσις alone determine Being in its structure. These elements are the basic determinations which make it possible for beings to maintain themselves as constant.

Yet, remarkably, the idea of the ὑποκείμενον is not discussed in relation to these phenomena themselves. Why the question does not arise is connected to the unclarity of the concept of motion. Motion is merely blending and separating and is reduced to the ἀεὶ ὄν. Empedocles excludes the concept of φύσις in the sense of growth. Nevertheless, standing for στοιχεῖα we find in him the designation ῥιζώματα (frag. 6), "roots," and in Anaxagoras σπέρματα (frag. 4), "seeds." The orientation toward the principle of sufficient reason leads back almost to the level of pre-Parmenidean philosophy: elements—water, earth, fire, air.

Anaxagoras: "Everything comes from everything" (cf. frag. 6). The conventional view of his theory (that the world is structured out of ultimate elements which consist in like parts, like the atoms of Democritus or the four elements) is false. These elements "of like parts" are qualities, not matter (smallest things), qualities that modify themselves (cf. Descartes[55]). Every individual thing is merely a determinate constellation of the whole, a stage of the continual blending relation, πανσπερμία: the conjunction and intermingling of the elements. A thing is always a totality of present-at-hand and pos-

54. See above, p. 65, n. 91.
55. See above, p. 189, n. 53.

sible qualities. The names are not arbitrary; on the contrary, they are related, in their meaning, to the being itself, inasmuch as the latter is nothing but a form of change based on what is constant. Cosmogony (Empedocles, frag. 26[56]): four stages of the world: 1. σφαῖρος, homogeneous equalization of all oppositions, 2. κόσμος, everything bound by law, but still blended together, 3) νεῖκος, "strife," 4) return to the σφαῖρος. We are now in stage 2.

Democritus and Leucippus. The totality of motion itself is interrogated regarding its presuppositions. One presupposition is an ordered whole, within which motion is possible. Also the κενόν, the "void," a free space, into which the physical thing can withdraw at any time. But then the void itself must exist. That is a positive determination, dimensions of space. The κενόν has its own φύσις. Frag. 156: "Beings do not exist in a higher degree than do nonbeings." Plato's thesis: even nonbeing, the void, is. Democritus does not yet ask how that could be possible. He attempts to discover positive ontological conditions for nonbeings, just as Kant seeks the conditions of nature in general.[57] Question of what must be in order for nature to exist. Parmenides has in view the whole of Being, but for him that means undifferentiated Being in its sameness. Democritus seeks an intrinsic structural articulation, and he thereby finds the constitutive elements of motion.

34. (Relates to p. 67.)

Also for him {Democritus}, λόγος, νοῦς, the "concept," has priority over αἴσθησις. But that is not without all justification. Something can be known only through something similar to it. Knowledge is merely the assimilation of like to like. Already Parmenides: the Being that is known and the Being of knowledge are the same. Being in the sense of the Being of nature has repercussion on the ontological structure of knowledge. Empedocles, frag. 109: "We know only that which we are physically like." The apprehending subject must already be like what is apprehended (frag. 106). Democritus develops this theory of knowledge into a doctrine of εἴδωλα: images which come loose from things and wander over into the soul. Democritus cannot represent knowledge otherwise than as a transfer of atoms, ἐπιρυσμίη (frags. 7, 8, 9, 10). Frag. 7: "We have actual knowledge of nothing, but the influx into each one is his opinion." Frag. 8: "All we have in the soul are images loosed off from things." Repercussion of the conception of the beings to be known onto the Being of knowledge. Despite this purely naturalistic interpretation of knowledge, the peculiar functional accomplishment of λόγος is maintained. Yet that accomplishment is not grasped in its Being.

This discrepancy continues in Plato and Aristotle, even where they are able to grasp the soul and spirit more accurately. The mode of Being of life or of the soul does not come to be delimited against the mode of Being of nature or of the world. The same for Descartes. Even in Kant, the concept of the subject, of consciousness in general, remains ontologically indeterminate. Likewise for Hegel: he also grasps the spirit as substance, to be sure in a very broad sense. That is connected to the domination of Greek ontology.

56. See above, p. 66, n. 102.
57. *Kritik der reinen Vernunft,* B 165.

35. (Relates to p. 70.)

The theory of the Being of the world in general is carried over to humans, who are constantly changing. The content of perception has no connection with the content of thought (Protagoras, frag. 7[58]): "Even perceived lines are not the ones the geometer, in the theoretical attitude, speaks of and intends." The perceived line is basically a surface; the geometer means something else. Likewise, there is in reality no absolute straight line and no geometrically exact circle. Even the fact that a tangent touches a circle at *one* point cannot be established in sense perception. What is true and existent is only what is considered from the standpoint of a determinate mode of experience. No one mode is privileged.

Reflection on the laws of linguistic expression and meaning. Protagoras divides propositions into four (sometimes seven) forms: εὐχωλή, "plea," ἐρώτησις, "question," ἀπόκρισις, "answer," ἐντολή, "command." Plato and Aristotle investigated the various propositional forms and the structure of assertions (λόγος in the strict sense). Protagoras also seems to have been the first to distinguish the genders (masculine, feminine, neuter). Frag. 4: position regarding the gods and religion: "I have no knowledge of the gods, neither that they are, nor that they are not, nor how they are constituted; for there are many hindrances making the knowledge of the gods impossible, such as their imperceptibility as well as the shortness of life." Cf. Socrates and his being condemned to death.

36. (Relates to p. 71.)

Gorgias: Περὶ τοῦ μὴ ὄντος ἢ Περὶ φύσεως, title of the work he is supposed to have written. Opinion of some: examples of an overdone dialectics; opinion of others: serious philosophical deliberations. The latter is no doubt correct. Aristotle wrote against him,[59] which shows that Gorgias was not a mere babbler. Sextus Empiricus (*Adversus mathematicos*)[60] transmitted the propositions of Gorgias. Three theses: 1. There is nothing, οὐδὲν ἔστιν. 2. If there were something, it would not be knowable. 3. And if there were something, something knowable, it could not be communicated to another person; it would be, ἀνερμήνευτον, "not interpretable." 1. Denial of Being, 2. denial of knowability, 3. denial of communicability.

Regarding 1: argument on the basis of consequences (cf. Zeno and Melissus). "If is," εἰ γὰρ ἔστι (not: if something is), then "either beings, or nonbeings, or beings as well as nonbeings." But neither beings, nor nonbeings, nor the one as well as the other. a) Nonbeings are not: τὸ μὲν μὴ ὂν οὐκ ἔστι. If nonbeings are, they are and they are not at the same time. Insofar as they are thought as nonbeings, they are not. But insofar as they are nonbeings, they *are* once again. It is quite absurd that something is and at the same time is not. Therefore nonbeings are not. Another proof: if nonbeings are, then beings are not, for they are opposed to each other. Therefore neither beings are not, nor nonbeings are. b) Beings are not: if beings are, they must be either eternal, or having to come to be, or both. If they are eternal, they have no beginning. But

---

58. See above, p. 70, n. 121.
59. See above, p. 71, n. 126.
60. See above, p. 71, n. 130.

then they are unlimited. And if they are unlimited, they are nowhere. For if they are somewhere, then there is a place where they are, and so beings are encompassed by something other, something which they are not. For what encompasses is greater than what is encompassed. This impossible consequence shows that beings are not eternal. It could be shown similarly that beings have not come to be and that they cannot be *both* eternal and having come to be.

Regarding 2: if beings are knowable, then everything that is known would have to be. Thought is also known. Everything thought of would have to be. But that is not the case. If beings are knowable, then nonbeings would have to be unknowable and unthinkable. Thus the second thesis is also proven on the basis of its consequences.

Regarding 3: if something is communicated, it must be communicated in λόγος. The latter is different from the ὑποκείμενον; e.g., I cannot communicate colors in speech, because they cannot be heard. But λογός must be heard. Furthermore, how are different subjects supposed to mean the same thing? That which is grasped is multiple and diverse. The many changing subjects do not grasp the unity of an object.

The dialectic, which stands behind these theses, made a great impression on Hegel, and he saw in Gorgias an especially deep thinker.[61]

Foundation of logic begun. Gorgias explicitly takes up the problem of Being. Question of the relation of λόγος to the thing meant in it. Beginnings of Plato's theory of Ideas. λόγος, in the sense of a verbal whole, is something present-at-hand, but it does have a relation to what is meant, although the meaning as such still remains hidden and one apprehends the word only as a verbal formation and linguistic expression. This superficial way of questioning was, in a certain respect, overcome by Plato and Aristotle.

37. (Relates to p. 74.)

Socrates was as critical as the sophists. Yet he did not distinguish between the value and content of individual propositions but, instead, between what can, or even primarily must, be understood and what is not understood. He emphasized ignorance versus omniscience, methodological prudence versus the rashness of common understanding. He asked what knowledge in general means. Critical and positive reflection on ignorance and on genuine knowledge. Consideration of what is immediate and self-evident, and precisely in this way he emphasized its questionableness. He considered knowledge without any preconceived theory, without restricting theory to the ontological doctrine of Parmenides or of Heraclitus. He examined knowledge in itself and sought what is intended in the striving after knowledge and what belongs to the foundation of genuine knowledge.

Previous to him, a consideration of the origin of the world as of something produced. Socrates' reflection, too, is based on the notion of production. But he does not ask about the produced work and its ontological possibilities; on the contrary, he inquires into the productive activity, e.g., that of a shoemaker. ποίησις, τέχνη. Question: what must the craftsman primarily understand? The individual steps of the productive activity are preceded by an

61. See above, p. 72, n. 131.

understanding of that which the craftsman properly wants to produce. Constant Socratic question, τί ἐστιν; Later, the question of the εἶδος, the "outward look," of what is at issue. This τί is the ground for what will actually be produced. Prior to every actuality of a produced thing is its possibility. The possibility comes first. For every actuality, its possibility is its essence, its τί. The possibilities of beings determine the sphere of what can be attained. Primarily, it is the "what" that must be known and understood. Production, as a comportment, receives its transparency from the knowledge of the essence.

In his reflection on human activity, Socrates has moral action in view. All action is genuine action only if it is not blind, if the gaze is alive to that for the sake of which the action is carried out. The ability to act is ἀρετή (poorly rendered as "virtue") and has a very wide meaning: "suitability," e.g., that of a knife for cutting. Usefulness for something. Thus there also belong to human Dasein various suitabilities, which are to be developed. Reflection on the possibilities of human Dasein. ἀρετή is primarily determined through reflection on the possibility of the human mode of Being. "Reflection": φρόνησις. "Virtue" is knowledge, ἀρετή is φρόνησις. Virtue not understood as a property of humans, which would arise through a subsequent reflection. ἀρετή is ἀρετή only insofar as it actualizes itself in φρόνησις.

38. (Relates to p. 74.)

Socrates does not want to impart determinate knowledge, nor to establish moral principles (system of morals). His reflection does not bear on determinate contents but, instead, is concerned only with bringing individuals to face the task of understanding themselves. The instinct for this new kind of knowledge is planted by Socrates. Shaking of the current science through the radical call for a new knowledge; preparation of a new science of the grounding of science and knowledge. Genuine methodological reflection has foundational significance for the progress of science. The genuine movement of science lies in the disclosure of new possibilities of questioning, of method, in the sense of inquiry into the ground of the pre-given matters at issue and of the necessary way to apprehend and determine them.

Aristotle: "Two things must rightfully be attributed to Socrates: 1. ἐπακτικὸς λόγος ['logos that leads on'], 2. ὁρίζεσθαι τὸ καθόλου ['circumscribing the universal']. Both of these concern the principles of science in general" (cf. Met. M 4, 1078b27ff.). Regarding 1: "leading over" to something; often translated as "induction," which is erroneous, since it means just the opposite: leading over to the τί, the essence, and that is precisely not an inductive, empirical gathering of extant properties, but a primordial apprehension of the "what" itself. Not αἴσθησις, but λόγος. Grasping of that which precisely precedes all induction. All inductive gathering of natural objects presupposes the idea of nature. That was first demonstrated by Socrates, though without insight into the conditions of possibility of such a priori knowledge. Socrates himself is always carrying out this grasp of the essence factually, when, in dialogue, he leads individuals away from accidental properties and shows them that they already intend the essence, without knowing it, even as they submit mere accidental properties in answer to his questions. Regarding 2: the task is to circumscribe this essence. Analysis of the constitutive elements of the essence. 1. Essence, 2. concept.

Both are always already co-intended in every empirical assertion, which already—unawares—includes an understanding of the essence. The method can only go so far as to free, deliver, this essence that is already lying there in the individual person. That is why Socrates characterizes his trade as the art of midwifery (μαιευτική). The empirical consideration is only an occasion for seeing the essence. Thereby the basic requirement of science is captured: λόγον διδόναι (Plato). λόγος here as "ground," that which is primarily "addressed" in a being.

"Socrates turned from the philosophy of nature to ethics": this characterization is narrow-minded. Knowledge in general is what Socrates wants to tear away from contingency, by exposing that which every grounded science necessarily presupposes.

Socrates is not to be characterized as a theoretician, or a moralist, or a prophet, or indeed a religious personality. He cannot be pigeonholed. What counts is not a reconstruction of the so-called historical personality of Socrates, but an understanding of the influence he had on Plato and Aristotle.

39. (Relates to p. 79f.)

Plato's philosophy is usually characterized by the theory of Ideas, and that is not accidental. Aristotle already spoke of the Platonic school as "those who teach the Ideas and treat of them" (*Met.* A 8, 990a34f.). The theory of Ideas seems to present something completely new, and yet it is only an expression for the same problem: the question of Being itself. The ἰδέα is what answers the Socratic question, τί ἐστιν; This question is posed not in regard to a being but in regard to the universality of beings in general. What beings are is accessible in the Idea. εἶδος, ἰδέα, root ϝιδ, "to see"; the εἶδος is what is seen, what shows itself in seeing. The question is: how do beings as beings look? How do beings show themselves, if I consider them not with respect to a determinate property, but only as beings? The question of Being is fundamentally posed by taking up the Socratic question: τί ἐστιν; Methodological character of Socrates' investigation. The way is thereby given to characterize Plato's research: we do not intend to see in the "theory of Ideas" something new but, instead, to expose, on the basis of what has preceded, Plato's more radical position.

The ground of beings, Being, should not be subjected to mystical speculation, but to scientific demonstration. A question that is so universal presupposes a corresponding, experiential orientation with respect to beings as a whole: an orientation with respect to the totality of beings and the entirety of the current directions and methods of the scientific knowledge of beings themselves.

At bottom there lies an understanding of what is meant by Being. If Being is characterized as εἶδος, then the question of Being is oriented toward seeing, grasping, knowing; seeing in the broad sense of intuition, insight. εἶδος signifies not only outward look, but also Gestalt. The Gestalt is not the juxtaposition of the parts of the whole, but is the law of the fitting together, and of the mutual fitness, of the parts. The Gestalt is not a sum and a result; on the contrary, it is the law and the antecedent, with respect to which an individual "this here" is configured. The Gestalt is principle, standard, rule, norm. Hence there are manifold determinations in the concept of Idea. For every individual configuration, the Idea is always already there; it is the antecedent and the constant. It is what remains and is unchangeable and thus, for the Greeks, knowable in the strict and only proper sense. Only what always is can be known. This basic constitution of order manifests itself everywhere in experience: the heavens, the earth, etc., and also in medicine, where health is that toward which medical investigations are oriented. Health is not a contingent state; it is the Idea. In the same way, geometry deals with relations among beings, though it is not directed to experience. The laws of geometry are valid for spatial things but have not been acquired from them

The Idea is the ὄντως ὄν, the "genuine being," that which is all that a being can be. The Being of beings themselves is here necessarily taken as a being, necessarily on the basis of the way of questioning. But Being is not located here or there under the heavens; instead, it is at some "hyperheavenly place," ὑπερουράνιος τόπος (cf. *Phaedrus,* 247C3). It does not belong in the region of beings accessible in experience. It is transcendent. Being is distinct from all beings. On the basis of this κρίνειν, Being pertains to the task of critical science, philosophy.

Being is distinct from beings. The Idea is itself a being, but of a very different mode of Being. The Idea is something like the meaning of Being. Since it is distinct from all beings, there exists between the Idea and beings a "separation," χωρισμός. Between them there exists an utter difference of place. To be sure, in such a way that all beings as beings do "participate" in the Idea, μετέχει: μέθεξις. Between the separated things, of which the one participates in the other, there exists precisely the "between," the μεταξύ.

So-called Platonism as a philosophy and as a world-view is characterized according to this outline: the totality of beings is partitioned into two worlds, which are then always designated by oppositions: change–constancy, individual–universal, accidental–lawful, temporal–eternal, graspable in sense perception—graspable in conceptual knowledge. In these oppositions, the world, the whole of beings, is partitioned such that two worlds result, of which the second is always the genuinely positive one, on the basis of which the other is at all and is knowable.

40. (Relates to p. 81ff.)

1. Ground and domain of the problem of Being.

The question concerns the Being of beings. Beings must be given in experience. What does this pre-givenness look like? The questioning already includes an understanding of Being. For, everything I question I already know in advance, even if only in a dim way. Thus two things: pre-givenness of beings and pre-understanding of Being. What domain of beings does Plato have in view when he asks about Being?

First of all, the things of nature, living beings, but also the things we produce, utensils, etc. With these beings, there is also given at the same time nature, not only as in prescientific experience, but already as understood scientifically in a certain sense; that refers, in Plato's time, especially to medicine, which has organic nature for its object. Besides knowledge of nature, there is mathematical (geometrical and arithmetical) knowledge: spatial and numerical relations. Beings also include human persons, taken as acting theoretically and practically, but also as acting in the realms of politics and morals. This totality of beings, acting persons, nature, is given concretely in the πόλις, where the individual human exists together with others. That is the domain of beings which stands under Plato's gaze. These beings must be determinable in their Being and as Being. Something can be experienced as a being only if the meaning of its Being is understood in some way. Humans, who comport themselves to these beings and to themselves, are not blindly delivered over to things, as if humans were simply other occurring things; on the contrary, to humans, beings are given *as* beings: humans understand Being. Only on that account can there awaken in humans the question of what Being is, according to its concept. Plato, in the Πολιτεία, presents an outline of the totality of beings and of the modes (corresponding to the various realms) of apprehending beings.

Republic 6, 507Bff.:[62] Plato begins this consideration by indicating that there is a multiplicity of beautiful things, a multiplicity of good things, and in general a multiplicity of whatever, πολλὰ ἔκαστα. At the same time, there is the αὐτὸ καλόν and the αὐτὸ ἀγαθόν, the "beautiful as such," the "good as such." Multiplicity is posited with respect to *one* Idea, κατ᾽ ἰδέαν μίαν. The Idea provides the ὃ ἔστιν, that which in every case the individual member of the multiplicity "*is.*" τὰ μὲν ὁρᾶσθαι, "the individuals are seen," but τὰ δὲ νοεῖσθαι, "the other is apprehended in νοῦς," is understood. For the apprehension of multiplicity, Plato deliberately uses the mode of seeing, but he also refers to ἀκοή and the other αἰσθήσεις, the other modes of sense perception. The multiple things are perceptible through αἴσθησις, whereas ὃ ἔστιν is grasped in νόησις. αἴσθησις and νόησις: this distinction is encountered in all subsequent philosophy.[63] αἴσθησις in the sense of seeing has a preeminence over all other modes of experience (primacy of seeing). Even what is not accessible in αἴσθησις, but only in νόησις, counts in a certain way as something seen: intuition as the mode of the apprehension of Being and of the principle of all beings.

What distinguishes ὄψις? The fact that things are visible only if there exists something like light. This light, which makes possible the visibility of what can be perceived by the senses, is the "sun," ὁ ἥλιος. It is the αἴτιος ὄψεως, the "cause of seeing." Therefore ὄψις is ἡλιοειδές ["of the same *eidos* as the sun"], it has the mode of Being of the sun, and the eye is "sunlike" (Goethe). Only on that account are colors, for example, visible. The seeing and grasping of the Being of beings also requires a light, and this light, whereby Being as such is illuminated, is the ἀγαθόν, the Idea of the "good." To light in the case of αἴσθησις, there corresponds in the case of νόησις the highest Idea, the ἀγαθόν. Thus there is a connection between the apprehension of the Ideas and the apprehension of sensuous beings. Beings must be illuminated through ἀλήθεια and ὄν. Only insofar as there is an understanding of Being, are beings accessible in their Being. This understanding of Being, according to Plato, is possible only because there is the Idea of the good. Therefore, just as αἴσθησις must necessarily be sunlike, so νόησις must be

62. See above, p. 81ff.
63. Cf. Kant, *Kritik der reinen Vernunft,* Einleitung, A 2/B 2.

related to the good, ἀγαθοειδές ["of the same *eidos* as the good"]. This ἀγαθόν is ἐπέκεινα τῆς οὐσίας; it resides, so to speak, "beyond Being."

The question is how to understand, in accord with this schema, the articulation of beings themselves and the articulation of Being itself. The multiplicity of beings can be grasped as the ὁρατόν. Inasmuch as Being is accessible in νόησις, it is the νοητόν. Within each of these two regions Plato makes a division. This division produces an articulation within the ὁρατόν and within the νοητόν. The mode of apprehension proper to each side is articulated in correspondence.

Within the ὁρατόν: 1. εἰκόνες, 2. ᾧ τοῦτο ἔοικεν, that which these images "resemble," that of which they are illustrations. 1. Shadows cast by things. In a man's shadow, I see him, but not him himself, only images of him, φαντάσματα (root φαίνω, φῶς), and specifically ἐν τοῖς ὕδασι, reflections in "water," and also the reflections on the surface of smooth and shiny bodies. 2. Beings themselves, which can reflect themselves and cast their shadow. Regarding 1: the images possess the lowest degree of Being. They do not provide the ὁρατόν in itself. Regarding 2: here belong the ζῷα, φυτευτά ("plants"), and the entire domain of things produced with tools, namely: furniture, utensils. These things are μιμηθέντα, "imitated," in shadows and reflections.

Within the νοητόν: the previous beings, which were imitated, can now become an "image," εἰκών, for the Being residing in them. Plato refers to geometry: there the objects are the figures of triangle, circle, angle, etc. In a geometrical consideration, we do not mean the circle drawn on paper but the circle as such. The drawn circle is now an εἰκών for the circle in itself. To the sensibly seen figures there correspond the figures apprehended in διανοεῖσθαι: εἶδος ὁρατόν–εἶδος νοητόν. The geometrical objects are graspable because the mathematician proceeds from basic concepts he himself postulates. He no longer considers what lies in these postulates. If the postulates were for their part to become the theme of the consideration, then the question would be about the ἀνυπόθετον ["the non-postulated"], and one would arrive at the point of departure and the ground for everything: the εἴδη, the "Ideas" in the strict sense. Mathematics is εἰκόσι χρωμένη, it "still uses images," and is therefore not in touch with the beings considered by the philosopher in λόγος.

Four kinds of apprehension: the ὁρατόν is the object of δόξα ("opinion" [»*Meinung*«] is a very inadequate translation, for the notion of seeing must be included). Images become accessible in εἰκασία, image-apprehension. Sense perception itself is called πίστις, "trust." Amid the multiplicity of individual things, any one of them is accepted in good faith, but without complete certitude regarding its Being, for it can indeed change in the next moment. νοητόν, grasped through νόησις, "understanding," and, to be specific, 1. inferentially: διάνοια. 2. On the other hand, that which shows itself as the Being of beings is not grasped inferentially but, instead, immediately: νόησις in the strict sense, λόγος. Mathematical thought employs postulates and therefore does not attain the ground of Being: διάνοια. In contrast, philosophical νόησις uses no postulates and goes back to the ἀνυπόθετον, to the ground of all postulates, and does not use images, either. Just as δόξα receives its light from the sun, so does νόησις (in the broad sense) from the ἀγαθόν.

In this way, beings are uncovered in their being such and such and in their

Being. Four kinds of apprehending, and at the same time four forms of truth, in unitary gradation, in levels of truth. According to the respective source of the light and the apprehended being, and also according to the kind of grounding and the certitude, there are levels of truth. Plato did not clearly expound these levels. He availed himself of a μῦθος ["mythical story"].

μῦθος

ἥλιος	ἀγαθόν
δόξα	νόησις
εἰκασία	διάνοια
πίστις	νόησις-λόγος

41. (Relates to p. 84.)

Cave allegory at the beginning of bk. 6 of the Πολιτεία (514Aff.). From the very outset, it is to be understood in reference to the mode of Being of humans themselves: we find ourselves under heaven in something like a cave. Humans are dwelling in a subterranean cave-like abode; a long path leads up toward the light. The cave dwellers have been chained there since childhood, are unable to turn their heads, and their backs are to the entrance of the cave. Far behind them is a light, and between them and the light is a path, along which a partition has been built, the way conjurors enclose a space for their shows. All sorts of carvings, σκευαστά (cf. 515C2), are carried along this partition, and they cast shadows on the wall seen by the people in chains. These people are like us. "Do you now believe that the ones in chains have ever seen, of themselves and of other things, anything except shadows on the wall?" (515A5ff.). One thus enchained cannot even see the things carried along the partition, only their shadows. If the prisoners could διαλέγεσθαι with one another, then they would take the shadows on the wall for beings themselves, since they have known nothing else since birth. If there were in the cave an echo of the voices of those who are carrying the things along the partition, then this echo would be referred to the shadows on the wall. Now, if the shackles were removed from a prisoner and his lack of understanding cured, i.e., if he were allowed to turn around, then everything would bring him pain, and, on account of the glare of the light, he would be unable to see the things whose shadows he had previously been looking at. He would take these things themselves for nullities. If someone said to him that he was now closer to the things themselves, he would be totally at a loss. He would maintain that the shadows were more real. If he was forced to look at the light, he would turn away to that which he was able to see and would take the shadows to be clearer and more graspable. A fortiori, he would experience pain if he were dragged out into the sunlight. It would take him a long time to get acclimated to it. It would be easiest for him to see at night: the light of the stars and moon. Eventually he would come to see the things themselves and to distinguish the shadows from genuine beings, and finally he would see the sun itself as that which determines the course of the seasons. And what if the man were suddenly brought back to his old place in the cave? The others in the cave would laugh at him. The ascent out of the cave would be to them the most ruinous thing there could be, for it spoils the eyesight. Those in the cave would even endeavor to put to death anyone who was again supposed to be led out.

To the cave and its prisoners, there corresponds the place of sense perception, where we find ourselves every day. To the light in the cave, there corresponds the sun; and to the ascent out of the cave, what corresponds is the way of the soul εἰς τὸν νοητὸν τόπον ["toward the intelligible place"] (517B4f.), where that which is specifically understandable can be sighted. The last thing visible is the Idea of the good, μόγις ὁρᾶσθαι (517C1), "scarcely to be seen." It reveals itself as the cause of the sun and of all other beings. The eyes can be blinded in two ways: by moving from the light into darkness and from darkness into the light. In both cases, the possibility of seeing is disturbed. The soul requires a conversion, represented allegorically by the removing of the shackles. The soul then freely sees beings in their Being: what is clearest in beings, namely, Being. Being is not accessible in δόξα; seeing is corrupt.

Phaedo 99Dff.: the Being of beings is not to be sought ἐν ἔργοις, "in produced things," but is to be apprehended ἐν λόγοις, "in conceptual interpretations." Beings are to be made thematic as they show themselves in λόγος, in "assertion" about them. A is B. λόγος is not to be understood as "concept," but as full "assertion." Socrates already does not ever think of λόγος as *mere* concept. Beings as they reveal themselves in the understanding, not as in αἴσθησις.

The cave is an image of our Being, namely inasmuch as we move in a spatial surrounding world.

Question: how to understand the connection among the various levels of truth? That which immediately shows itself is what is accepted as a being. Dasein is always in a cave, surrounded by beings. A light necessarily belongs to this cave. Dasein can indeed see something, even if only very confusedly and even if only shadows. The experiencing of beings requires an understanding of Being. Yet the people in chains see nothing of the light and know nothing of it. They live in an understanding of Being, without knowing that they do so, without seeing Being itself. The first level of truth, of disclosedness, requires: a) the pre-givenness of the world as a whole, b) an understanding of Being in general, c) a determinate mode of experiencing beings, here the apprehending of the shadows in motion, d) and a διαλέγεσθαι, a "speaking" about beings, about the beings encountered. e) Furthermore, Dasein itself, to which this world is pre-given, must already be disclosed and revealed to itself: those in chains see themselves and the others—as shadows. With Dasein, not only is the surrounding world given, but Dasein is also uncovered to itself.

42. (Relates to p. 87.)

The ἀγαθόν is the principle of all beings and of all truth about beings. Later, this was altered. The Idea of the good was again understood as a being. Indeed, there are leanings in that direction in Plato. The same happened to the concept of God in Augustine and in the Middle Ages, and to Hegel's concept of absolute spirit.[64] Being refers beyond itself to the ἀγαθόν. However the

---

64. *Enzyklopädie der philosophischen Wissenschaften*, §553ff.

connection of the ἀγαθόν with Being itself is to be understood, and no matter how obscure it is, nevertheless Plato's questioning does intend to go beyond beings and attain Being.

Only in his later period (*Sophist, Parmenides, Philebus*) did Plato himself understand this and recognize its difference from all previous philosophy, which always inquired solely into beings. No matter what kinds of beings there may be, the prior question concerns the meaning of Being in general. That is the problem posed in the *Sophist* (242Cff.): retrospective on the preceding philosophy, very similar to Aristotle's retrospective. Clear distinction between his own and the earlier questioning: "It appears that each of the earlier philosophers told us a story (μῦθον) about beings" (242C8). Plato, on the contrary, will provide the λόγος. The ancients told a story about the origin of beings and said that beings are threefold, that there is love and hate among them, etc. "Whether they were speaking the truth or not is difficult to decide; but it would be very easy to raise objections against them" (243A2ff.). "Each of them told a story about beings without regard to whether we could understand it" (243A6f.). Plato recounts that in his youth he believed that he understood the words of the ancients and that he knew what Being means. Now all this has become questionable to him: what beings are and what nonbeing signifies. "What do you mean when you say: 'to be'?" (244A5f.).

43. (Relates to p. 87.)

2. The center of the problem of the Ideas.

Being[65] becomes accessible through νόησις, and its highest determination is the ἀγαθόν. Relation between νόησις-λόγος and ἰδέα-ἀγαθόν. The understanding is in itself already related to Being. The question is: how and where does this relation exist? The place of this relation, according to Plato, is the soul. The soul is the basic determination of Dasein. There resides in the soul, in accord with its very structure, an essential relation to Being. The essential definition of the soul includes the soul's comportment to Being. *Phaedrus* 249E4f.: "Every human soul has by nature already seen beings." Human Dasein is such that it already understands Being. If Being is ultimately determined through the ἀγαθόν, then this means: Dasein has an immanent relation to the good. ἀνάμνησις: "recollection" of the already seen and understood beings: an understanding of Being precedes every concrete experience of beings. That is the formulation of the later doctrine of the a priori character of Being and of the essence, over and against beings. How then is the soul to be determined, such that it can comport itself to Being? In a certain sense, Plato poses this question naively, and he answers in the *Phaedrus* by presenting a myth. It is the same as the later question of consciousness in its relation to Being, of the I to the not-I. In all these questions, there resides an immanent relation of Being and Dasein, Being and life. That is to be considered together with the basic problem of Platonic ontology, namely, the problem of the dialectic.[66]

65. [Reading *das Sein* for *das Seiende* ("beings"). —Trans.]
66. See next excerpt, no. 44.

44. (Relates to p. 88.)

3. Basic problem of Platonic ontology: the dialectic.

The essence is always one, over and against the multiplicity of its possible in-stantiations. But there are many Ideas. Every Idea, however, is *one* and distin-guishes itself from the others in virtue of ἑτερότης, "otherness." ἑτερότης is in a certain sense "alteration." From one Idea to the other there is change, μεταβολή, "motion," κίνησις. Unity itself is something other than otherness. On the basis of difference itself, the Ideas are connected to one another. Ques-tion: how is the multiplicity of the Ideas possible, since multiplicity is pre-cisely a characteristic of that mode of Being which is distinct from the mode of Being of the Ideas? The question is how the Ideas could be, and are, in their multiplicity and their interweaving. At the same time: how are the Ideas graspable at all? In conversation, Socrates attempted to lead other people to the τί through διαλέγεσθαι, through the "sense of dialogue." What Socrates here practiced is grasped by Plato as a fundamental method: διαλέγεσθαι becomes methodological dialectics, the working out of the Ideas and their connections. This λόγος, too, has the basic structure of ἐπαγωγή. The inves-tigation, once it penetrates into the realm of the Ideas, remains therein. "The philosopher uses Ideas alone in traversing the realm of the Ideas." By exhibit-ing the Ideas in λόγος, the philosopher runs through their connections. Only by traversing the Ideas does he attain their inner nexus; "by remaining with them he finally comes to grasp their commonality," κοινωνία (cf. *Republic,* 511C1f.). Thereby, for the first time, its own proper domain is predelineated to philosophy. That has been especially forgotten today. It is believed that Ideas, kinds, etc., can be seen by acquiring them through the procedures of natural science. But the requisite method here is completely different from the natural scientific one. Plato deals with this problem most comprehen-sively in the later dialogue, the *Sophist,* and most profoundly in the *Parmenides.* In the *Philebus,* the problem is related to the ἀγαθόν. The *Statesman* takes up a middle position.

Plato's "dialectic" must be kept distinct from all modern, confused ver-sions. Being itself is to be exhibited. The basic determination of λέγειν is to be preserved in dialectic. Already for Plato, λόγος and logic are nothing other than ontology. The coupling of logic and ontology returns in Hegel's *Logic,* but in a very different form.

45. (Relates to p. 90.)

Clarification of these two great problem-areas in the *Theatetus.* This dialogue is aimed at a more precise grasp of the problem of the dialectic. At first glance, the theme seems to be a special question, that of knowledge. But it is not a matter of epistemology; on the contrary, the question of the Idea of science here stands in the closest connection to the question of Being itself.

46. (Relates to p. 91.)

Theatetus appears again in the *Sophist.* That is not accidental: connection of geometrical knowledge with the νόησις of the Ideas.

Socrates begins (143D8ff.) by paying Theodorus a compliment: Many young people seek your company. Socrates himself is seeking young people who excel in scientific work. Then Theatetus comes out from the gymnasium. Socrates is eager to meet him and explains why he wants to engage Theatetus in dialogue: the young man is very gifted but, like Socrates, is not handsome. Socrates wants to see in him what he himself looks like.

Socrates asks Theatetus what he is occupying himself with and what he is learning from Theodorus. Mathematics, astronomy, harmony. (In the *Theatetus*, Plato himself is implicitly criticizing his earlier method of penetrating through to the Ideas and to the ἀγαθόν.) Socrates replies that he too is fairly knowledgeable in these subjects; yet he has a difficulty, one which does not concern the content of the disciplines named but, instead, concerns learning itself. Is learning not gaining more understanding with regard to that which is learned? Thus is it not σοφία, "understanding," that makes those who are knowledgeable what they are? ἐπιστήμη = σοφία? Does not the knowledge of something imply an ultimate understanding of it? Connection of knowledge and understanding? Question of knowledge itself. Knowledge in the broadest sense: not only theory, but also to have a knack for something, e.g., for some handcraft.

Theodorus refers Socrates and his question to Theatetus. Theodorus himself cannot get accustomed to the new method (and that is significant). So Theatetus responds, and his first account of what knowledge is is an enumeration of various kinds of knowledge: geometry, shoemaking, and all τέχναι. Socrates: you were asked for *one,* and you give back *many.* Socrates is asking for the ἕν (146D3). The ἰδέα is always *one,* over and against the multiplicity of concrete types and forms and ways. Socrates was not asking about the things to which knowledge can be related but, instead, about knowledge itself, what it *is.* Clay: that with which the potter has to do, that with which the brickmaker has to do, etc. This is a ridiculous explanation of clay, for it presupposes that the other person already knows and understands what clay is. The question of knowledge must be posed without reference to the respective object and content of any knowledge. That is the kind of διαλέγεσθαι Plato formerly used, following Socrates' example. Theatetus is unsure in the method and attempts to withdraw from the discussion. Socrates stops him by indicating that he himself is just as unsure and would like to arrive at the truth dialectically. This maieutic method, as presented here, will be abandoned by Plato precisely in the present dialogue and in the ones following.

47. (Relates to p. 93.)

The knowledge and apprehension of beings are not made thematic for their own sakes but, instead, with a view to clarifying that which at any time can be grasped in αἴσθησις and δόξα. The clarification of becoming and of nonbeing must also clarify Being itself. For, knowledge, perception, and opinion are not things for themselves, things that simply occur; on the contrary, knowledge is knowledge *of,* perception is perception *of,* having an opinion in having an opinion *about.* Insofar as knowledge is thematized, beings are co-thematized. The consideration bears on the known beings themselves. The phenomenon of knowledge includes an essential relation to beings. That which is known by me is in itself uncovered to me; the being is disclosed to me.

48. (Relates to p. 95.)

Already from the beginning, Plato speaks not of knowledge, but of Being, becoming, nonbeing. Theatetus now attempts a definition of knowledge: "It
seems to me that one who knows something comports himself, to what he
knows, in the mode of perception" (151e1f.). Knowledge = perception. Refer-
ral of this statement back to Protagoras: *homo mensura* (152A1ff.). What is is
what shows itself. What shows itself is a being. To grasp beings is to let them
show themselves in the mode of perception. But the fact is that a thing shows
itself one way to one perceiver, another way to another. One person finds the
wind cold, another not; one finds it very cold, another slightly cold. What
then is the wind itself? The question of φαίνεσθαι is coupled to the question
of the self-sameness of beings. Can something be the same and yet show itself
differently to different perceivers? What is the genuine Being of the being: its
self-sameness or its otherness, its becoming? Question of the relation between
Being and becoming: whether Being in the sense of constancy is what constitutes Being, or whether change and becoming are to be called that which
genuinely is. In contrast to the earlier dialogues, Plato here tries to demonstrate, at least hypothetically, that at bottom the things that are becoming are
beings in the proper sense, and the things at rest, on the other hand, properly
are not. In question is not αἴσθησις but, instead, beings in the sense of the
changeable. Since becoming is the transition between Being and nonbeing,
there resides herein the question of the μὴ ὄν: to what extent are nonbeings
fundamentally beings? The question ("What is knowledge?") should not be
interpreted away. But that question rests on the question of Being.

First thesis: knowledge is αἴσθησις. Perception is perception *of*. This structure is today called the intentional structure of comportment. Comportment
is structurally directed to something. It is not the case that first of all there
would be a soul present, which, by means of perception, would then direct itself to something; on the contrary, perception as such is perception *of*. Two
basic philosophical approaches: comportment could be considered 1. according to its intentional structure, or 2. in an objectivistic, naturalistic sense, i.e.,
as a process, in a psychic subject, which unfolds in parallel with something
physical outside. The latter is the approach characteristic of psychology and
naturalistic philosophy. In Plato, 1 and 2 tend to coalesce.

1. αἴσθησις, always directed to beings: intentional character of perception. By its very meaning, every perception includes an understanding of the
perceived as a perceived being, even if the perception is an illusion. It pertains
to the meaning of perception to intend—even if erroneously—the perceived
as an actual being. Perception is always related to something present.

2. Yet Plato's way of expounding the fundaments of perception has a different
orientation: he attempts to prove that perception arises only inasmuch as the
psychic is somehow affected by the physical. Natural scientific explanation of the
causes of perception. Plato: the perceived cannot itself be in the eyes, but it also
cannot simply be something present-at-hand outside the eyes. For if the perceived itself were lying fixed somewhere, then it would not be different for each
perceiver; so it must necessarily arise through an encounter between the perceiver and the being. 152D2ff.: there is not a One, a being in itself, nor can you
address anything as such and such and as having these or those qualities, be-

cause it never remains as something but, instead, always arises only at the moment of perception. Protagoras's proposition is based on this general thesis: nothing remains, everything is in motion. If what I encounter in perception were, in itself, white then it would have to be so for every other perceiver. In order for the established facts to hold good, there must be change and the perceived as such must be determined by change. The perceived is reduced to κίνησις.

Example of the ἀστράγαλοι (cf. 154C1ff.).

49. (Relates to p. 97.)

In these theses, there lies the problem of relation, and indeed as still unarticulated: being-other in the sense of difference and becoming-other in the sense of an event. The meaning of Being perhaps includes relation in general, a thesis unprecedented at this stage of Plato's philosophy and first conceptualized in the *Sophist* and only within certain limits. Beings are always relative to the perceiver in the way they show themselves. The perceived itself can arise only through motion. Two moments are thereby necessary: acting and undergoing. Only from the connection of what acts and what undergoes can something ever arise. Neither of these two moments is for itself; on the contrary, acting is what it is only in connection with an undergoing, and vice versa. This thesis signifies: nothing is one and self-same in itself; that which is is determined through motion, both active as well as passive. Therefore we must do away with the expressions "is" and "Being." They derive merely from habit and lack of understanding. Our language must not include any expression that means something constantly present-at-hand. Everything is moving, and motion alone characterizes Being.

180Cff.: here the positive content of the discussions comes forth. 157D–180C is a confrontation of Plato with the contemporaneous philosophy. Plato shows that its attempts to refute Protagoras are insufficient and will remain so unless the phenomenon of motion is apprehended.

50. (Relates to p. 99.)

General character of the perceived: the indeterminate. It will become determinate only if it is determined in λόγος. Kant: the manifold of appearances is indeterminate over and against the determinateness provided by the judgment of the understanding.[67] Exhibition of the connection between Being and λόγος and of the relation of διαλέγεσθαι to the self-showing of Being itself.

51. (Relates to p. 100f.)

The essence of perception resides in the perceiver, and so the latter must be determined first of all. Otherwise something frightful would result: there would be a multiplicity of perceptions juxtaposed to one another like individual men in a wooden horse. Instead, all the perceptions strive together toward one Idea (ἰδέα here in a broad sense) which sees through the organs. The perceiver cannot be determined as the sum of the perceptual organs. What we perceive belongs to us ourselves. We ourselves are the perceiver, and this perceiver is something self-same and remains constant throughout the changes in the perceived. From this something that is self-same, the organs first receive their meaning.

---

67. *Kritik der reinen Vernunft*, A 20/B 34.

The earlier discussion posited an interplay between the eyes and the things out-side. That consideration is now abandoned. In the phenomenal content of per-ceiving, nothing of that is given; in perceiving, I know nothing of the vibrations of the aether. 1. The organs through which we perceive belong to our body. 2. What I perceive through one faculty I cannot perceive through another (cf. 184E8f.). How does it happen that I discern something about the seen and the heard *together*? How do I *see* the *chiming* clock as *unitary*? How can both determi-nations be integrated? The *whole* object is what is primarily given to me, and out of it I can then extract the individual moments. But that still does not explain how I can discern something about *both,* how I can say: something heard *and* seen. I do not perceive the "and." It is already given that the heard thing *is* and the seen thing *is:* both *are.* If they are two things, I can say: each is other in rela-tion to the other. Likewise, each is the same in relation to itself. Both are two, and each is one. 185B7: διὰ τίνος; Through what do I apprehend that? With none of the senses, and yet all this is already grasped with natural perception: sameness, difference, etc. Something is salty—I establish that through the tongue. But the fact that something *is* and is different: through what do I estab-lish such a thing? Obviously not with a faculty comparable to the sense organs; on the contrary, the soul itself seems to have these determinations in view, and indeed without an organ.

By way of an analysis of what is already given in perception, we arrive at the problem of the connection of Being with the soul. The soul sees Being in ad-vance and understands determinations such as equality, numerical relations, etc. Being is a determination that in the highest degree accompanies every-thing given in perception. It is the soul itself, according to its very meaning, that tends toward Being and thus also toward all other determinations, even ones such as "ugly," "beautiful," "good," "bad." The ἀγαθόν is now one charac-ter among others, and its disclosure is something in which the soul as such participates. The soul can bring about a correspondence, within the perceived, among the past, present, and future. I cannot hear something past, but I can understand, for example, what is expected as something futural, etc. Even the determinations of time accompany those qualities. The comportment by which the soul grasps similar things is ἀναλογίζεσθαι: λόγος grasps the similar. The ψυχή considers these determinations and compares them, sees them in rela-tion to one another, distinguishes one from the other, etc. κρίνειν: the soul "differentiates." It can make stand out from beings the moments proper to Being. Plato names these characters in perceived Being ἀναλογίσματα (186C2f.), and these are things that pertain to every (human) perception. To be sure, this is only the initial stage. At 186C, the decisive question: is it possible for someone who has no apprehension of Being whatsoever to attain to the dis-closure of beings? It is impossible. Anyone who in principle cannot attain truth cannot attain knowledge. Perception as such is incapable of apprehending be-ings, i.e., Being. If perception cannot apprehend Being, then it cannot disclose anything similar: αἴσθησις is *not* ἐπιστήμη. Admittedly, that is only a negative result, but it is positive in relation to Plato's earlier dialogues, since now the dif-ference becomes clear and does so within beings themselves.

The perceived contains more than mere sensation; it also includes deter-minations such as otherness, which we do not sense and yet do perceive.

Perception can be true only if there is more to it than mere sensation. Only where truth is attainable can knowledge be acquired. Perception cannot be knowledge: negative result. But the positive problem: how is there a connection between sensation and the apprehension of beings in the unity of a full perception? There is an understanding of Being only where the soul itself sees and, as we will learn, speaks, where λόγος is also at work. Natorp: Plato is thereby close to Kant: ordering of sensation by the understanding, theory of categories.[68] Plato would have been the first to uncover the categorial determinations of beings.[69] It is correct that the ontological determinations of beings refer back to λόγος, but this is not an interpretation of knowledge in Kant's sense.

Distinction between sensuous and categorial intuition (Husserl, *Logische Untersuchungen*,[70] pt. 2, Sixth Investigation; to be sure, not without intending to forge a connection with Kant). "The board is black": this assertion is not completely fulfilled in the object; I cannot sense "the" and "is" in the black board. They are meanings which cannot be sensuously exhibited; they are non-sensuous, categorial. I have already attributed to what is given, to the black, a determinate meaning, that of property. Straightforward perception involves sensuous as well as categorial (apprehension of something as a thing and in its Being) intuition. Plato takes up these phenomena in the *Theatetus*, without mastering them. Discovery of the categorial versus the sensuous.

52. (Relates to p. 103.)

The grasp of ontological determinations is characterized as δοξάζειν, "having a view or being of the opinion" about something, taking something for something. That is an abandonment of the earlier position, where Plato placed δόξα in sharp opposition to νόησις: δόξα as connected to nonbeing. Here: something positive must reside in δόξα itself. What is δόξα itself? If it is supposed to be knowledge, then it must be δόξα ἀληθής, for truth is essential to knowledge.

Yet Plato does not proceed to question δόξα ἀληθής but, instead, false δόξα. That is no accident: 1. it is historically conditioned; Antisthenes: οὐκ ἔστιν ἀντιλέγειν ["there is no contradiction"], "it is impossible to say something false": οὐκ ἔστιν ψευδῆ λέγειν.[71] It is with this in mind that Plato thematizes false opinion. 2. Substantive motive: in general, the false counts as a nonbeing, and the true as a being. False opinion in related to a nonbeing. Problem: how can there be a relation to a nonbeing? The latter must then, in some sense, *be*! Question of the Being of nonbeing, question of Being itself. The second part of the *Theatetus*, too, is centered ultimately on the question of Being. Plato must have already at that time possessed the solution given in the *Sophist*.

Positive consequences of the first part of the dialogue. That is to be emphasized against Natorp, who characterized it all as an accessory, mere critique of the contradictions held by others. A definite epistemological approach guides

68. See above, p. 103, n. 54, and pp. 135f., 233.
69. Natorp, p. 76.
70. See above, p. 101, n. 48.
71. See above, p. 103, n. 51.

Natorp's interpretation of the *Theatetus:* Plato exhibits λόγος next to αἴσθησις; critical concept of knowledge over and against the dogmatic concept; the latter would be represented in δόξα; the object, and beings, are posited by thought; and thus the two parts: 1. critical concept of knowledge, 2. refutation of the dogmatic concept.[72] But it is exactly the reverse: it is precisely the second part that moves toward the positive. δόξα as dogmatic representation is Natorp's interpretation, from taking Plato's examples too literally.

1) 187B–189B: δοξάζειν ψευδῆ is impossible. Plato first of all confronts his opponents. 2) But 189B–190E: false opinion means that one's opinion is directed to something else, confusion with something else: ἑτεροδοξεῖν. Phenomenon of otherness. Otherness means *not* to be like that one. Included therein is a moment of negation: again the problem of nonbeing. 3) 190E–200: δόξα as σύναψις αἰσθήσεως καὶ διανοίας, "conjunction of the perceived with what is meant."

53. (Relates to p. 104.)

Can a person see something and yet see nothing? A person indeed sees something, if he sees a *one*, for unity is of course something. Thus whoever has an opinion about something does necessarily have an opinion about a one, hence about a being. Whoever has an opinion about a nonbeing has an opinion about nothing; and if his opinion is about nothing, then he does not have an opinion, for having an opinion is always having an opinion *about*. False opinion does not exist. This is playing with the phenomenon of intentionality. For the Greeks, it was excluded a priori that opinion could be false. Of course, this consequence is brought out only for the sake of a sharper fixing of the problem: whether in this way the phenomenon of δόξα is touched at all? As long as these are the alternatives, it is not touched.

54. (Relates to p. 105.)

It must be shown that in δοξάζειν there is λόγος, which apprehends something *as* something. λόγος is conceived as a determinate kind of speaking about beings; as having these or those qualities. This conception of λόγος was obscure up to then. Antisthenes: we can never assert more than that something is self-same: the horse is the horse; not: the horse is black.[73]

δόξα = λόγος. This definition is something new within Plato's thinking; it is established in the *Sophist*. In Greek philosophy, Aristotle was the first to acquire a more precise concept of λόγος in the sense of "assertion." Phenomenologically, assertion is the showing of something as something. For such a λόγος to be possible, a first "something" must be pre-given. This pre-given something is specified in the assertion as this particular something, the determinant something. The structure of λόγος is characterized by the "as." This phenomenon of the "as" needs to be disclosed. Plato still does not see it. Even Aristotle does not grasp it conceptually. Question: in an assertion, how can two things (the pre-given something and the determinant something) be related to a one? That is a difficulty for the Greeks, because of a purely theo-

72. See above, p. 103, n. 54.
73. See above, p. 105, n. 60.

retically (not phenomenologically) acquired preconception of λόγος (Antisthenes, influenced by Parmenides): if "is" is to have a meaning, then I can say only: the board is the board; not: the board is black. Antisthenes conceives of λόγος as identification, and specifically of something pregiven with itself.[74] That is why the *Theatetus* is constantly discussing the ἕτερον, the "other," and its determination.

Now as to false δόξα: an assertion is false if something pre-given is addressed as something it is not, e.g., the board is red. Something is addressed as a nonbeing. If the Greek theory of λόγος is maintained, then it would have to be possible to identify a being with some nonbeing. But that is not possible, and so there is no false opinion. Assertion is identification. This thesis is always already at the foundation. A mistaken seeing, a mis-seeing: something pre-given is addressed as something it is not. If I say someone approaching me is so-and-so, then that means: something I encounter is addressed as something known to me. Thereby the assertion can indeed be false. The Greek thesis fails. Nevertheless, Plato's result is not purely negative; there is the insight that assertion is not simply a matter of identification but, instead, that *two* things are asserted in relation to each other.

55. (Relates to p. 105.)

Otherness: the one is other than the other. The fact that the other is not the one does not make it nothing, as had always been said. Otherness must not be posited as nothing, but as an actual other, as something. ἐναντίωσις: contradictory opposition; ἀντίθεσις: this opposition does not posit nothing against something but, instead, some one thing against another. The ἑτερότης is determined as ἀντίθεσις; versus the sophists, who used the word ἐναντίωσις. In Aristotle, the *terminology* is reversed.

These phenomena have still not been clarified today. We have no right to disdain Plato.

56. (Relates to p. 106.)

False opinion serves as the guideline for the discussion of the second thesis, ἐπιστήμη = δόξα ἀληθής. It is shown first of all that false opinion is impossible. Then a discussion of this phenomenon as ἀλλοδοξία, "mis-directed opinion" = ἑτεροδοξεῖν. The discussion begins at 189C. The question is whether false opinion amounts to our positing one thing for another, ἕτερον ἀντὶ ἑτέρου (cf. 189C2f.), "something *for* something else." Plato does not say "as" but, rather, "for." To posit one in place of the other is impossible, because that would be to identify things that utterly exclude each other. Question: what comportment is it by which in general I address or determine something pre-given? That which, in perception, is more than αἴσθησις is related to the soul and is now to be determined more precisely. This διανοεῖσθαι is nothing other than λόγος. "This 'speaking all the way through' is what the soul carries on with itself regarding what it sees" (cf. 189E4ff.). This speaking is, more precisely, a discourse of the soul with itself, taking place in silence. The soul makes beings, as they are, explicit in their determinations. Discourse of the soul with itself regarding what it

---

74. See above, p. 105, n. 60.

sees. δόξα = "fully carried out discourse," λόγος εἰρημένος (cf. 190A5). Socrates: if δόξα is such a speaking all the way through, then I say that ἕτερον ἕτερον εἶναι: "The one is the other" (190A8). But can I say that? The ox is the horse? Impossible! But in fact I do not say anything like that. Therefore ἕτερον ἕτερον εἶναι is impossible. It is impossible to say in λόγος two things as different. On the other hand, if I say only one, I can never address it as something else, never utter anything mistaken. ἑτεροδοξεῖν is impossible. An attempt to determine λόγος more precisely. Now the positive phenomenon breaks through in Plato, though he does not put it into effect.

57. (Relates to p. 109.)

The distinction is now expounded further, at 192A. Distinction between what is perceived and what is merely represented. In mis-seeing, Socrates in a certain sense hovers before my mind. I know many things, though I am not now beholding them in the flesh, and perhaps have never seen them in the flesh. How is it possible to know something without presently perceiving it? Retention, memory. In our soul, there is a wax tablet—Democritus already uses this image—with impressions that are retained longer or more briefly, according to the quality of the wax. I can see something, and I can also, on account of the wax, know something I am not presently seeing. X is brought together with Socrates, who has already been impressed on the tablet. Socrates relates the following possibilities (192Dff.): 1) I can know you both, Theodorus and Theatetus, but do not perceive you; both are only preserved on the wax tablet of my soul. In that case, it will not happen that I take the one for the other. 2) I know the one, but the other not at all. And I do not perceive either of you. Also in this case, I will not take the one I know for the one I do not know. 3) I know neither of you, and I perceive neither one. Here, again, no mistaking is possible. 4) I know both, you both hover before my mind. If I now see you both unclearly in the distance, I will endeavor to discern who you both are. This desire to know, to prove, is carried out in this way: I try to attribute to X and Y the corresponding image in my soul. If I attribute to X the corresponding image, then I recognize him. But I can also mistake the two images, so that I mis-see both X and Y. But both must be given to me, for such a mis-seeing to be possible, and at the same time the "image," σημεῖον, of each must be given, if only so as to mistake the two images. False opinion therefore does not merely float in the air; on the contrary, it is possible only on the basis of αἴσθησις and διάνοια. For a mis-seeing to be possible, there must exist perception and memory.

But this definition also fails, for we can be mistaken even in realms where perception is out of the question: e.g., the realm of numbers.

Antisthenes: λόγος is tautology. Plato: ἀλλοδοξία in opposition to ταὐτόν. σύναψις αἰσθήσεως καὶ διανοίας ["Conjunction of perceptions and thought"]. To be sure, the phenomenon of the "as" still remains obscure for Plato and Aristotle. In Plato, it is at first the ἀντί, the "in the place of": thus I indeed have two things, but not both at once; instead, I exchange one for the other. On the other hand, however, in genuine λόγος, both are given unitarily and at the same time.

58. (Relates to p. 110.)

The definition of knowledge as true opinion cannot be maintained. True and correct opinion, e.g., in courts of law, is correct conviction about the state of affairs, although the judge was not present at the deed; still, there is correct judgment. Yet this correct conviction cannot be called knowledge. I must have the possibility of testing and establishing what I know by turning at every moment to the things themselves. What is the difference between correct opinion and knowledge?

59. (Relates to p. 112.)

Naming is not knowledge in the genuine sense. It is impossible in λόγος to determine any one of the elements. For the essence of λόγος is the composition of one thing with another. For such λόγος to be possible, the being must also be composite, so that out of it a component can be drawn out. But the στοιχεῖα are un-composed; they are ultimate parts, and are therefore unknowable, scarcely perceivable, and are accessible, in a broad sense, only to a simple onlooking. The elements of writing are the letters. What is combined, συλλαβεῖν, out of them are "syllables," συλλαβαί (203A3). At issue are formal structures: elements and combinations.

It is indeed possible to have an opinion about beings, even elements, just as they are, but not to know them. For what is knowable is only what is a composite and on that account can be taken apart (cf. *Sophist*). Only on the basis of this new version of the concept of Being is it understandable how Plato can say that something is self-same, one. Determinations such as "this," "that," "it itself," and "one" are characters that belong to every being, περιτρέχοντα ["things running around loose"] (202A5): they are formal determinations of Being. Analogy between the soul and a dovecote: the doves that have no fixed place and can determine every single thing are περιτρέχοντα. Result: what is knowable in λόγος is only what is determinable in a combination, such that it is graspable with respect to something else.

60. (Relates to p. 113.)

The parts of a whole have a very different relation to the totality than do the parts of a sum. Need to distinguish between a sum and a whole, though they both have the formal character of a totality. A totality consists in, or is related to, parts. Kinds of totalities: a) sum, *compositum*. Parts here are pieces; adding pieces together = a sum. b) Whole, *totum*. The parts that correspond to a whole have the character of moments. Plato shows that a whole, versus a sum, has its own Gestalt, its own εἶδος. This Gestalt cannot be attained by starting with the parts but, instead, already precedes them (203E). Distinction between "sum," πᾶν, and ὅλον, "whole." Indeed Plato's terminology is still uncertain. The word-whole is in itself a one and cannot be resolved into elements without being destroyed. Consequence: then the unitariness of the εἶδος is also inaccessible and can be apprehended only through αἴσθησις. Yet Plato attempts to show that the εἶδος can be removed from its isolation. The question is whether the ontological determinations of beings are perceivable only for themselves or whether they can be delimited in λόγος. Problem of the dialectic as the purely ontological problem of apprehending the ontological connections of the Ideas among themselves. By upholding the thesis that the elements are unknowable, Plato comes to rectify the thesis. In learning, we proceed from the elements; so they are in fact accessible. Thus the elements are knowable. The whole also has a unitary character. Plato's discussion stops at these two propositions.

61. (Relates to p. 114.)

At 206D, λόγος is determined as "assertion," in the sense of something expressed. What the soul thinks for itself, in silently speaking to itself, can be made visible for others by means of φωνή, an "utterance," "expression," of the words. Plato also calls such λόγος, in the sense of an expressed proposition, an "image," εἴδωλον.

Second determination of λόγος at 206E: the λέγων ["speaker"] speaks when he answers the question, "What is that?" Reappropriation of the Socratic determination. Nevertheless, λόγος has a relation to a ἕτερον. This λόγος, the one that shows what something is, has the character of traversing the individual determinations of beings and aiming at the whole.

Third definition at 208C: λόγος is the assertion in which what is distinctive about a being is exposed in such a way that this being is utterly distinguished from all other beings.

Here Socrates abandons the discussion of the question of what knowledge is. The question remains open. Yet the result is not negative. The problem of dialectic has been prepared.

62. (Relates to p. 114f.)

The first definition shows that an apprehension of beings is impossible without λόγος. λόγος itself is then discussed. In the treatment of the second definition, λόγος is characterized as σύν, ἄλλο, ἕτερον. Third definition: the σύν is a composite. Beings themselves have the structure of συλλαβαί. Ontological structure and the structure of language: a strict correlation (for the Greeks) between beings and expressed discourse. The structure of beings is reflected in discourse about them.

First appearance of the phenomenon of the specific difference. Cf. Aristotle: εἰδοποιὸς διαφορά ["the *eidos*-making difference"] (*Topics* Z 6, 143b7f.): the difference that makes the genus a species, *differentia specifica*, the difference that alone constitutes the species as such.

Plato's procedure can make clear only the distinction between what is known and what is not known. Socrates: *art of the midwife*. The conclusion of the dialogue indicates very well that the discussion ought to be taken up again as soon as possible and shows that Plato is already in possession of the resolution worked out in the *Sophist*.

What is thereby acquired regarding the two main questions? The soul has a primordial relation to Being. The basic comportment of the soul is λόγος. λόγος—ὄν. This relationship belongs to the soul itself. A being is as such related to an other. ὄν is at the same time ἕτερον. Question: how is it possible for λόγος to be related to ὄν, and how can ὄν (grasped as ἕν ever since Parmenides), as the One, be essentially the other? Being is the one self-enclosed whole. Parmenides' constructive concept of ὄν must be modified according to the phenomena. How is Being to be grasped such that λόγος, which is itself an ὄν, stands related to another ὄν? And how is it possible that the structure of Being includes a relatedness to what is other? Only if Being is apprehended differently, is διαλέγεσθαι possible: the exposition of the general characters of Being itself. Already in the *Theatetus,* Plato names "sameness," "thisness," "otherness," etc., as characters of *every* being. The result, versus Plato's position in the *Republic,* is that Being in itself is multiple. ὄν itself is determined as same, other, this, that, individual. There is a multiplicity of Ideas. How can we conceive of the basic determinations in their connectedness?

Plato's *Sophist:* the modification of the concept of Being resides in Plato's claim that Being is δύναμις κοινωνίας τῶν γενῶν, i.e., that there is the "possibility of a connection among the highest determinations" belonging to Being in general.

Among the original determinations of Being, there exists such a κοινωνία, "clamping together." Plato demonstrates that with respect to five basic determinations. Pertaining to Being itself are "sameness," ταὐτόν, "otherness," ἕτερον, "motion," κίνησις (and in addition ἔρως, ψυχή, λόγος), and "rest," στάσις.[75] Everything self-same is, as the same, Being and is also, as the same, other. Possibility of co-presence with one another: παρουσία. Co-present in Being are already sameness, otherness, motion, and στάσις. (Being itself is one of the five determinations!) That makes it possible for λόγος to be related to a ἕτερον, μὴ ὄν. Therefore λόγος is not tautological, and dialectic is ontologically possible. To be sure, difficulties remain.

63. (Relates to p. 116.)

Let us mention only one question. In the *Republic,* the connection of all the Ideas culminates in the highest Idea of the ἀγαθόν. The latter has disappeared from Plato's dialectical project. Question: how can the ἀγαθόν play a fundamental role in the clarification of Being? This also applies to Plato's late dialogue, the *Timaeus,* and to Aristotle. Possibility of a solution: knowledge is a κίνησις of the soul, an action. Every action is related to something which is to be made actual. Beings are that for the sake of which I place myself on the path of knowledge. Being is characterized as that for the sake of which I have knowledge: relatedness of Being to an end for the sake of which it exists. This end is naively grasped as a being and as the ἀγαθόν. Insofar as knowledge is conceived as an action, Being must be characterized as ἀγαθόν. This "for the sake of which" is apprehended as something higher in relation to Being. But that is no longer a character of Being as such; instead, it is relative to knowledge. The ἀγαθόν is not a purely ontological determination.

64. (Relates to p. 117.)

Relation between Being and value. Values as such are fictive. To bring in values is to misunderstand the Greek way of questioning. The "validity" of values is a modern invention (Lotze[76]). The concept of value must be reduced to ὄν. If the analysis purely and simply thematized the ὄν, then the step to an ἀγαθόν would be avoided. To address Being as ἀγαθόν is to misunderstand

75. See above, p. 115.
76. Cf. H. Lotze, *Logik.* Leipzig, 1843, p. 7.

Being. It is no accident that later in Plato the problem of the ἀγαθόν, in its original function, disappears. Yet Plato did not adhere to the purely ontological problematic but, instead, tied it again to the Being of nature and then explained the Being of beings in terms of a creation (by a *demiourgos*).

Relapse from the height of the *Sophist*. Aristotle tries to sustain the height of the ontological problem.

65. (Relates to p. 117.)

To speak of Plato's philosophy as a system is out of the question. But that is not a drawback. Everything is open, under way, approach, obscure; which is precisely what makes it productive, leading further on. No system; instead, actual work on the matters at issue. That is why such a philosophy is ageless. The meaning of scientific research is not to disseminate finished truth, but to pose genuine problems.

That is also the character of Aristotle's philosophy, which is traditionally taken to be even more of a doctrinal edifice. Aristotle attempts to appropriate positively the impulses driving Plato's philosophy. Three basic questions:

1. The problem of the distinction between the formal and the concrete determinations of Being. Every being is self-same and other. But it is questionable whether every being is moving, or is rather at rest. Beings in the mathematical sense are not determined through κίνησις, but also not through στάσις.

2. Still unresolved is the question of the connection of the dialectical schema itself with Being. Being remains the guiding idea, to which the other categorial determinations of Being are related.

3. Is it possible to work out the problem of Being in such a way that Being is apprehended as having *one* sense, or is the concept of Being polysemic?

66. (Relates to p. 118.)

Opposition Thales–Plato: Being conceived as a being versus the attaining of the difference and even of λόγος as the mode of grasping Being. In opposition to Parmenides, Plato sees the ἕτερον. Being is the "possibility of mutual belonging together," δύναμις κοινωνίας (*Sophist*).

κατηγορεῖν: "to assert" in an emphatic sense. The category is preeminent λόγος. λόγος as "assertion" is at the same time determined by truth. δύναμις, "potentiality": what does potentiality signify in relation to Being? σύν ["together with"]. In this way, various aspects of λόγος are expounded, ones that lead to Aristotle's ontological problematic.

67. (Relates to p. 122.)

The young Hegel was already very occupied with Aristotle and found there his own philosophical impetus. Schleiermacher stimulated the editing of Aristotle's works. Trendelenburg and Bonitz: historiographical research into Aristotle. Brentano: beginning of the systematic elaboration of Aristotelian philosophy. On the other hand, Neo-Kantianism was a hindrance. There Kant was seen essentially as an epistemologist, and the discussion centered on the relation between idealism and realism. Aristotle was then characterized as a realist, i.e., as taking up a backward and naive standpoint. In fact, however, there is neither idealism nor realism in ancient philosophy. Absolute authority of Aristotle in the Middle Ages: *philosophus dicit* ["the philosopher says"]. The Middle Ages now seem a time of darkness. Aristotle was viewed as an apothecary. Here in Marburg was the main opposition against Aristotle, and yet important works also originated here. Then came more openness to Aristotle and the recognition that he has a closer connection to Plato than to Thomas Aquinas or to the realism of the nineteenth century.

68. (Relates to p. 124.)

1. *The question of Being. Met.* Γ. Ontological questioning arrives at a double concept of ontology and so must pass through a stage of oscillation. To understand beings as beings, to achieve a genuine grasp of beings, can mean, on the one hand, to expose that particular being which most adequately satisfies the idea of Being. Question of that which most properly is, the original being, from which all the others are derived. For this, the idea of Being does not need to be made explicit. On the other hand, the question of the Being of beings in general, inquiry not only into the one most proper being, but also into the derived beings—with respect to their Being. Even this latter questioning does not need to survey the entire horizon. Aristotle does not manage to surmount this double concept. Philosophy is for him: 1) πρώτη φιλοσοφία ["first philosophy"], 2) science of the most proper being, of the divine being, with which all other beings have a certain connection: theology.

Met. Γ 1: here the genuine concept of philosophy as science of Being is to be exposed. "There is a science, a science is possible, which considers beings as beings, just inasmuch as they are, with respect to their Being" (1003a21). This science thematizes Being "and those determinations that pertain to Being as such" (1003a21f.). The idea of the science of Being is here formally fixed once and for all. Delimited against the other sciences: it coincides with none of them. The other sciences thematize beings; they cut out a region of beings to consider. Nor does this science investigate the *sum total* of beings, all beings. None of the other sciences take into view what is to be said about Being in general, as a whole. All other sciences cut out a region from the universal realm of beings and investigate what belongs to this ontological region, what is co-given with it. Geometry treats of a determinate being, space. But now the question is about Being. Insofar as the question is scientific, it is about the principles that constitute Being as Being. Whatever is expounded about Being must necessarily be brought into relation with something that in a certain sense is φύσις. Being, its principles, and its characters are also still something else. Predicament: Being is not nothing but is also not a being; it is "something like that which persists in itself." φύσις is not "nature" but, instead, in a formal sense is "that which exists on the basis of itself," persists in itself. This science of Being, whose domain can nowhere be lodged within the realm of beings, does nevertheless not treat of nothing. The ontic explanation of beings on the basis of a preeminent being is distinct from an ontological interpretation of beings as beings.

"If even the questions posed by the ancients, who were investigating the elements, implicitly aimed at the basic determinations of beings as such, then these elements must be thought as determinations of beings in general and not merely as pertaining to a region of beings" (1003a28ff.). Task of the science of

Being: to grasp the first causes of beings, the latter taken precisely as beings, τὰς πρώτας αἰτίας τοῦ ὄντος (cf. 1003a31). This science is the science of the first causes. These causes, however, are principles and are themselves powers, etc., and thus they themselves *are*. This science deals with ultimate principles, not those of beings, but the ones of Being. That formulation is full of contradiction, inasmuch as the causes are always taken as beings. Thus Being is reduced to a being; it happens already in Aristotle, and especially in scholasticism.

69. (Relates to p. 125.)

Regarding 1: in what sense can Being in general be the object of a science? Central question of ontology. A step beyond Plato; total revolution of the idea of ontology. Seemingly, a dogmatic answer, yet this is only a response to the problematic of *Met.* B: what is (and can be) the object of the fundamental science? Can the highest genera of beings constitute the principles of Being? In other words, is Plato's approach to ontology tenable, if it is cut to the measure of the interpretation of Being itself (995b16ff. and b28ff.)? Plato: basic determinations, γένη, from which all other beings originate. Example of the dovecote. The γένη are διὰ πασῶν (*Theatetus,* 197D8), determinant of every being. They are connected among themselves; they stand in κοινωνία. Aristotle's critical question: can the γένη also represent the principles of Being? Put more pointedly: does Being have the character of a genus at all? Can Being, sameness, unity be characterized as genera?

70. (Relates to p. 126.)

In *Met.* B 3, 998b14–28, this question is posed: "If the genera, γένη, most of all have the character of basic determinations, then which of the genera function as principles: the highest ones or the lowest (the final ones, that have no further genera under them)? If the most general (most widespread) determinations possess more of the character of basic determinations, then the most universal of the genera are obviously the basic determinations. For these are asserted in regard to each and every thing. Thus there will be as many basic determinations of beings as there are first genera. Therefore ὄν, 'Being' as well as 'unity' will be such basic determinations. They constitute the basic structure of Being, οὐσία." These basic determinations are always already co-intended, even if they are not made explicit.

"But it is impossible that either Being or unity constitute a genus of beings" (998b22). This is Aristotle's negative formulation: Being can never have the character of a genus. Negative proof: "The differences of every genus must necessarily *be* and in each case must be *one* (difference). But it is impossible for the species of a genus to be attributed to the appurtenant differences, and, moreover, there is no genus without its species. Therefore, if Being or unity had the character of a genus, then no difference could be or could at all be *one;* but if, as in fact is the case, Being and unity are not genera, then they could not be basic determinations either, presupposing that every principle has the character of a genus" (998b23ff.).

What needs to be proved is the claim that the basic determinations of beings as beings, and Being itself, cannot be genera. Being is not a genus. The proof is worked out indirectly on the basis of the impossibility of the ὑπόθεσις; if its consequences are impossible, then the thesis is untenable as well. *Homo animal rationale:* teaching example, to clarify the proof. *Animal* possesses, in its methodological significance, the character of a genus. It is the general determination, "living being," which is here further determined by *"rationale,"* a new character that is not already contained in *"animal."* That further determination, which effectively differentiates the genus *"animal,"* is *"ratio." Ratio* is the difference; it introduces a division into the genus. It produces a species; it is εἰδοποιός. I pertain to the species *"homo." Ratio* is not included in the idea of the genus, *animal.* Furthermore, the species, *"homo,"* cannot be asserted of *"ratio"; ratio* is possible not only as a human mode of Being, but it also pertains to the Being of God. The difference is not included in the genus. Now, to apply this example, ὄν (Being) is substituted for *"animal."* If Being were a genus, then the differences, which differentiate the genus into definite species, should not have the determination by which we say "they *are."* The difference as such cannot already possess the character of Being. If so, then there are no differences and thus also no species. If Being is supposed to be a genus, then the differences and the species necessarily have the determinations that already reside in the genus itself. That contradicts the very meaning of species. So there are two possibilities: 1. either Being is a genus, one to which no species correspond, for in that case species cannot be. But a genus that excludes the very possibility of species is not a genus. 2. Or differences and species indeed *are,* but then the result is that Being cannot be understood as a genus. Now, there are in fact differences and species. Therefore ὄν is not a γένος. This proof, however, is merely negative. The universality of the basic determination of all beings has become questionable. That is Aristotle's advance beyond Plato. In what sense is Being? In what sense are the categories of Being principles of beings? What constitutes the principle-ness of these principles? The answer to this question and the supplement to the negative solution are presented in the first paragraph of *Met.* Γ 2.

71. (Relates to p. 127f.)

All these meanings are related to health, but not in the same way. Likewise, the various meanings of Being are modifications of the relation to *one* basic meaning. This ἕν constitutes the unity of the manifold meanings of Being. In all the meanings of "healthy," "health" itself is co-intended in some way or other. "Analogical meaning," κατ᾽ ἀναλογίαν. This ἕν is also called a μία ἀρχή (cf. 1003b6), a "single, primary principle," on the basis of which the various existing objects are grasped as existing. The problem of the relation of the meanings of Being among themselves only now comes to the fore.

Aristotle uses the expression πολλαχῶς in reference to the word "Being" in three ways: 1. multiplicity of Being (cf. *Met.* E 2, 1026a33ff.): four basic meanings, and according to them Being is articulated as: a) the ὄν of the categories, b) the ὄν κατὰ συμβεβηκός, c) ὄν ὡς ἀληθές, and d) ὄν δυνάμει καὶ ἐνεργείᾳ. ὄν κατὰ συμβεβηκός (b) is roughly translated: "Being in the sense of co-givenness." This is *one* kind of πολλαχῶς, one kind of the "multiplicity" of Being.

2. *Met.* Z 1, 1028a10ff.: Τὸ ὂν λέγεται πολλαχῶς: a) τί ἐστιν, b) ποιόν, c) ποσόν, d) πρός τι. This second multiplicity is a multiplicity within the meaning 1a. The ὄν of the categories breaks down into a new πολλαχῶς.

In *Met.* Γ, Aristotle intends neither 1 nor 2 but, instead, both pressed together. This doubling of the πολλαχῶς has been overlooked previously, in particular by Jaeger. The problem to be exposed is how these two kinds of πολλαχῶς are connected to each other. In the πολλαχῶς of the categories, the other three are included.

Example of health: just as the various meanings of "healthy" are related to the bodily state of health, so the meanings of Being are related to a basic meaning. We say of a being that it is: 1. ὅτι οὐσίαι,[77] because "it is in itself something present-at-hand," 2. because it is a πάθη οὐσίας, a "state of something present-at-hand," 3. ὁδὸς εἰς οὐσίαν, the "way toward the presence-at-hand" of something, 4. φθορά, the "disappearance" out of presence-at-hand, 5. ποιότης, because it is a "quality," 6. ἀπόφασις, nonbeing. The meanings 1 through 6 all have a relation to οὐσία. All these meanings of Being are πρὸς ἕν. That one basic meaning is οὐσία. 1. οὐσίαι, plural of "present-at-hand." οὐσία in the singular means "presence-at-hand in general"; in the plural: "present-at-hand things," ones that are in the mode of presence-at-hand. 2. οὐσία, "some *one* thing present-at-hand." 3. τί, the "what," the essence. If now all the basic significations are related back to a ἕν, then that means back to οὐσία in the sense of presence-at-hand. *Met.* Γ 2, 1003b17: "that on which the other meanings of Being depend, the basic meaning through which all other meanings of Being are asserted." I do not understand "healthy" if I do not relate the expression to "health" in the sense of the health of the body. Yet this basic meaning is not a genus. The kind of modalization proper to presence-at-hand, the basic meaning of Being, is different than that of genus and species and is fixed in the term "analogical meaning." Aristotle did not clarify its precise structure, one which is still obscure today.

Now, insofar as we expose the relation to the basic meaning, we thereby acquire the unitary sphere of the thematic object of this science, namely, Being itself. All ontological structures refer back necessarily to the basic meaning, which is accessible though an αἴσθησις. Just as in geometry all individual objects and nexuses presuppose space and refer back to space, so here with regard to Being. Space is already understood in a basic apprehension. So also Being is accessible in a primordial αἴσθησις, which is not a sense perception but, instead, a pure direct apprehension of the object itself. Aristotle showed only that this is required as a matter of principle.

Inasmuch as the fundamental science has Being in general as its object, the structure of ontology can also be clarified by delimiting it against the ontology of beings in the sense of nature, i.e., against mathematics and φυσική ["physics"]. How does the universality of the domain of the object of ontology relate to the universality of mathematics and physics? The problem is formulated more pointedly in *Met.* K 4ff. It is a matter of the same problem treated in *Met.* B and E. *Met.* K used to be considered spurious. Jaeger[78] showed that it must be attributed to Aristotle, at least chaps. 1–8; but chaps. 8–12 are genuine as well.

The question of Being must be posed independently of any question concerning determinate beings. For this reason there comes at first (*Met.* K 3,

77. For the citations, see above, p. 128.

78. Jaeger, *Studien*, pp. 63–88; and *Aristoteles*, p. 217ff.

1061a26ff.) an orientation with respect to two sciences that have determinate beings as their objects: mathematics and physics. Just as mathematicians carry out their investigations within a sphere of things they have acquired by adopting a determinate perspective, so it is the same with regard to Being as such. ἀφαίρεσις = "abstraction." Mathematicians indeed consider what is sensuous, but they abstract from everything, so that what remains left over is merely the "how much," the pure extension in its amount and its continuity. They then consider this extension according to one, two, or three dimensions, but only with respect to quantity and continuity—in no other respect. Meaning of the abstraction: positive freeing up of pure space in its extension and continuity. It is only within this secure region of pure space that mathematicians receive their various problems. A unitary region is given, that of geometry. In this way, the elaboration of pure space as such is carried out: whatever belongs to pure space as such. Physics, on the other hand, the science of nature in motion, considers all objective nexuses with respect to motion. Physics indeed considers beings, but not with respect to their Being as such. To consider them in *that* respect is to pursue philosophy.

In *Met.* K 3, 1061b7, Aristotle arrives at his positive determination of philosophy, and it stands opposed to Plato. Dialectics and sophistry are concerned only with things that are co-given precisely in beings, properties that are encountered by chance. They do not treat of beings with respect to their Being; only philosophy does. Thereby Aristotle, and his ontology, are delimited against Plato. Plato's διαλέγεσθαι lacks a unitary perspective on Being as such. Plato also includes in his dialectical schema κίνησις and στάσις. For Aristotle, κίνησις and στάσις do not pertain to pure Being. Aristotle has thereby fixed for all time the idea of a pure science of Being. This delimitation occurs at *Met.* Γ 2, 1004b17. Dialectics and sophistry are, so to speak, dressed in the same garments as philosophy, but they fundamentally are not philosophy. Sophistry merely appears to be so. On the other hand, the dialecticians indeed take their task seriously and positively, they treat of the κοινόν, but they lack an orientation toward the idea of Being. Both move in the same domain as philosophy. Dialectics is distinguished through its kind of possibilities: it has only limited possibilities, it can only seek. Philosophy, on the contrary, allows an understanding to arise. The sophists are distinguished through their peculiar decision with regard to scientific research: they are not serious, they merely want to win people over.

Thus philosophy treats of Being as Being. This orientation is carried out in λόγος, in assertion, in the way beings are spoken of as beings and as such and such.

72. (Relates to p. 130f.)

It is in Aristotle that λόγος first comes genuinely alive. λόγος = "assertion." In Aristotle, to "assert" (= κατηγορεῖν) receives its meaning in relation to κατηγορία. How does it happen at all that in philosophy κατηγορίαι are the theme of the investigations? λόγος = "expressing" of something as something. Aristotle had a sharper vision of this structure. λέγειν τι κατά τινος, with respect to an other; the same κατά as in the word κατηγορία. We today reverse the construction:

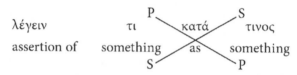

How can something like categories be acquired at all on the basis of λόγος? What are categories? What was the guiding principle for Aristotle's acquisition of the categories? That question is still controversial today. Kant and Hegel maintain that Aristotle simply snatched the categories out of the air.

Which categories does Aristotle recognize? Difficult to say with certainty, since different passages list different ones: ten, eight, three (*On the categories:* first work in the *Organon*, *Cat.* 4, 1b26f.[79]). Of the things that, from no possible point of view, can be determined through combination, each one means either: 1) οὐσία, 2) ποσόν, 3) ποιόν, 4) πρός τι, 5) πού, 6) ποτέ, 7) κεῖσθαι, 8) ἔχειν, 9) ποιεῖν, 10) πάσχειν. Regarding 1: "presence-at-hand." Regarding 7: "how one bears oneself." I can attribute presence-at-hand pure and simple only to a thing. ποσόν: categorial determination for two cubits long, three cubits long, etc. πρός τι: for half, double, greater. πού: in the marketplace. ἔχειν: shod, armed. πάσχειν: to be cut, to be burned. The last nine categories all have the basic determination of relatedness to the first.

The concept of category is indeterminate. In appropriating Kant, the categories were understood as forms of thinking which give order to the content of thought; as forms of thinking, the categories are subjective; question of their objective bearing. For Kant himself, the categories originally have nothing to do with forms of thinking in this sense. According to their own meaning, the categories signify modes of Being. It is remarkable that their name was chosen from the word for assertion, λόγος. The Greek question of Being is carried out in the question of λόγος: the determinations of Being are characterized on the basis of λόγος. Orientation of the question of Being toward λόγος. Showing of beings themselves: then that has nothing to do with subjective forms of thinking but, instead, with determinations of beings as beings in themselves. The categories are not subjective, although the sphere of the categories has a peculiar limit, inasmuch as the only beings they include are the ones we designate as present-at-hand: the αἰσθητά. Hence Plotinus's reproach that Aristotle did not question the νοητά. To be sure, Plotinus himself did not advance very far. With regard to all things, what is always asserted in advance is their Being (*Met.* K 2, 1060b4). Being is the most universal predicate whatsoever. How is the connection among the categories to be determined, and how are they acquired?

Synopsis of Aristotle's conception of the categories:

1. *Met.* Θ 10, 1051a34f.: The categories present τὸ ὄν {. . .} κατὰ τὰ σχήματα τῶν κατηγοριῶν. τόδε ὄν signifies: the "this here," or "quality," or "quantity" (cf. *Met.* Z 4, 1030b11). The κατηγορίαι are determinations of beings, as the beings are shown in assertion. The categories are also properties of propositions, *not* primarily, but only because they are determinations of beings themselves.

---

79. See also p. 132, n. 61.

2. Cf. *Cat.* 4, 1b25: The categories are such that, according to their content, they allow "no combination." In their meaning, they are utterly simple and irreducible, but they do indeed have an essential relation to something other. They are determinations of which it cannot be said what they are beyond this. They are that on whose basis an assertion can be carried out. "The stone is hard": I must already have an understanding of quality. "The tree is along the path": that requires an understanding of place, perhaps not an explicitly conscious understanding at the moment. "The stone is too big": quantity. I would be blind to all these determinations of Being, if they were not understood in advance.

3. *Met.* Δ 7, 1017a22ff.: "Being in itself is spoken of and understood in as many ways as there are categorial forms." There are as many possibilities of assertion as there are meanings of Being. Here it is evident that the multiplicity of the categories corresponds to a multiplicity of possible assertions. λόγος must be understood here as λέγειν τι κατά τινος ("assertion of something as something"). The various possible basic modes of the "as such and such" result in the possible categories.

4. *Anal. priora* A 37, 49a6ff.: "The attribution of something (namely, this) to something else (the co-presence-at-hand of something with something else) and the disclosure of this one thing in relation to another (the 'this-here' as something) is to be taken as manifoldly as there are manifold categories to be distinguished." Here it is evident how beings, which are exhibited in λόγος, are apprehended in their structure: the co-presence-at-hand of stone and hardness is the presupposition for the exhibition of the stone with respect to this one of its qualities. The ontic moment of the category is here apparent.

5. *Met.* Γ 2, 1003b9: The categories are what can be said πρὸς τὴν οὐσίαν, "with reference to," the first category, namely, "that which is present-at-hand in itself." All categories are, by their very sense, related to οὐσία: quality is always quality *of* something, etc. In every category, there resides a relation to something present-at-hand, which is then determined in a particular respect. ὑποκείμενον (οὐσία) ἐμφαίνεται: "in every category, what lies at the foundation comes to appearance" (cf. *Met.* Z 1, 1028a26ff.). Each of the nine categories (other than οὐσία) contains relations to οὐσία itself. On that is grounded the unity of the categories.

6. Aristotle's characteristic names for the categories: διαιρέσεις, πτώσεις, πρῶτα, κοινά, γένη. διαιρέσεις: most fundamental "differentiations" within beings as regards their Being. The term refers not so much to the mode of differentiating but, instead, to that which is differentiated. πτώσεις (cf. *Met.* N 2, 1089a26): "bendings," "inflections," modifications, diversifications of the general idea of Being. τὰ πρῶτα: the determinations already lying at the foundation of every being, ones every being must have if it is to be at all. κοινά: the "most universal" determinations. The idea of "quality" is what is most universal for all individual qualities. γένη has the same meaning: the "stem" out of which every particularization originates (cf. *De anima* A 1, 402a23). This latter is unclear, since Being does not have the character of a genus; thus not to be pressed too hard; stem but not genus in the logical sense.

73. (Relates to p. 133.)

2) In these types of co-presence-at-hand, there is expressed the mode of Being of what is gathered together, the one with the other (fundamental discovery of Plato versus Parmenides. The one is not the one, but is the one *and* the other.) Aristotle apprehends this more sharply: every ontological character includes a co-being with an other.

74. (Relates to p. 133f.)

All categories, by their very essence, are πρὸς ἕν. They do not first obtain this relation through their employment; on the contrary, they possess it already in themselves. οὐσία is what is primary and holds sway in all the categories; cf. the meanings of "healthy." This analogy, the correspondence of every category to Being, was understood in the Middle Ages as *analogia attributionis,* as the analogy of the univocal assignment of the categories to the first one, *substantia*. The Scholastics then exhibited a second analogy: *analogia proportionis,* "analogy of proportionality." Yet the essential one is the *analogia attributionis.*

All the individual categories have a proportional relation to their concretization. The mode has a relation to the respective being that exists in this mode: *analogia proportionis.*

Thus there is, in the case of the *analogia attributionis,* an *identitas termini.* The *terminus* is always the same. In addition, there is a *diversitas habitudinis.* Scholasticism recognized still another analogy: the analogical relation between the *ens infinitum (increatum)* and the *ens finitum (creatum)*. God is infinitely different from what is created. What common meaning of Being is foundational in these two cases: "God is" and "the chair is"? There is no highest *genus* of beings which could encompass both. Instead, both kinds of Being stand in a relation of analogy, one which is ultimately reducible to the *analogia attributionis,* since God is apprehended as the *ens infinitum,* the highest concretization of the concept of οὐσία.

Plotinus, *Enneads* 6, 1.1f.: limit of Aristotle's philosophy: he does not consider the νοητόν, which is determined by Being just as much as is the αἰσθητόν. They are ταὐτόν simply through ἀναλογία.

If God is substance in the proper sense, then are other beings only qualities or quantities? Descartes: *res cogitans—res extensa* ["thinking thing—extended thing"].

The problem of Being in Aristotle's philosophy is oriented toward the Being of the categories.

75. (Relates to p. 135.)

The meaning of Being, as understood by the Greeks: Being in the sense of presence [*Anwesenheit*], the present [*Gegenwart*]. Inasmuch as beings are not single, but multiple, presence means togetherness and, in this togetherness, being with one another, unitarily in the present. Every being includes a possible relation to an other, with which it is there. Being is always a lying-together, συγκείμενον. Structure of λόγος as σύνθεσις. Referred back to the structure of beings themselves. The categories are possible forms (kinds) of the co-presence of something with something. Of course, a being can also be co-present-at-hand with something that does not constantly and necessarily belong to it: e.g., a tree that is offering shade to some particular man. The tree is still the same without the man.

76. (Relates to p. 136.)

Another being can supervene upon the being which is in itself: ὂν κατὰ συμβεβηκός, "Being with respect to what supervenes, with respect to supervenience." Supervenience is a possibility that belongs to every being but does not constitute Being—it cannot be determined, or even traced out, in advance. The beings which are in themselves can, in λόγος, in ἐπιστήμη, be known, disclosed, apprehended, spoken of. Yet they still are, without my knowing them. Being includes the possibility of disclosedness. To be true, to be uncovered, is a possibility of what is present-at-hand.

77. (Relates to p. 136.)

The fates of those who live in the house do not pertain to οἰκοδομικὴ ἐπιστήμη ["the science of house building"]. The mathematician is not interested in the accidental differences between right triangles and other triangles but, instead, in triangularity as such. *Met.* E 2, 1026b13ff.: accidental circumstances are merely a name. Aristotle says Plato was correct to emphasize that the sophists busy themselves with μὴ ὄν. For they busy themselves with accidental fates. 1026b21: supervenience appears to stand very close to nonbeing. Yet it is not nothing; on the contrary, it is a definable mode of Being. That is why its essence is to be discerned along with the ground on which something like that mode of Being is possible. The essence of supervenience needs to be determined. The being which is in itself is present ἐξ ἀνάγκης (1026b28), "necessarily," and αἰεί (1026b30), "constantly." "Necessity" here means: cannot be otherwise. There are beings which are constantly, always, and necessarily what they are. In addition, there are beings which indeed are not absolutely always what they are, but are so for the most part (as a rule). The change of day and night happens as a rule. But we cannot say it occurs in the same way that $2 \times 2 = 4$. Over and against these two modes, there is the way of Being of the occasional, of what happens out of nowhere, without any possibility of determining its whence, its whither, or its duration. The ground of supervenience is nothing other than what is constant. Otherwise, there would be no accidentality. Constancy is the ontological possibility of accidentality. Otherwise, the accidental would have no whither. 1026b30f.: constancy is the ground for the possibility of something accidental, and the accidental transpires in the sphere of what is constant or is as a rule. Only as standing out from that background, does something accidental show itself. The mode of Being of supervenience is for the Greeks far different than Being in the proper sense.

Met. E 2: this mode of Being κατὰ συμβεβηκός is close to nonbeing, because it lacks the essential characters of the αἰεί and the necessary. Nevertheless, there can be the accidental, but only inasmuch as there is the constant. Hence this mode of Being is by essence (i.e., not accidentally) non-autonomous and derived from Being in the sense of the constant.

If, during the dog days, a cold storm blows in, that is accidental and improbable, neither expected nor the rule. Likewise, it is arbitrary and not necessary if a man is blond. He could just as well have dark hair. But a man cannot fail to be a ζῷον, a "living being." That is always and necessarily there, wherever a man is. To cure the sick is something accidental for an architect. But in itself it is the aim of a doctor. Likewise, a cook can, by means of food, cure someone; yet that is not the essential function of a cook. The supervenient cannot become the domain of a particular pursuit, handcraft, or activity, for these go by rule. There can be no systematized understanding, no τέχνη, of that which merely supervenes. Because the supervenient is not a possible object of determination and calculation, it also falls outside of θεωφία, scientific "consideration." Therefore the mode of Being of the accidental must be excluded from the theme of the science of Being, which investigates Being in the proper sense. Being in the sense of supervenience is derivative.

78. (Relates to p. 137.)

The same holds, in a certain sense, for the third mode of Being: Being ὡς ἀληθές (*Met.* E 4). To be sure, the proof proceeds very differently. The concept of Being as truth needs to be determined more precisely. *Met.* E 4 is textually uneven, both as regards content and diction. Jaeger has read into this a double concept of truth, as well as a development of the concept of truth, on Aristotle's part.[80] ὂν ὡς ἀληθές and μὴ ὂν ὡς ψευδές: "Being in the sense of uncovered-ness" and "nonbeing in the sense of coveredness." Question: in what and in which way do uncoveredness and coveredness have their Being?

    Met. E 4, 1027b19ff.: uncoveredness and coveredness depend on σύνθεσις and διαίρεσις, "conjunction" and "disjunction." Both belong to the unitary structure of λόγος, of "assertion," which may be characterized as either true or false. How do σύνθεσις and διαίρεσις make possible the structure of truth and falsity? Uncoveredness involves κατάφασις, the "attribution" of something to something else, and specifically ἐπὶ τῷ συγκειμένῳ (1027b21), "with respect to what is present-at-hand together." The showing in the mode of attribution with respect to what is present-at-hand together, or the showing in the mode of denial with respect to what is not together, what lies apart. Coveredness is characterized by the corresponding opposites: it is "showing in the mode of attribution" with respect to what is not actually together, or "showing in the mode of denial" with respect to what is actually present-at-hand together. κατάφασις and ἀπόφασις = positive and negative judgment.

79. (Relates to p. 138.)

In order for uncovering and covering to be carried out as assertions, the structure of conjunction and disjunction must be in assertion itself, whereby it can be true or false. I must take apart, διαίρεσις, run through and take apart, διανοεῖσθαι, what is straightforwardly pre-given, so as to separate what is present-at-hand, "board," and how it is qualified, "black." Question: how is such a unitary assertion possible, one by which I take apart the determinations ("board" and "black") and indeed *within* a σύνθεσις and *for* a σύνθεσις? How is it possible that the determinations can be at once ἅμα and χωρίς? A unitary act of assertion, in which something is at once disjoined and con-

---

80. See above, p. 137, n. 96.

joined, and specifically at the same time! This problem is treated more pre-cisely and *De anima* Γ 6ff. and *Met.* Z 12.

We are now asking for the ground of uncovering and covering. They are ways of carrying out διανοεῖσθαι, ways of carrying out λόγος, and are pos-sible only insofar as διάνοια, "understanding," is assertion. Uncoveredness and coveredness do not pertain to Being as such; instead, they arise only if there is assertion. Truth and falsity are grounded in the fact that 1. beings exist as possible objects of assertion and 2. διάνοια exists. Truth and falsity are ἐν διανοίᾳ and not ἐν τοῖς πράγμασι, in beings, "in the things" them-selves. Insofar as the categories constitute the ontological structure of the πράγματα, truth and falsity are different modes of Being in relation to Being in the proper sense. *Met.* E 4, 1027b31.

80. (Relates to p. 139.)

These two modes of Being, the accidental and the true, are dependent. Thus both refer back to an original Being and do not themselves belong to the sci-ence of Being and of its ultimate, fundamental grounds. *Met.* E 4, 1027b33: supervenience and uncoveredness are to be excluded from the fundamental consideration of Being. The reason, with respect to the accidental, is the ἀόριστον (1027b34); it is "undeterminable," inconstant, nothing I can be certain of at every moment. With respect to the true: it is a state of thinking, of judging, of determining, not a character of Being itself as it is in itself.

Both of these ontological modes affect the remaining stem of Being. They constitute that which, of the four modes of Being, does not pertain to the fundamental consideration. In *Met.* K 8, 1065a24, this ἔξω seems to be used in a different sense: "outside" of the understanding, thus identified with the πράγματα, which are in themselves. That is erroneous, even disregarding the fact that the Greeks did not have a concept of consciousness in this sense. These two ontological modes do not manifest a Being or the nature (one that would reside outside of Being in the proper sense) of a Being. ἔξω means that the accidental and the true are not modes of Being outside of Being in the proper sense. ἔξω means unfounded. The true as well as the accidental are founded, essentially grounded in genuine Being. That is why ἔξω in *Met.* K is placed together with χωριστόν (1065a24). General character of Being in the proper sense: autonomous constancy. The accidental lacks the character of constancy, the true the character of autonomy.

81. (Relates to p. 139f.)

The task is to expose the ἀρχαί, the "ultimate grounds," of autonomous con-stancy, which is founded in the basic category, οὐσία. This mode of Being is called ὂν κυρίως, "genuine, pre-eminent Being," and for Aristotle it does not include the Being of the true or of the accidental. Yet at *Met.* Θ 10, it is ἀληθὲς ὄν that is characterized as the κυριώτατον, the "most genuine" Being (cf. 1051b1), which seems to run counter to what has just been said. In fact, that is not a contradiction, but it can be understood only on the basis of an original interpretation of the Greek concept of Being.

How is the idea of the συμβεβηκός connected to the Being of the catego-ries? The categories are subject to a basic articulation: they are related to οὐσία by way of analogy. The categories are the possible modes of the co-presence-at-hand of beings; specifically, what is thought of here is a being that is in the genuine sense, that is therefore constant and follows a rule. Supervenience is merely a determinate mode of co-presence-at-hand, and, as accidental, it is not genuine Being. An extreme form of co-presence-at-hand.

The term κατὰ συμβεβηκός is used in two ways: 1. as above, it is a mode of Being; 2. Aristotle also calls the categories, as categories, the συμβεβηκότα. Are the categories then accidental conceptions of substance? No; that would be counter-sensical. Rather, it is to be understood in a completely formal sense: the categories are possible forms of being-together in general. A distinction must be made between συμβεβηκός in the sense of the accidental and this formal meaning of it. The idea of ὂν κατὰ συμβεβηκός is conceived on the background of being-together. Just as the Being of the categories is conceived under the guidance of λόγος (something pregiven exhibited with respect to the co-givenness of something else in it), so also is the second kind of Being (ὂν κατὰ συμβεβηκός) oriented toward λόγος. Greek ontology, especially in Aristotle, is approached and carried out with λόγος as the guideline.

Truth is attributed to λόγος. Truth is a determination of an assertion and is possible only on the basis of διάνοια, i.e., on the basis of λόγος. λόγος is now considered not with respect to the possible modes of beings shown in it but, instead, with respect to the kinds of showing, namely the true and the false. Met. Θ 10: truth is attributed not only to διάνοια, but also to νοεῖν as such, to the pure and simple "apprehension" of something which has as its opposite not falsity, but ἄγνοια, "ignorance." All direct, straightforward apprehension of something, e.g., the apprehension of the categories, does not grasp a composite but, instead, something which is graspable only in itself. Here no σύνθεσις is involved. Thus it cannot also be apprehended as something it is not. It can only be encountered straight on. That is the most original kind of apprehension: disclosure in pure and simple beholding. Met. Z 4: the λόγος which addresses something in itself and not *as* something else, the λόγος which purely and simply shows the thing. Inasmuch as Being is presence, straightforward uncovering of a being signifies something like an enhancement of the being with respect to its Being and its presence. It is now present in a genuine sense; previously it was there only in an improper way. Now, as something present-at-hand, it is brought into the immediate presence of the one who is apprehending it. When it is grasped, the being is present in a higher sense than it was when ungrasped and hidden. Its uncovering confers on it a higher mode of presence. Therefore, ὂν ὡς ἀληθές is a higher mode of οὐσία. Accordingly, Aristotle is right to attribute to truth the highest mode of Being: truth is genuine Being. Something *is* when it is uncovered. ὂν ὡς ἀληθές as κυριώτατον ὄν (cf. Met. Θ 10, 1051b1). But, in the ontological sense, truth is still not the most original mode of Being, for it presupposes οὐσία. Double connection of ὂν ὡς ἀληθές with οὐσία. παρουσία, "the present," "presence."

82. (Relates to p. 150.)

δύναμις and ἐνέργεια are two basic modes of presence-at-hand, of οὐσία. Thus they refer back to genuine Being, the Being of the categories. ἐνέργεια is the highest mode of Being. ἐνέργεια is prior to δύναμις, "actuality" before "possibility": to be understood on the basis of the fact that Being means presence. Possibility = preparedness for, which requires that ἐνέργεια or ἐντελέχεια exist. δύναμις and ἐνέργεια also have meanings that function by analogy.

The task is to grasp together the four basic meanings of Being. The center of the *science of Being* lies in the Being of the categories. Yet Aristotle says that the first science is *theology;* it deals with the highest being itself. How are these to be reconciled? Is the science of Being not supposed to be indifferent to every particular domain of objects? Jaeger: Aristotle was here not equal to the problem of Being.[81] That is a superficial interpretation. On the contrary, the two concepts of ontology (science of Being–theology) necessarily belong together. Science of beings as beings: that necessarily includes the question of the particular being in which genuine Being is most purely demonstrated. In such a being alone can one acquire the idea of Being. Thus a discipline is necessary that studies the being which is conceived as a being in the most proper sense. Whether this being is the first mover or the first heaven is a secondary question. Such an orientation to the most proper being is not a special science; on the contrary, it is an ontologically oriented science. It is the science of that which Being genuinely means and also the science of that being which genuinely is; science of Being and of the highest being. *Met.* E 1, 1026a29ff.: "If there is a being that is utterly unmoved but always is in the sense of pure ἐνέργεια, then this being is prior and the science of it is the first." Hence this science is also an investigation into beings as beings.

Aristotle adds a third moment that had never been taken up previously: every ὄν is one, ἀγαθόν, ἕτερον, μὴ ὄν, etc. "Unity," "otherness," "opposite," "nonbeing," ἀγαθόν: these are determinations that pertain to every being just as a being. They are "formal" determinations of Being, the object of "formal ontology." Therefore: 1. ontology of the most genuine being, 2. ontology of the categories, 3. formal ontology. How these are connected Aristotle did not say.

83. (Relates to p. 153.)

De anima:

Bk. 1: exposition, critical retrospective on the previous philosophy.
Bk. 2: positive determination of the concept of the soul:

  Chaps. 1–4: general ground-laying;
  Chaps. 5–6: αἴσθησις, perception;
  Chaps. 7–11: forms of perception;
  Chap. 12: more precise determination of the structure of αἴσθησις.

Bk. 3:

  Chaps. 1 and 2 properly belong to bk. 2.
  Chap. 3: analysis of φαντασία, *imaginatio.*
  Chaps. 4–6: νοῦς, understanding, διάνοια.
  Chaps. 9–13: concluding analyses of the constitution of life, basic relation between thought and conation; approach to an analysis of the lower levels of life.

81. Jaeger, *Aristoteles*, pp. 223–27, 379.

Supplementary treatises:[82] *parva naturalia,* small works on biology: Περὶ αἰσθήσεων καὶ αἰσθητῶν; *On memory and recollection; On sleep and waking; On life and death;* in addition: *On the self-motion of living beings:* Περὶ ζῴων κινήσεως; genuinely Aristotelian, as Jaeger has shown.[83]

84. (Relates to p. 155f.)

De anima B 2, 413a21ff: ἄψυχον versus ἔμψυχον, "unsouled" versus "ensouled": the latter is distinguished by the presence of τὸ ζῆν. Life is the very mode of Being of that which is living. ζῆν is a basic ontological concept. The soul is also to be understood in this sense. We say something is living where we find that: it moves in a oriented way, i.e., in a way oriented by perception; it moves itself and can stop itself; it was young and ages; it takes in nourishment and grows; etc. A physical body moves in only *one* direction. Plants, in contrast, extend themselves, through growth, in *all* directions simultaneously. The basic determination of such a living thing is the capacity of θρεπτικόν (413b5): "it can feed" and thereby is in communication with the beings around it. To this is added αἰσθητικόν (417a6), the possibility of orienting oneself, even if only as touching and grasping out for something. What is alive, and also stands in a determinate communication with something, is such that it has a world, as we would say today. Many living beings are tied to a certain place, others can move about. And their motion is different than the change of place to which lifeless things are subject: κίνησις πορευτική (cf. 432b14), to move oneself *toward* something which matters to life in one way or another; an oriented motion in the respective surrounding world.

Bound up with the phenomenon of κινεῖν is the phenomenon of κρίνειν, "distinguishing" in the sense of a formal orientation in general. κρίνειν: αἴσθησις and νοῦς. κινεῖν and κρίνειν constitute life.

De anima Γ 9ff.: every motion is motion ἕνεκά τινος: the motion, as a conation, proceeds toward the ὀρεκτόν (433a18), the "desired." Question: how is this ὀρεκτόν, the "desirable," made accessible, and what are the basic modes of conation? φεύγειν and διώκειν (cf. 432b28f.), on the one hand, to "make for" something, to pursue an object, and on the other hand, to "avoid" it. With the living being, what is, formally speaking, the mover itself, the ἀρχὴ κινήσεως? Aristotle shows that the point of departure for the motion is not the pure and simple observation of a desirable object. This object is not grasped through αἴσθησις but, instead, through ὄρεξις: the "conation" has the function of disclosing. Only on the basis of the ὀρεκτόν is there deliberation, κρίνειν, διάνοια. It is not the case that the living being first observes things disinterestedly, merely looks about in a neutral attitude, and then moves toward something; on the contrary, ὄρεξις is fundamental. The ἀρχή is the unity of κρίνειν and κινεῖν; that is the principle of motion for living beings. αἴσθησις for animals, νοῦς for humans. The αἴσθησις of animals is not a theoretical capacity; on the contrary, it exists in a context of pursuit and flight.

De anima B 6: the general structure of αἴσθησις is threefold (418a9ff.): 1. αἴσθησις ἰδία, 2. αἴσθησις κοινή, 3. αἴσθησις κατὰ συμβεβηκός. Regarding

82. See above, p. 154.
83. See above, p. 154, n. 162.

1: the "perception" that relates to its *own* proper object. Every sense is true in its "own" field. Every perception is disclosive within its own field. Other phenomena are not determined through these sense-qualities, e.g., change of place, which is perceptible through several senses. Regarding 2: phenomena that are "common" to determinate perceptions, κοινά. Regarding 3: Furthermore, we always see some determinate moveable thing, not mere qualities such as colors. I see first that this is chalk and only then that it is white and has such and such a form, etc. The co-givenness of accidental properties is not for the Greeks of essential significance. Chalk can be white, but so can paper and other things.

Humans are distinguished from animals by their possession of νοῦς (cf. 433a9ff.) or, more precisely, λόγος. λόγος belongs necessarily to the definition of the ζῷον, human being: ζῷον λόγον ἔχον, "a living thing which can speak," which can ἀποφαίνεσθαι ["let be seen"]. The world is not then known only in the horizon of pursuit and flight; instead, beings in their being such and such are spoken of, determined, understood, conceptualized, and thereby grounded in their "what" and their "why." Humans have the possibility of understanding the ὀρεκτόν as the basis of their action and the motive of their decisions (cf. 433a17ff.). Such a being is called human Dasein. κρίνειν is determined through λόγος, i.e., νοῦς. The unity of κινεῖν and κρίνειν, ἄμφω (433a13), is determined through προαίρεσις (cf. 406b25), the possibility of "anticipating" something as the basis of action and decision. Thereby humans face the possibility of an opposition between ἐπιθυμία (cf. 433b6), sheer "appetite," impulsive life, which is blind, and understanding, action grounded in reasons. *De anima* Γ 10: this opposition between impulse and genuinely chosen, rational action is a possibility open only to those living beings which can understand time. Insofar as a living being is delivered over to impulse, it is related merely to what is immediately there and stimulating, τὸ {. . .} ἡδύ ["the pleasurable"] (433b9). Impulse strives unreservedly toward that, toward what is present and available. But humans, because they possess an αἴσθησις χρόνου ["sense of time"], can presentify τὸ μέλλον ["the future"] (433b7f.) as the possible and as that for the sake of which they act. This capacity of a double comportment—toward the future and toward the present—allows conflict to arise. Aristotle does not clarify the extent to which time makes something like that possible. It is difficult to grasp fundamentally the connection between time and λόγος; likewise, it is difficult to determine whether animals have the capacity to perceive time.

85. (Relates to p. 157.)

Here we have the first general laying of a foundation for a description of human Dasein. Question: what is the specifically human mode of Being? κρίνειν is not limited to αἴσθησις but is also found in νοῦς. Thereby arise various possibilities for disclosing beings (*Nic. Eth.* 6), five such possibilities: 1) τέχνη (chap. 4), 2) ἐπιστήμη (chap. 6), 3) φρόνησις (chap. 5), 4) σοφία (chap. 7), 5) νοῦς (chap. 8). Five modes of ἀληθεύειν, of κρίνειν, of orienting oneself, incorporated into the corresponding comportments of the movement of life: 1) τέχνη–ποίησις, 2) ἐπιστήμη; to it no further movement corresponds, since ἐπιστήμη is theory and simply beholds. 3) φρόνησις, πρᾶξις, 4) σοφία, 5) νοῦς: this latter is not attained by humans; it determines the first mover.

The modes of κίνειν are doubled: ποίησις, "manipulating," and πρᾶξις, "acting" (*Nic. Eth.* 6, 4, 1140a2) in the genuine sense: something done for reasons, which is distinguished from producing by the fact that the ἔργον does not lie outside the doing, like the nest of a bird, but resides in the doing itself. The goal of acting is the action itself, i.e., the acting being as such. Definition of a human being: ἄνθρωπος is the ζῷον to which belongs πρᾶξις, and also λόγος. These three determinations conjoined: ζωὴ πρακτικὴ τοῦ λόγον ἔχοντος (cf. *Nic. Eth.* 1, 7, 1098a3f.) is the essence of human beings. Humans are those living beings that, according to their mode of Being, are able to act. The same conception appears again in Kant (*Kritik der reinen Vernunft; Grundlegung zur Metaphysik der Sitten*): humans are the ones that can speak, i.e., act for reasons.

The Greeks' determination of the highest mode of action depends on their conception of Being and of the possibilities of Being. Such a life is not mere ζωή, but βίος, "existence." In the course of history the meaning of this concept changed completely; βίος became that which humans have in common with other living things. Various possibilities of βίος (βίοι). Which is the highest βίος, the highest possibility of existence, the mode of Being in which a person satisfies to the highest degree the proper human potentiality for Being, in which a person genuinely *is*? All practical comportment is directed to something outside the person, something determined as this or that temporally circumscribed thing. All action is carried out within the καιρός, the "practical moment." Such an existence is a specifically human possibility: βίος πολιτικός (cf. *Nic. Eth.* 1, 5, 1095b18), "life in community." Orientation toward something temporally determinate and historically pregiven, thus toward a mode of Being that in the Greek sense, is not genuine Being. The merit of action is to adapt itself to change.

In contrast, however, the highest mode of Being must be directed toward the ἀεὶ ὄν, which is not a possible object of manipulation; on the contrary, it can only be contemplated and investigated: θεωρεῖν, "pure research" into Being as such, which aims at no practical consequences and is merely for the sake of exposing beings as they are (cf. *Nic. Eth.* 10, 8, 1178b3f.). The researcher is the one who comes closest to Being and to beings, to νοῦς itself. In θεωρεῖν (cf. 1178b28), a person attains the greatest possible closeness to the highest mode of Being meted out to humans. To be sure, this comportment is possible for humans only occasionally; they fall back again. But that was not something Aristotle merely taught; he also lived it. At that time, philosophy did not need to be *brought* close to life.

86. (Relates to p. 158.)

Decline of Greek philosophy; this high level of research could not be upheld. In the modern period, Kant became a Greek of the first rank, if only for a short time.

So it happened that the basic question of Being was gradually loosened from its primitive stages. First understanding of the question of Being in Parmenides and Heraclitus; methodological inquiry in Socrates and Plato; comprehensive elaboration in Aristotle.

Greek ontology is an ontology of the world. Being is interpreted as presence and constancy. Being is conceptualized on the basis of the present, naively on the basis of the phenomenon of time, in which, however, the present is only *one* mode. Question: how is it that the present has this privilege? Do not the past and future have the same rights? Must Being not be apprehended on the basis of the whole of temporality? Fundamental problem taken up in the question of Being. We will understand the Greeks only when we have appropriated this question; i.e., when we have confronted the Greeks by vigorously countering their questioning with our own.

BRÖCKER TRANSCRIPTION

1. (Relates to p. 141.)

We broach now the most difficult phenomenon within Greek—and especially Aristotelian—ontology: the ὂν δυνάμει καὶ ἐνεργείᾳ. Aristotle was the first to disclose these characters of Being, and he thereby achieved a fundamental advance beyond Platonic ontology. To be sure, Aristotle did not clarify these concepts so fully that the problems connected to them are now transparent in every respect.

We will attempt to grasp the main determinations of these concepts and, at the same time, their genesis. Aristotle treats of δύναμις and ἐνέργεια in *Met.* Θ, of δύναμις especially in *Met.* Δ 12. These two categories doubtlessly developed in the analysis of the phenomenon of motion. Aristotle analyzes motion itself in *Phys.* Γ 1-3, E, Z, and also somewhat in Θ.

Let us first gain our orientation from the pre-ontological concept of δύναμις, from δύναμις as an ontic concept. There δύναμις signifies a being and not a mode and structure of Being, and it is laid open in *Met.* Δ 12, 1019a15ff.:

1. First meaning of δύναμις: it is the ἀρχὴ κινήσεως ἢ μεταβολῆς ἡ ἐν ἑτέρῳ ἢ ᾗ ἕτερον. "Potentiality is the point of departure of a motion or a change in another as the moved, the changed, or insofar as the moved is an other." Such δύναμις is, e.g., a craft one is *capable of*. This capability is the possible principle of a determinate motion, and specifically this δύναμις is carried out in an other, namely in that which arises through the motion or, expressed more prudently, *insofar as* this is an other. For it can happen that whoever disposes of such a capability applies it to *himself*. The doctor can treat himself medically, but only insofar as he takes himself as someone ill.

2. Correlatively, δύναμις is a potentiality to *undergo* something, to be influenced by something other, by something insofar as it is other. This is the correlative reversal of the first, and Aristotle establishes it as a basic concept.

3. Potentiality in an *emphatic* sense. For instance, if we say of a runner that he *can* run, we mean he runs well. Potentiality in the emphatic sense of leading something correctly to its end or carrying it through with resolution; thus, not just any arbitrary acting and moving, but a preeminent one, having the character of the καλόν.

4. Counter-concept to 2: the ἕξις according to which something is insensitive to influence. Capacity in the sense of *power to resist* something. All perishing and destruction occur because the thing did not have this potential, because a certain capacity, or power, of resistance was missing. This that is lacking in destruction, but that is there in self-conservation in vitality, is δύναμις in the sense of resistance.

You see in all these four notions that the ontic concept of potentiality is oriented toward the phenomenon of *motion* (acting, doing in the widest sense) or toward its correlate: toward that which is affected by the activity, what resists it or not.

In a similar way, Aristotle now determines the derived concepts of δύναμις: δυνατόν, "to be capable of something," completely analogous to the first four concepts; likewise, ἀδύνατον, "not to be capable," or in other terms, δύναμις and ἀδυναμία. Here Aristotle mentions a concept of impossibility which we also use: something is impossible whose opposite is necessarily true: 2 × 2 is not 4. Thus potentiality here related to truth; more precisely, potentiality here means non-contradiction. This concept of *potentia* then plays a major role in modern philosophy. The principle of non-contradiction becomes an ontological principle. All the concepts we have enumerated were spoken of in relation to the first determination: i.e., in relation to potentiality in the sense of the point of departure of a change in that which is other. Therefore even these concepts, with respect to their meaning-structure, have the character of analogical meanings.

The question now arises: what is the transition from this ontic concept of δύναμις in the sense of "ability" to the ontological concept of δυνάμει ὄν, or its correlate, ἐνεργείᾳ ὄν? The use of the concept of δύναμις in the ontological sense develops out of the analysis of *motion*. Let us now pursue that analysis; obviously we can do so here only in broad strokes.

2. (Relates to p. 142.)

How in general does Aristotle manage to grasp δύναμις and ἐνέργεια ontologically? How do potentiality and actuality fall under the basic determinations of *Being*, under which they then have remained in the subsequent ontology up to today? The task is to see whence these basic concepts have been drawn and how they then expand so that they enable the basic category, οὐσία, to be determined. If they do this, then it is proved that they must be reintegrated into the Being of the categories.

The ground for acquiring them is the phenomenon of motion. Therefore we must first consider that phenomenon and bring it into a fundamentally ontological horizon. Hence the question now is: how are δύναμις and ἐνέργεια connected to the phenomenon of motion? Motion in a broad sense was always already a problem for the Greeks, inasmuch as the pre-Platonic philosophers already saw that motion is a basic determination of the world. It was seen that the things of the world come to be and pass away. And coming to be and passing away are possible only if there is motion. This first way of posing the question of motion has an ontic character and neglects to investigate what motion in itself is. Aristotle was the first to pose explicitly this latter question, and he answers it in his *Physics*.

3. (Relates to p. 143.)

Physics: Γ 1-3: Aristotle begins by presenting an outline of the basic structures involved in the phenomenon of motion. Motion, in the Greek sense, refers to any change from something to something. Thus for a thing to move, taking the simplest phenomenon of locomotion, means that a point changes its place. At every moment it passes from one place, as it were, to the next. Spatial motion is therefore change of place, passage from one place to the next. Thus the phenomenon of motion—if we take our orientation from "locomotion," φορά—immediately includes the moment of succession, ἐφεξῆς (*Phys.* Γ 1, 200b16), "succession," the "one after the other," the constant passage through places one after the other.

Along with that, motion possesses another character: συνεχές (200b18), "continuous," without leaps, continuous transition. The phenomenon of the συνεχές, the continuum (in the Greek sense of "holding together," such that there are no gaps in between) contains, according to Aristotle, the more original phenomenon of the ἄπειρον (cf. 200b19), the "unlimited": i.e., not infinite in every direction, but unlimited in the sense that there is no limit between the individual places. A continuum is pre-given, and I can mark it out de facto by two points; but, between these, there are always more points. That is, I never arrive at an ultimate simple which cannot be divided further. In other words, the course of a point (and space in general) is by essence a continuum, not something composite but, instead, something primordially simple.

Moreover, τόπος is among the further determinations of motion. For something to move, it must be in a *"place."* Also, it must have room, which refers to the κενόν, the *"void,"* space in the sense of the "space between." And there must be *"time,"* χρόνος (cf. 200b21). Motion is carried out in time.

In this outline of the most general structure of motion, you see already the basic concepts that were later appropriated by modern physics and were fixed for the first time by Galileo's determination of motion and of the moving body in general. As a young man, Galileo made a thorough study of Aristotle, something which is only today coming to be appreciated. It is beyond question that the impulse driving Galileo's formulation of the basic physical concepts derives from Aristotle's *Physics*.

We now want to see the extent to which Aristotle succeeded in grasping the phenomenon of motion and how his definition is essentially a philosophical-ontological one, versus the definition of motion in modern physics. There motion is merely given a definition and is not grasped in its essence.

Physics Γ 1–3. Aristotle characterizes the following phenomena as essential determinations of the domain in which motion is possible: συνεχές, ἄπειρον, τόπος, κενόν, χρόνος. How is motion itself now to be determined, such that the character of motion can be connected to Being in general? It must be stressed that Aristotle demonstrates κίνησις is not something παρὰ τὰ πράγματα, *"beside* the things," existing for itself as a being. This is to be understood in the positive sense that the determinations of beings as beings can, for their part, undergo modification through motion, so that there are only as many kinds of motion as there are basic possibilities within beings that allow motion at all. On the basis of this joining of the modes of Being with the characters of motion, Aristotle comes to say: there is motion only with respect to οὐσία, ποιόν, ποσόν, and τόπος. With respect to οὐσια, there is motion from nonbeing to Being: coming to be. The inverse: passing way. With respect to ποιόν: increase and decrease. With respect to ποσόν: alteration, becoming other. And finally there is motion with respect to place: locomotion, spatial motion. Thus the kinds of motion are oriented toward the basic categories. Motion itself is therefore fundamentally understood as a modification of these ontological determinations themselves.

But how must motion now be apprehended on its own part? To anticipate the definition: ἡ τοῦ δυνάμει ὄντος ἐντελέχεια, ἧ τοιοῦτον, κίνησίς ἐστιν (201a10f.). That means, to translate at first very traditionally: "Motion is the actuality of the potential as potential." Let us clarify this statement by referring to the states of affairs on which Aristotle bases his definition. Example: a determinate comportment, the production of a table. Wood, of a determinate kind and size, is pre-given. It contains this potential, namely, that out of it a table can be produced. Production therefore necessarily requires something pre-given, δυνάμει ὄν, something, namely, the wood, which is in itself *prepared* to become a table. The wood is at hand for the handcraftsman, it lies there before him. If the wood is taken up by being worked on, if it comes under the hand of the handcraftsman, then it is in motion, i.e., the table comes to be, *becomes*. What does this becoming mean? Becoming, coming to be, means here that this wood is now *present* precisely in its preparedness to become a table, and with respect to such preparedness. It is no longer simply lying around as a piece of wood but, instead, is now there as this determinate thing prepared to be a table. The preparedness now becomes, in the production, real, actual. This preeminent presence of the preparedness of the wood to become a table is what Aristotle calls motion, i.e., the change from mere wood to table.

As long as this preparedness is *there*, the motion is occurring. When the wood is finished with its preparedness, then the table *is;* it has become, it is a finished ἔργον, and the motion is no more. Up to the moment the wood is a finished ἔργον, the wood is, so to speak, *under way* to the table. In this manner, the wood, with respect to its preparedness, can be grasped as under way toward that which is supposed to result from the producing. This being-under-way of the δυνάμει ὄν, the wood, to the ἔργον, the table, characterizes the motion as ἀτελής (cf. 201a6). What is moving is necessarily under way to something, to that which it will come to "at the end." The wood is being worked on as long as the table is not finished. When the table is finished, then the motion stops; the table has come to be.

Motion necessarily includes this indeterminateness, the unfinishedness, the not-having-come-to-the-end. This character of being under way to something is essential for motion. But when the table is finished, the end has been reached. The moment the table is finished, some *new* present-at-hand thing is there, one that is now at rest. The motion, on the basis of which and in which the table has become, stops and is no more. The motion is thus the preeminent presence of a determinate piece of wood with respect to its potentiality to become a table. Aristotle explicitly stresses, in *Phys.* Γ 2, 201b24ff., that this phenomenon of motion, namely that it is ἀόριστον ["indefinite"], is difficult to see. For there is a tendency to focus only on the two end stations, to allot the main accent to the ends. But the essential task is to see the "between the two," to determine ontologically the transition from the one to the other. This transition, in the case of the wood, is nothing other than the presence of its potentiality to be a table, precisely as potentiality.

4. (Relates to p. 144ff.)

The question now arises: how do these two characters Aristotle uses to define motion, δυνάμει and ἐνεργείᾳ ὄν, acquire a fundamental *ontological* function? We see already from the analysis of motion that the translation of δύναμις as "potentiality" is erroneous, for the potential is also something that is not yet, but can be, something to whose actuality nothing is in the way, though it is not yet actual. On the other hand, in the definition of motion, δυνάμει is not understood in the sense of something purely and simply possible, something possible only in the formal sense, as it were, but, instead, is a character of something *already present-at-hand*. The wood is actual. That is why δύναμις is better translated as "preparedness for" something. Preparedness for something belongs to *all* the things we use. Every utensil, tool, and material has a preparedness for something. Preparedness is a character pertaining to something present-at-hand. It characterizes this something with respect to the fact that it has not yet been taken up explicitly into use. When it is used, it is preeminently present, it achieves a preeminent presence. Previously, it was merely available to me. In use, however, it comes closer to me in a certain way. In coming to be used, it becomes especially *actual*.

Thus "actuality" would be a very apt translation of ἐνέργεια, except for the fact that the philosophical tradition comes to employ it for something else. The distinction between actuality and preparedness consists in this: in both cases it is a matter of something present-at-hand, but while the wood is indeed something there in both cases, it is so with a different explicitness. This difference is thus to be understood as a difference in the insistence of the object. The δύναμις of wood means that it can be, as matter, insistent with respect to its preparedness, and it is actually insistent when it enters into the process of production. Both concepts, that of δυνάμει ὄν as well as that of ἐνεργείᾳ ὄν, are modifications of what is present with respect to its presence.

These concepts are now transferred from what is produced to what is self-moving. And here again we see exactly the same distinction. A thing at rest—and this is something essential, which Aristotle was the first to see clearly—is not cut off from every character of motion. Rest is merely a limit case of motion. What can be at rest is only what has the potentiality to be in motion. That is why rest is a limit case of motion. If something is self-moving, then that means phenomenally: it of itself is more properly insistent on what it *can* be than when it is at rest. Thus self-motion is a higher mode of insistence, i.e., a higher mode of the presence of something present-at-hand. And this self-insistence of a being, from itself, as self-moving, is something Aristotle finds especially marked in *living* beings.

The basic ontological determination of ζωή is that it is self-insistent of itself, not accidentally, but necessarily. That is because motion itself belongs to its essence or, in other words, because the τέλος (the "goal," that whereby the motion comes to its end) resides, in the case of a living beings, in themselves. In the case of manipulation, production, etc., the τέλος resides outside, as the finished work; and the same can be said about that which has been manipulated. A table no longer has anything to do with the manipulation. When the table is finished, it is something present-at-hand in itself, just as the carpenter continues to exist for himself after producing the table. Quite to the contrary, however, the self-moving of living beings means that their τέλος is in themselves, such that this τέλος is not an ἔργον which arises out of, and then resides next to, the motion but, instead, is a mode of the motion itself.

What is decisive for understanding the concept of motion is to grasp that δυνάμει ὄν and ἐνεργείᾳ ὄν represent two different modes of the presence of what is present-at-hand. Motion has always played a fundamental role in the question of φύσις, i.e., in the question of beings.

5. (Relates to p. 147.)

The question now is: what does Aristotle gain, with this answer to the question of the essence of motion, for the clarification of beings as a whole, i.e., the beings we call "nature"? Motion is eternal, and that is fundamental to Aristotle's position. There *never* was *not* motion. The question is how Aristotle proves this claim. He shows that motion is eternal and that it is a preeminent character of all beings 1. from the idea of motion itself and 2. from the phenomenon of time. On the basis of this proof, Aristotle arrives at the ultimate determinations of beings in general. He argues: if motion is eternal, then there must necessarily be something constantly *moved*. For there is motion only if there is a moved being. Hence the question: how must motion be constituted such that it can be eternal, and how must the moved be constituted, such that it can move itself eternally? This question is the ontological question of the condition of possibility of eternal motion as such. This purely ontological intention of clarifying the eternity of motion leads Aristotle to a first unmoved *mover*, πρῶτον κινοῦν ἀκίνητον (*Phys.* Θ 6, 258b12). Now, insofar as motion presents a higher kind of presence, and insofar as motion determines the Being of the world and, as this determination, is eternal, we then have to see *in motion and in movedness the highest kind of Being*, out of which alone can rest then become understandable.

Inasmuch as the mover, as the eternal mover,[84] is the most genuine being, the τιμιώτατον ὄν, Aristotle also determines it as the θειότατον (cf. *Met.* Λ 9, 1074b26), the "most divine" Being. This ontological meaning of the θειότατον, however, has nothing at all to do with God or religiosity. As a correlate, we can already see that, although Aristotle designates the science of this highest being "theology," it has nothing to do with any sort of interpretation or clarification of the religious relation of mankind to God. Therefore what is most important to see is the completely unmistakable and univocal orientation of the problem of motion and of the divine to this purely theoretical problem of Being. This meaning of the Aristotelian concept of motion and its ultimate interpretation were later transformed in Scholasticism and were incorporated into the Christian conception of the relation of God to all other beings. This scholastic transformation led, in turn, to a retrospective interpretation of Aristotle in a Christian sense, which is completely wrong.

6. (Relates to p. 147f.)

The task is therefore to prove that motion is eternal. Coming to be and passing away appear constantly. For them to be possible, motion must *be*. Every motion, however, presupposes at the same time a being, δυνάμει ὄν, which, as something present-at-hand, changes into something which is constituted in this higher presence of the potential as potential. Hence, for motion to be possible, there must always already be something present-at-hand which possesses the preparedness for it. But this present-at-hand, resting thing must be questioned as to the motion from which it itself originated and as to how it *came* to the stage of something present-at-hand at rest. Every motion is μεταβολή {. . .} ἔκ τινος

---

84. Bröcker's transcript is obviously mistaken here in saying: "the moved as the eternally moved."

εἴς τι (*Phys.* E 1, 225a1) "change from something to something." The from-which must already be, and it, in turn, owes its Being purely and simply to some other motion. Thus motion always already presupposes motion.

Aristotle bases the more precise proof on the phenomenon of time. In changing, a thing becomes something it had not been earlier. Change therefore involves the earlier and the later. But can the earlier and the later be possible, unless there is time? The earlier and the later *are* only inasmuch as time is. And how can there be time if there is no motion? Thus we are led to explicate, very concisely, Aristotle's concept of time.

We found: 1. motion requires the earlier and the later. 2. The earlier and the later imply time. 3. Time includes motion; time is founded in motion.

Time is the ἀριθμὸς κινήσεως (219b2), the "numbered of motion" as such. We heard that motion consists in the explicit presence of something prepared with respect to its preparedness. When I determine—in other words, *count*—a moved being with respect to the presence of its preparedness (loco-motion: an object's traversing a determinate expanse), then I say: the object has the potentiality to be at this place. At first such and such a point is at rest. If the point then moves over an expanse, i.e., if this preparedness of the point to be at different places becomes actual, present, if I can see it in its preparedness to occupy various positions, then I see it present *here*, present here, here, here, now there, now there, etc. Thereby I count, I count the motion. That which I count in the case of locomotion, in the case of the presence of the preparedness of the point, are the nows. The nows constitute time, and therefore time is "the numbered of motion."

From this it is clear that for Aristotle the basic phenomenon of time is the νῦν ["now"] (218a6). Consequently, there is time only where there is motion. Time is thus founded in motion. If it can be shown that time is eternal, then a fortiori that whereby time is possible, namely, motion, must be eternal. If the proof of the eternity of time succeeds, then it is also proved thereby that motion is eternal.

To what extent is time eternal? The basic phenomenon of time is the now. The now has a twofold character: the beginning of that which is just about to be and the end of that which just was. The now is at once ἀρχὴ ἐσομένου and τελευτὴ παρελθόντος (cf. 251b21f.). Every now is by essence the ἀρχή of the coming one. Even a now thought of as infinitely distant, the most extreme end point I can imagine, is by essence the ἀρχή of a future now, and so on into the infinite. I cannot make out any now that does not lead to a future one, that does not bear in itself a future one. That is why time is eternal in the direction of the future. Likewise, the same proof is possible in the direction of the past, *mutatis mutandis*. The series of nows going back to the past is just as indeterminate in its infinity. The most extreme now of the past is always the now of an earlier one.

Thus from the essence of time it is clear that time is eternal. Therefore motion is eternal as well. But if motion is eternal, this self-moving being must also be eternal by necessity. Eternal signifies for Aristotle: uniformly self-enclosed. What is eternally self-moving can, as such, have nothing outside of itself which it would not be in itself. The ideal of such a motion, which, at every stage, can be both beginning and end, is circular motion. Every point of the circle is in itself beginning and end, i.e., beginning and end of the same uniform motion.

This is therefore the explication of motion, of what is self-moving, purely on the basis of the phenomenon itself.

7. (Relates to p. 149f.)

So the question arises: is there such a motion? In fact, there is: the course of the πρῶτος οὐρανός (*Met.* Λ 7, 1072a23), of the "first heaven," thus the course of the most outer sphere, in which are incorporated the other spheres, the ones that bear the fixed stars and the planets. This first heaven is that according to which all other motions are ruled and measured. Yet that does not complete the analysis of motion in its eternity. For, according to Aristotle, what is moved, what is self-moving, also has a τέλος, and "end." We know, however, that an eternal motion, which, as circular motion, is self-enclosed, can have no end, can have nothing, to which it draws closer and closer in any way. For, in such drawing closer it would no longer be ὁμαλής (*Phys.* E 4, 228b16), "uniform"; on the contrary, as it draws closer to its τέλος it would always be different at every stage, since it would have a different relation to the τέλος. It would be proceeding toward its end and would stop when it reached its τέλος. On the other hand, if a motion is to be eternal, it must have a τέλος from which its distance is eternally and constantly uniform.

Aristotle calls this τέλος, from which the uniform motion is always uniformly distant, the *first mover,* which for its part is not moved. As the τέλος of what is self-moving, it must be of a higher mode of Being than what is self-moving. Is there such a being? Indeed there is! The particular being which, in its motion, is not directed to a goal but, instead, is complete in itself, at every moment of its Being, and in which there is no ἀτελής, this being is pure energy, pure ἐνέργεια, pure presence, which purely in itself is unchangeable and eternal. Aristotle again seeks a concretion for this being of utter presence, and he finds it in pure θεωρεῖν ["contemplation"] (cf. *Met.* Λ 7, 1072b24).

When I *have* seen something, I say: I am now seeing it. With the having-seen, the act of seeing does not stop but, on the contrary, genuinely *is* only then. The other kinds of motion, viz., hearing, walking, etc., stop when they reach their τέλος; they are completely over, once they reach their goal. νοεῖν, on the contrary, is by essence always in activity, and as activity it is perfect in itself; furthermore, insofar as it is perfect, it genuinely *is. The most genuine being must have the mode of Being of* νοῦς, *must be* νόησις. Insofar as νόησις is directed to something, that toward which it is directed can here only be itself, and that is why the highest being is νόησις νοήσεως (*Met.* Λ 7, 1074b34), pure knowing of itself. In this formula, νόησις νοήσεως, Aristotle is not thinking of spirit, of person, of the personhood of God, or the like, but is simply attempting to find and determine a being which satisfies the highest sense of Being; Aristotle does not mean the spirit's thinking of itself, in the sense of something personal. This becomes clear in the fact that Aristotle establishes no connection between this highest being and the world, and it can also be seen in the fact that Aristotle is very far from saying anything about how the world would be created by this highest being. Aristotle, and the Greeks in general, know nothing of the idea of creation or conservation. The relation between this highest being and the world is left indeterminate. The world does not need to be created, because, for Aristotle, it is eternal, without beginning and without end.

Accordingly, this whole connection between what is properly moved and the original mover is a purely ontological one and is not oriented toward a personal God or a creator God. Aristotle is simply attempting, though to be sure in a radically philosophical way, to make ontologically understandable only what lies in the phenomenon of motion itself. In doing so, he remains steadfastly consistent. He finally speaks only, as it were, in images, when he says: This first mover moves ὡς ἐρώμενον (1072b3), "like something which is loved" and, as such, attracts. Aristotle does not say how it attracts. This attraction, however, is not to be understood in the sense of Plato's concept of ἔρως; on the contrary, the circular motion is self-enclosed and keeps a uniform distance from the first mover.

This explication cannot be represented more precisely, but that is not essential. On the contrary, the decisive question is how the problem of Being is necessarily impelled toward a *most genuine* being: can there at all be an ontology constructed purely, as it were, without an orientation toward a preeminent being, whether that is thought of as the first mover, the first heaven, or something else?

Aristotle's approach contains a fundamental problem, one that has been covered with debris by the traditional reinterpretation of these things in theology and in Christian anthropology. The same misunderstanding occurs in Hegel, who famously placed at the end of his *Enzyklopädie* what Aristotle said in his *Metaphysics* about the νόησις νοήσεως. Hegel is thereby expressing his opinion that what Aristotle calls the νόησις νοήσεως is the same as what he himself designates in his concept of spirit, which he also connects to the Trinity of God.

Eternal motion, according to its very sense, must be circular motion (demonstrated in *Phys.* Θ). The basic idea of this motion does not derive from factual observations; i.e., it is not on the basis of empirically observed motions in the world that we conclude there must be a mover, a higher being, which sets all motion going. On the contrary, motion itself in its own structure requires motion in the sense of circular motion, which Aristotle also sees as factually given in the motion of the first heaven.

Thus Aristotle can conceive of the possibility of the τέλος of motion only by placing the unmoved mover, in a certain sense, utterly outside of every connection with motion. Aristotle does not provide a more precise ontological elucidation of the connection between this τέλος and motion; he only offers images to the effect that the τέλος, the eternal mover, moves in the manner of something desired. The desired attracts as such and holds in motion, ὡς ὀρεκτόν (cf. *Met.* Λ 7, 1072a26), as something all beings strive for. This highest being, which represents the idea of the Being of movedness in the genuine sense, this first mover, is, in its connection with eternal motion, outside of every relation to the world and to mankind. Therefore on purely ontological grounds the idea of creation is excluded, and so is every sort of guidance or providence in the sense of a divine principle ruling the world. The νόησις νοήσεως is a basic character of this first mover and must not be grasped in the sense of the concept of spirit in the subsequent philosophy. That philosophy did indeed interpret Platonic notions into this Aristotelian concept. An example is Augustine: the absolute spirit, in self-contemplation, generates the models of the things, and, in accord with these models, the absolute spirit then, as God the creator, created the actual things.[85] Of all this, Aristotle says nothing.

8. (Relates to p. 150.)

On that basis, we are now prepared to specify the connection of this fourth determination of Being with the Being of the categories. We saw that δυνάμει ὄν and ἐνεργείᾳ ὄν are two basic modes of Being (even pure potentiality is understood as a mode of presence-at-hand). Thus they are basic modes of presence-at-hand and thereby two basic modes of οὐσία. Accordingly, δύναμις and ἐνέργεια, as modifications of οὐσία, refer back to the genuine Being of the categories. The categories themselves are anchored in οὐσία on account of their analogous relation to it. ἐνέργεια represents the highest ontological mode that can fall to οὐσία. Therefore Aristotle says at *Met.* Θ 8, 1050b3f.: ἐνέργεια is *prior* to δύναμις, prior to potentiality in the sense of purely neutral lying-there-about. Prior to all that is presence in general. Only by understanding that the implicit sense of the Greek concept of Being is presence, can this apparently paradoxical thesis be clarified, namely, that actuality is prior to potentiality.

---

85. Cf. Augustine, *De civitate Dei* 11, 10; *Confessiones* 1, 6, 9; *De diversis quaestionibus* 46, 2; *Tractatus in Johannis Evangelium* 1, 17.

Editor's Afterword

Martin Heidegger offered the lecture course, "The basic concepts of ancient philosophy," at the University of Marburg. The course met for four hours each week in the summer semester 1926.

The main text is based exclusively on the Marbach photocopy of Heidegger's original handwritten manuscript. The original includes eighty-two numbered pages in folio format, some unnumbered pages in the same format, a numbered page in smaller format, and numerous inserted slips. The numbered pages bear the numerals 1–77. P. 10 is missing. P. 49 is in a smaller format. Seven manuscript pages in folio format are numbered 12a, 19a, 19b, 50a, 59a, Regarding p. 66, Regarding 70b. Three sheets of the same format bear small numerals. Amid the pages in folio format, a total of sixty-five slips of various sizes are inserted here and there. Five of the slips indicate their proper place in the manuscript: Regarding 59a, Regarding 61a, 61b, 62a, Regarding p. 76.

The handwritten pages in folio format are in small German script; the pages are in landscape orientation. As a rule, the main text is on the left half, interpolations on the right. Sometimes—specifically in the case of diagrams of keywords and graphically ordered notes—the main text covers the whole page. Heidegger wrote on both sides of thirteen of the slips. In nine of these cases, one side contains texts that could not be attached to the content of this course. Heidegger was evidently re-using these slips, for the sake of saving paper, to write down thoughts related to this course; thus the sides that could not be incorporated are mere "versos." Seven of these versos contain excerpts from a draft of *Sein und Zeit*, whose first division Heidegger had already finished and sent to the printer at the time of the composition of these lectures. One of the slips with writing on a single side contains a text that still could not be inserted in these lectures. It is obviously a variant of a passage from the treatise, *Vom Wesen des Grundes* (6th ed., Frankfurt, 1973; in *Wegmarken* GA 9, Frankfurt, 1976). The four versos connected to the lectures have been placed in the supplements, although Heidegger crossed out three of them.

The title of the lectures in the manuscript is "Sketches for the course on the basic concepts of ancient philosophy" (see above, p. 1). A close study of the manuscript confirms the use of the word "sketches." In many parts, the text is not formulated in complete sentences but, instead, varies from a laconic style characterized by missing verbs to mere lists of key words serving as a basis for oral delivery. The clearly lesser degree of elaboration, in comparison with the other courses that are close to it in time, that of winter semester 1925–1926 (GA 21) and summer semester 1927 (GA 24), presumably has extrinsic reasons. In the summer of 1926, Heidegger was still at work finishing the second division of *Sein und Zeit* and that task was pressing on him. It is especially passages in the first part of these lectures, and in the first section of the second part, that indicate this was an introductory, survey course for students from all the departments. A decree from the ministry of culture in Berlin obligated the university docents in philosophy to present such introductory courses, for which a specific curriculum was prescribed. That also accounts for the fact that Heidegger, in treating the individual philosophers, provides purely biographical data, even if very summarily. Such mere indications, without deeper philosophical significance, run counter to Heidegger's understanding of the meaning of a course in philosophy, and in the present course itself, Heidegger clearly expresses his dissatisfaction with them: "No intention of filling the class sessions with anecdotes about the lives and fates of the ancient thinkers or rambling on about Greek culture. There will be no mere enumeration of the titles of the writings of the ancient authors, no synopsis of contents which contributes nothing to the understanding of the problems" (p. 9).

To reconstruct the text of the lectures I had available a typewritten transcription of Heidegger's handwritten German script. Hartmut Tietjen produced this transcription in 1976.

Also at hand were the following notes taken down by students:

a) A typewritten transcription of the entire course by Hermann Mörchen. According to a brief note on the cover, this transcription was typed out in 1976.

b) A typewritten transcription, presumably the work of Walter Bröcker, found amid the literary remains of Herbert Marcuse in the library of the city and university of Frankfurt.

The work of editing began by my checking, word for word, the Tietjen transcription against the photocopy of Heidegger's manuscript. I corrected obvious errors and attempted to decipher passages that had not been transcribed. This latter task presented considerable difficulties, mainly in those passages which consist of little more than keywords, for there the context was meager or nonexistent. Despite repeated efforts, passages remained which either could not be decided with sufficient certainty or which had to be judged illegible if the deciphering proved to be too vague or altogether impossible. A question mark in braces {?} indicates misgivings about the deciphering of the word or words. If a passage had to be omitted on account of a corrupt text or illegibility, that is indicated in a footnote.

Heidegger wrote a limited number of passages in Gabelsberger shorthand. These vary in extent from a single word to a sentence, and Guy van Kerckhoven was able to decipher a large part of them. Since Heidegger evidently used here his own modified version of Gabelsberger, some passages could be deciphered only with a certain probability, while others were quite doubtful. The latter are again indicated in the present text with a question mark. Shorthand passages that could scarcely be deciphered have been omitted.

I could not altogether avoid introducing conjecture into the text. Only in that way could the manuscript, which is characterized often by the use of keywords and ellipses, be readable. But I interpolated conjectures only where they were completely beyond doubt and did not influence the intended content. I did *not* interpolate conjectures in the form of the auxiliary verbs, to be, to have, and the like, nor verbs which were without a doubt missing simply because of the telegram style of the manuscript. On the other hand, I did interpolate, in braces, concepts that were taken up again after some remark had broken the continuity.

I articulated the main text (i.e., the text of the manuscript, not including the appendices) into chapters, sections, and subsections primarily by following the numerous indications and hints in the manuscript itself. The table of contents should make clear the main lines of the course of thought. The manuscript affords a few footholds for the division into paragraphs, but for the most part, the content was what was decisive. Emphasis through italics stems in part from the editor. I re-punctuated according to the sense.

Regarding the mode of citation in the text of the manuscript: the first citation of a work was placed in a footnote. The editions cited are, as much as possible, those of Heidegger's own copies. (Cf., in this regard, the afterword to the Marburg lecture course, *Platon: Sophistes* GA 19, ed. I. Schüßler, Frankfurt, 1992, p. 661.) In the case of a repeated citation, the procedure varied: the citation was placed in parentheses and run into the text in the case of a rather long passage referring to one and the same work of a particular Greek philosopher. In the case of other repeated citations, the title is abbreviated. Suspension points (. . .) indicate ellipses within the original Greek text. When Heidegger's Greek quotations deviate from the original text, the citation is preceded by a "cf." In comparison to the other volumes of the *Gesamtausgabe* the footnote apparatus is here noticeably more extensive, and the references inserted in the text are also more numerous than usual. The manuscript itself for the most part contains abridged and meager citations and references to the secondary literature. It was not enough simply to take these up and complete them bibliographically. Instead, I attempted to identify and provide the references for every citation from the texts of the Greek thinkers, even when only a single word was quoted, as is not seldom the case in the parts of the manuscript consisting of keywords alone. These copious citations, although they may at times give the impression of weighing down the book, should help in determining more precisely Heidegger's choice of texts, their relative importance for him, and the interpretation he gives them. As a matter of principle, I decided not to indicate whether a particular reference is already found in the manuscript, since references occur there haphazardly and such indications would not contribute to an understanding of the matters at issue.

The use of the student notes posed a special editorial problem. Since Heidegger's manuscript is scantily elaborated in many places, it might have seemed appropriate to work the notes into the main text, so as to make it as readable, fluent, and consistent as possible. On the other hand, Heidegger did not authorize these notes. Hermann Mörchen wrote on the cover of his transcription: "In transcribing my notes, which I took down in telegram style, I have on occasion made small clarifications, by, for example, inserting copulas or other such parts of speech, but only ones that were obvious from the meaning. As a rule I did not eliminate stylistic rough spots (it cannot be determined whether these arose precisely in the act of transcribing). Abbreviated words were written out in full, and the punctuation was altered in conformity with the sense. Lacunae in the text (sentences or phrases that were missed in the note-taking) are indicated, if I could tell that something was missing, by three dots. Repetitions, peculiar to Heidegger's lecture style, were preserved, provided they had not been omitted in the notes." Thus the Mörchen transcription is by no means an exact stenographic record, as is also clear from a comparison with the Bröcker transcription.

According to the strictures regulating the *Gesamtausgabe*, student notes cannot be incorporated if their style does not attest to their authenticity. With the Mörchen transcription, complete certainty is unattainable. This judgment does not denigrate its quality, but it does have consequences for a careful reconstruction of the text according to established editorial principles. That is why I did not incorporate the excerpts from the Mörchen transcription into the main text and relegated them, instead, to the appendix.

These excerpts include: a) ones for which there is nothing corresponding in the manuscript, b) ones whose corresponding place in the manuscript consists of mere keywords and brief remarks, or c) ones whose fullness and whose presentation of the context go well beyond the manuscript and thereby contribute essentially to a better understanding of the entire course of thought. Thus, wherever the manuscript and the transcription exhibited the same degree of fullness, the former had the priority.

I was careful not to introduce too many divisions into the excerpts, so that, even there, conceptual connections and relations would be visible. To adhere to this principle of overall intelligibility, some repetitions with respect to the main text were unavoidable.

The following principles were the basis for the subdivision and enumeration of the excerpts. A new number was assigned: a) when the previous excerpt did not need to be carried on and thereby introduced an interruption. Accordingly, the length of the omitted excerpt played no role in the enumeration; b) when the corresponding passage of the manuscript included the beginning of a new section or a subsection with its own title. My intention was to further the correspondence between the manuscript and the excerpt from the transcriptions.

The transcription by Walter Bröcker corresponds to only three class sessions—content-wise, from §58 to the second paragraph of §62. This transcription is somewhat fuller than Mörchen's, and its diction unmistakably betrays a lecture style. Thus the Bröcker text has a priority over the Mörchen, when they overlap. The entire, unabridged Bröcker text is presented in the appendix.

I intruded only very slightly into the text of the transcriptions. A few small changes (such as expanding some colloquial abbreviations) seemed proper. In the Mörchen transcription, the ubiquitous semicolon was replaced by more current punctuation.

With regard to citations in the transcriptions: since these excerpts run parallel to the main text, there was no need to double the footnotes. Accordingly, the Greek citations were incorporated into the transcriptions, even in the few cases in which the main text does not already refer to the Greek. Furthermore, the citations in the transcriptions are not as expansive as in the main text and provide only enough detail that they can be identified and compared with the references given in the main text. In the case of references to non-Greek texts, the footnotes provide only whatever indications were not already mentioned in the manuscript. In the case of sheer repetition, I simply referred the reader to the earlier footnote.

Both transcriptions served an important function in helping to establish the order of the parts of the manuscript. Many of the supplements on the right side of the numbered pages as well as most of the annotated slips bear no indication of their proper place in the text. In many cases, the transcriptions offer valuable information on the progression of Heidegger's thought. I otherwise made decisions regarding the order of the text by basing myself on the content.

A few of the slips and unnumbered folio pages of the manuscript contain ideas that could not all—or only with difficulty—be fit within the flow of the thought of the lectures, to the extent that this can be reconstructed from the Mörchen transcription. Those fragments are presented as supplements, along with an indication of the corresponding passage in the main text.

This lecture course, "The basic concepts of ancient philosophy," seeks to show (through a discussion of the basic concepts developed by the leading Greek thinkers, concepts such as foundation, *physis*, unity-multiplicity, element, *logos*, truth, Idea, knowledge–science, category, motion, potentiality, *energeia*, life, and soul) that Greek philosophy is determined and permeated by the question of Being. The course breaks down into three parts:

In the preliminary remarks, Heidegger takes a position regarding questions of the intention, method, and acquisition of a correct basic understanding of philosophy. In contrast to the other sciences, which, as positive sciences, all treat of beings, Heidegger finds the essential feature of philosophy in "criticism," in the sense of distinguishing between Being and beings. The lecture course aims at "participating in and, as it were, repeating" (see above, p. 9) the beginning of philosophizing as the accomplishment that makes explicit the difference between Being and beings.

The first part, according to Heidegger, has the character of an *introduction* (see above, p. 112, n. 74; p. 122, n. 11; p. 168) to ancient philosophy. Heidegger allows Aristotle to "point the way" by taking up the analysis of knowledge and the interpretation of the previous philosophy as these are presented in bk. A of the *Metaphysics;* Heidegger, however, does not clarify the exact sense of this "pointing the way." What is characteristic of the Aristotelian presentation is the interpretation of the previous philosophies under the guideline of two of his own basic concepts, namely αἰτία and ἀρχή. Perhaps Aristotle leads the way in the sense that Heidegger appropriates the *formal* principle of interpreting the history of philosophy under the guideline of a pre-structure that one has projected for oneself, though not arbitrarily, in an attempt to understand the earlier thinkers "better" than they understood themselves. In any event, Heidegger's own guideline, with which he seeks access to an understanding of Greek philosophy, is the question of *Being* and of its difference from beings. In Heidegger's view, the phenomenon of foundation, in the form of the principle of sufficient reason, on which all later science is based, can be clarified in it-self, and in its relation to Being, only if Being is adequately understood in advance.

The second part is the genuinely main part of the course and is sub-divided into three sections. The first is a rather general evaluation of the more prominent pre-Platonic thinkers. The only text interpreted in detail is Parmenides' didactic poem. Sections two and three are each reserved for a single thinker, Plato and Aristotle respectively, al-though these sections are as long as the entire preceding one. The main intention of the first section is to show how, in the development of Greek thought in the form of an ever richer conceptuality, the phe-nomenon of Being, in its difference from beings, comes to light and is explicitly questioned. In the second section as well, Heidegger clarifies the central terms of Plato's philosophy in their intrinsic connection to the phenomenon of Being. At the same time, Heidegger shows, in his interpretation of the *Theatetus* and of dialectics, that, for Plato, the problem of Being is joined to the question of the Being of nonbeing and of becoming and thereby acquires new dimensions which remain decisive for the subsequent ontology. Section three takes Aristotle as the high point of Greek ontology, where the question of Being (in the double concept of philosophy as the question of the Being of beings and the question of the highest being) becomes the explicit object of scientific philosophy. The question of Being is then further differenti-ated in the formulation of four modes of questioning, radicalized in the ontologization of potentiality and *energeia* and opened to new on-tological dimensions with the inauguration of an ontology of life and of human Dasein.

I owe great thanks to Hartmut Tietjen for his generous and patient assis-tance in the deciphering of many difficult passages, for once again re-viewing the copy against the manuscript, for his careful examination of my ordering of the text and my choice of excerpts from the Mörchen transcription, and also for many very valuable suggestions. I am also grateful to him, to Hermann Heidegger, and to Friedrich-Wilhelm von Herrmann for carrying out the difficult task of deciphering passages in the manuscript that remained open until the last moment. I must thank Hermann Heidegger for his attempts to discover further transcriptions. His efforts were rewarded by the discovery of the valuable Bröcker tran-scription, so important for the corresponding passages in the text. I am grateful to him and to von Herrmann for a final examination of the fin-ished typescript. I also thank von Herrmann for advice on numerous matters.

I am indebted to Guy van Kerckhoven for the painstaking way he deciphered many passages written in shorthand. I very much thank

Mark Michalski for his extremely precise checking of the bibliographical references and Greek citations and for his careful assistance in correcting proofs.

My wife Maria devoted many hours to preparing the typewritten copy of the text, to incorporating necessary corrections, and to printing out the entire work. I offer her heartfelt thanks.

Franz-Karl Blust
Pfaffenweiler, June 1993

Greek-English Glossary

ἀγαθόν: good
ἄγνοια: ignorance
ἀδιαίρετον: indivisible
ἀδύνατον: impossible
ἀεί: eternal
ἀήρ: air
αἴσθησις: perception
αἰσχρόν: ugliness
αἰτιολογία: aetiology
αἴτιον: cause
ἀκίνητον: unmoved
ἀκοή: hearing
ἀλήθεια: truth, disclosedness
ἀληθεύειν: to take out of
  concealment
ἀλλοδοξία: mistaken opinion
ἀλλοίωσις: becoming other
ἀμυδρῶς: obscurely
ἄμφω: both
ἀναλογία: analogy
ἀναλογίζεσθαι: to grasp the similar
ἀνάμνησις: recollection
ἀντίθεσις: contrast
ἀνυπόθετον: non-hypothetical
ἀκριβεστάτη: most rigorous
ἀόριστον: indefinite
ἄπειρον: indeterminate
ἁπλῶς: simply
ἀπόκρισιν: answer
ἀπορία: impasse
ἀποφαίνεσθαι: to let be seen
ἀρετή: suitability
ἀριθμός: number
ἁρμονία: harmony

ἀρχή: beginning, principle
ἀρχικωτάτη: supreme
ἀρχιτεκτονική: architecture
ἀστράγαλοι: dice
ἀταξία: disorder
ἀτελής: incomplete
αὐτό: itself
γένος: genus
γῆ: earth
δηλοῦν: divulging
διάθεσις: disposition
διαίρεσις: disjunction
διάκρισις: disjunction
διαλέγεσθαι: dialectics
διάνοια: thought
διαφορά: difference
δόξα: opinion
δυνάμει: as potential
δύναμις: potentiality, preparedness
δύνασθαι: to be powerful
δυνατόν: able, strong
ἑαυτῆς ἕνεκεν: for the sake of itself
εἰδέναι: see
εἶδος: outward look
εἴδωλον: image
εἰκασία: image
εἶναι: Being
εἷς, μία, ἕν: one
ἕκαστον: the individual
ἐμπειρία: experience
ἕν: neuter of εἷς, q.v.
ἐναντίον: opposition
ἔνδοξον: esteemed
ἐνέργεια: actuality

251

ἐνεργείᾳ: as actualized
ἐντελέχεια: completeness
ἐντολήν: command
ἐνυπάρχον: constituent principle
ἕξις: comportment
ἐπαγωγή: to lead over
ἐπιθυμία: appetite
ἐπιρυσμίη: floating
ἐπιστάτης: one who understands
ἐπιστήμη: knowledge
ἔργον: finished product
ἔρως: love
ἐρώτησιν: question
ἑτεροδοξεῖν: opinion about something other
ἕτερον: other
ἑτερότης: otherness
εὐχωλήν: petition
ἐφεξῆς: succession
ἔχεσθαι: holding together
ζωή: life
ζῷον: living being, animal
ἦθος: comportment
ἥλιος: sun
θαυμάζειν: wonder
θεῖον: the divine
θεολογία: theology
θεός: God
θέσις: position
θεωρεῖν: contemplation
ἰδέα: Idea
ἴδια: proper
ἱστορία: research
καθόλου: universal
κακόν: bad
καλός: beautiful
κατά: against, according to
κατὰ συμβεβηκός: supervenient, incidental
κατηγορεῖν: categorizing
κατηγορία: category
κενόν: void
κίνησις: motion
κινοῦν: mover

κοινόν: common
κοινωνία: commonality, connection, communion
κόσμος: ordered world
κρίνειν: to separate, differentiate
κύκλος: circle
λανθάνει: to conceal
λέγειν: to say
λεγόμενον: the uttered
λογισμός: deliberation
λόγος: discourse, meaning, definition
μαθητικός: learned
μᾶλλον: more
μέθεξις: participation
μέσον: middle
μετά: with, after
μεταβάλλειν: to change
μεταβολή: change
μετὰ λόγου: with *logos*
μεταξύ: between
μέτρον: measure
μὴ ὄν: nonbeing
μία: feminine of εἷς, *q.v.*
μίμησις: imitation
μνήμη: retention, memory
μορφή: form
μῦθος: myth, story
νεῖκος: hate
Νεφέλαι: (Aristophanes') *Clouds*
νοεῖν: apprehension
νόησις: understanding
νόησις νοήσεως: knowing knowing
νοητόν: intelligible
νῦν: now
ὄγκοι: magnitudes
ὅθεν: whence
ὅλον: whole
ὄμμα: eye
ὁμοιομερῆ: of like parts
ὅμοιον: similar
ὁμοίωσις: assimilation
ὁμώνυμον: homonymous
ὄν: beings

ὁρᾶσθαι: see
ὁρατόν: visible
ὄρεξις: desire
ὁρισμός: delimitation
οὐρανός: heavens
οὐσία: presence-at-hand
ὄψις: sight
πάθος: affect
πάντα: all things
πάντα ῥεῖ: everything is flowing
παρά: beside
παράδειγμα: example
παρουσία: co-presence
παρώνυμον: derived in meaning
πάσχειν: undergoing
πέρας: limit
περὶ φύσεως: on nature
περιτρέχοντα: things running
  around loose
πίστις: trust
πλῆθος: quantity, amount
πλῆρες: plenum
ποιεῖν: to make
ποίησις: making
ποιόν: quality
πολιτική: politics
πολλαχῶς: in many ways
ποσόν: quantity
πού: place
πρᾶξις: doing
προαίρεσις: anticipation
πρός: toward
πρότερον: first
πρῶτα: first things
πτώσεις: inflections
σκοτεινός: obscure
σοφία: wisdom
σοφιστής: sophist
σοφός: wise person
σοφώτερος: wiser
στάσις: rest
στέρησις: deprivation
στοιχεῖον: element
σύγκρισις: conjunction

συλλαβαί: syllables
συλλαβεῖν: to combine
συμβαίνοντα: consequences
συμβεβηκός: the supervenient,
  incidental
σύναψις: conjunction
συνεχές: self-cohesive
σύνθεσις: combination
συνώνυμον: univocal
σφαῖρα: sphere
σχῆμα: configuration
τάξις: arrangement
ταὐτόν: the same
τέλος: end
τέχνη: know-how, understanding
τί ἐστιν;: what is it?
τόπος: place
ὕδωρ: water
ὕλη: matter
ὑπερουράνιος: hyperheavenly
ὑποκείμενον: substrate
ὑπόστασις: foundation
φαινόμενον: phenomenon
φαντασία: imagination
φιλία: love
φιλοσοφία: philosophy
φορά: locomotion
φρόνησις: prudence
φρόνιμος: prudent, insightful
φύειν: engender
φύεσθαι: grow
φυόμενα: plants
φύσει: by nature
φυσική: physics
φυσιολόγοι: investigators into
  nature
φύσις: nature, the self-emergent
φυτευτά: plants
φῶς: light
χαλεπά: difficult things
χρόνος: time
χωρισμός: separation
ψευδής: false
ψυχή: soul

CPSIA information can be obtained
at www.ICGtesting.com
Printed in the USA
BVHW031555170620
581748BV00007B/46